VINTAGE 'PORT

A Toast to Stockport County's Triumphant 1996-97 Season

TREVOR BAXTER

Trevor Baxter

Interleaf Productions Limited

© 1997 Interleaf Productions Limited

Published by Interleaf Productions Limited
Broom Hall
8–10 Broomhall Road
Sheffield S10 2DR
UK

Typeset by Interleaf Productions Limited
Printed in Spain by Edelvives

British Library Cataloguing in Publication Data
  A catalogue record for this book is available from the British Library

ISBN 1 9878070 5 7

Contents

To my dad David: you gave me my love of sport.
I wish we could have spent more time together.

To my mum Sheila: you've always been there when
I needed something . . . usually money!

Acknowledgements

AS WITH ALL BOOKS OF THIS type, the author himself could not have put it together without some help. I am indebted to Stockport County chairman Brendan Elwood for providing the Foreword and for taking time out to discuss the season in depth: thankfully, I got to him in time before the resignation of Dave Jones and the appointment of Gary Megson, otherwise the volume might not have come out.

Thanks to Dave Jones, not only for taking time out from his new job at Southampton to give me his input, but also for his time while manger at Edgeley Park. If every manager was as co-operative as him, the media's job would be so much easier. I envy my counterparts on the south coast. My gratitude also goes to Mike Flynn for allowing me into his home to obtain material for Chapter 7. On the field, Mike never pulls out of a challenge, and off the pitch he never ducks an interview. Many thanks.

Des Hinks and Richard Harnwell have been invaluable in providing background material: their knowledge of County and loyalty to the Hatters is staggering. Thanks to Matt Horn, Sports Editor of the Stockport Express, for allowing me to use photographs and for his company throughout the season. On the subject of pictures, thanks to club photographer Steve Southart for use of his snaps.

Others deserving a mention are: Dave Espley, editor of the County fanzine, The Tea Party; GMR reporter Paul Rooney; and Stuart Renshaw of Dawn Cover Productions, Ashfield Road, Davenport. Thanks to Pauline Climpson of Interleaf Productions for having faith enough to let me go ahead with this project, to Dean Bargh for putting it all together, and to Andrew Fyfe, my computer expert.

Last but by no means least, thanks to Adele, my wife. Your patience and loyalty is more than I sometimes deserve.

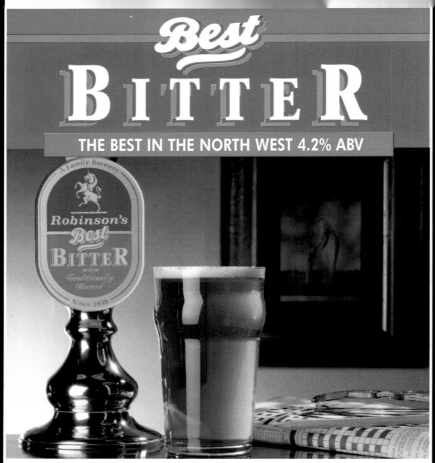

Foreword

Brendan Elwood, Chairman, Stockport County

THEY SAY IT'S A FINE LINE between success and failure and it only takes a second to score a goal. So it's perhaps odd to suggest a whole match could have wrecked the most successful season this club has ever known. Why do I believe that just ninety more minutes would have ruined the dreams of players, supporters and officials alike?

Quite honestly, if we had played one further cup match, I don't think we would have achieved promotion from the second division for the first time in sixty years, and this book would never have seen the light of day. Our end-of-season schedule was quite horrendous, and we certainly had sympathy for Alex Ferguson and Manchester United when they requested an extension to the season.

We had, quite simply, become the victims of our own success. Now, with the benefit of hindsight, I can truthfully say I was relieved when we were beaten by Carlisle United in the northern final of the Auto Windscreen Shield. At the time I castigated Chris Marsden for getting himself sent off—and I had a go at the manager for a lack of discipline in the side. But the 0–0 draw we got at Edgeley Park which meant we wouldn't qualify for a final against Colchester was among our best results of the campaign. Had we won, instead of losing 2–0 on aggregate, it would have meant the cancellation and rearranging of a league game at the expense of going to Wembley for what, with respect, is a Mickey Mouse trophy!

Don't get me wrong. I was grateful for the competition in the early days when we struggling to gain ourselves a better reputation after years of living in the doldrums, but it was never a great money-spinner and on this occasion we were pleased to be out of it. Publicly, the manager and the players were saying they still felt fit and full of energy. However, privately, they were worried about just what toll so many matches would take.

In the end, our worst fears proved groundless. We secured promotion, as everyone knows, on that unforgettable night at Chesterfield and went to Luton Town for the final game with the pressure well and truly off, probably for the first time in the season. Of course, it would have been the icing on the cake had we won the championship, but our aim was always to win promotion first. Anything else would have been a bonus.

We offer our congratulations to Stan Ternent and Bury for gaining the title. A lot of people said we were the best team in the division, but Bury sold their centre-half, Michael Jackson to Preston halfway through the season and still got more points than we did.

Both of us, plus Crewe of course, can now look forward to reaping the benefits of our labours. We've got some fabulous fixtures to look forward to and it promises to be another exciting season.

It's desperately sad that Dave Jones won't be taking us on to hopefully bigger and greater things; however, I understand his reasons for joining Southampton, and life must go on. We've got to show him now that we are every bit as ambitious as he obviously is. I wish him well for the future, but what matters now is the future of Stockport County.

Enjoy the coming season and enjoy this book.

Introduction

LET'S START THIS BOOK WITH A confession, which, hopefully, won't prevent you reading any further. The author is a Manchester United supporter. This affliction has been with me for exactly thirty years to the month.

My first trip to 'God's Acre' was for the Charity Shield against Spurs, and, even if my father had not been of the same persuasion, it would have been tough not to have been hooked after that match. A couple of Bobby Charlton scorchers, a Pat Jennings goal against Alex Stepney, and a 3–3 thriller all helped to make a starry-eyed seven-year-old see red for the rest of his life.

The stick didn't seem so bad in those days when you spoke of your allegiance to the United cause. The bitter Blues tried to rile you during their brief flirtation with success, but from the rest there was more sympathy than antagonism, especially as United went into decline, post-Busby. Now, owning up to having Stretford leanings makes you a target for abuse and derision. Even Kenny Boxshall, County's match-day announcer, gloats when, on the rare occasions, United slip up.

Having laid my cards on the table, here is the case for the defence. Unlike some of the more bigoted members of the tribe, I recognise there is life outside Old Trafford. That's why I and a few other enlightened teenagers (OK, saddoes without a Friday-night grope) found ourselves on the Edgeley

Park terraces in the mid-seventies. At the time, we were grateful to our mate Phil Jackson for this experience. While most of us were singing the praises of 'Pancho' Pearson or Dennis Tueart, Phil — later to become goalkeeper for Altrincham and Cheadle Town, among others — was raving about Barney Daniels and Eddie Prudham.

The exact game of our 'coming-out' remains shrouded in the mists of time, but I recall seeing all the great fourth-division sides of the day: Newport County, Workington, Southport. Whatever became of them? I also recall a visit by Fort Lauderdale Strikers and seeing George Best pull on a County jersey. Again, my powers of recollection aren't what they should be, but didn't Georgie-Boy score direct from a corner in a 3–2 victory over Swansea?

Eventually, though, trips to Edgeley became fewer and fewer: a combination of other attractions and three years working in Cumbria reporting on the fall and fall of Barrow FC.

In 1987, the call of home, a romance (later to fail) and the offer of another job became too strong. Had circumstances worked out differently, I could have been sports editor for the *Stockport*

SHAKERS ROCKED BY EARLY STRIKE

DEFIANT BUTLER SERVES UP LIFELINE

CAPTAIN MARVEL LIGHTS THE FUSE

ANDY'S GOAL IS ICING ON CAKE

Thanks very Mutch! Flynn firecracker

POLICE, STEWARDS MOVE IN AS RIVAL FANS SCUFFLE

ANGELL GRABS A GOLDEN CHANCE

LAST-GASP GOAL SEALS THE POINTS

By TREVOR BAXTER

Dazzling Port in a storm!

Durka

COUNTY BREAK STRANGLEHOLD

COUNTY ACE'S DOUBLE DELIGHT

DAVE'S BOYS STRIDING ON

Cooper's Angell wings in!

By TREVOR BAXTER

By TREVOR BAXTER

MANCHESTER EVENING NEWS

Express. Just think: Matt Horn's hat may never have been seen in these parts! Instead, I found myself still in the press box, alongside one of Matt's predecessors, Mike Brennan, working for local freelance, Joe Lancaster. Joe hired phones out to visiting scribes, and God forbid anyone who didn't make a transfer charge call: many an unsuspecting cub reporter has endured a Lancaster rollicking for 'running up the bill'.

Ten years ago, it was rare to see anyone from the 'nationals' joining the regulars for the unappetising fare that was fourth-division football. (At times last season it was standing room only.) County had hardly improved since I had watched from what is now the Vernon Building Society Stand, ten years earlier. At least it didn't cost me money to get in. Then, as Joseph Heller wrote, 'Something happened.' Brendan Elwood joined the board, Asa Hartford became another Edgeley managerial statistic and Danny

Bergara became the man to lead County to the Promised Land.

Messiahs come in all shapes and sizes. This particular one was a volatile bundle of Uruguayan energy whose pronunciation of English may not have been the best, but, then again, the 'f'-word has the same effect however it comes out. Under Bergara's leadership, Stockport were no longer a laughing stock. They were going places, usually to Wembley, but never quite into the old second division. Even this dyed-in-the-wool red was becoming hooked; I even began to hate Burnley, but don't ask me why!

There's nothing greater for stirring the blood than an exciting football match. Emotions take over; the referee suddenly has no parents and the opposing centre-forward couldn't hit a barn door from five paces. Whether you should make these comments from the press box, however, is debatable. Watching County was now a pleasure rather than a pain, and I genuinely felt a sense of sadness as one Wembley disappointment followed another.

The end of the Bergara era was as swift as it was a shock, and I wondered, along with many others, if the bubble had burst and whether an FA Cup victory over QPR was as good as it got.

Cometh the hour, cometh the man. Enter Dave Jones. In soccer-speak, the boy had already done well, graduating from youth team coach to coach, first team coach, and now manager. But was he the right man? History tells us that Elwood could not have made a better choice. At the start of the 1996–97 campaign, the County cognoscenti — i.e. Matt Horn, Des Hinks, Steve Bellis, etc. — were telling me this was going to be the season. 'Season to be relegated,' I opined after the opening few games. At this stage, I had begun to cover, thanks to the *Manchester Evening News*, a succession of away matches. Man. City Reserves seemed a more agreeable

proposition following a number of dire, dreary displays. However, as we now know, these games were the inedible appetiser to a season when County's cup ranneth over.

Due to other commitments, I didn't see every match — I even missed the final glory night at Chesterfield — but, thanks to contacts at Teletext and Ceefax, I always made an effort to find out the score as quickly as possible, wherever I was in the world. And I couldn't have been more delighted when County, after sixty years, finally reached their Holy Grail at Saltergate.

This book is an attempt to chronicle and bring back memories of the greatest season in the club's history. Hopefully, it won't be another sixty years before someone is writing the follow-up.

Trevor Baxter
August 1997

DES HINKS

DES HINKS

STOCKPORT EXPRESS

DES HINKS

THATTERS BEEN A BRILLIANT SEASON - WE'RE PROUD OF YOU COUNTY

DES HINKS

DES HINKS

THE FANS: A SEASON TO REMEMBER

One Elwood of a Season:
The Thoughts of Chairman Brendan

WHEN BRENDAN ELWOOD asked his wife Margaret whether it would be a good idea to invest his money and time into ailing Stockport County, he received a quick answer. 'She told me not to bother,' recalled the Sheffield businessman, smiling at the memory of his initial venture into the soccer industry. 'I don't often disagree with her, but on this occasion I did,' added Elwood, the Edgeley Park chairman of six years' standing.

Had he heeded Margaret's advice, there's every chance the most momentous season in the Hatters' 114-year history wouldn't have happened. At best, County might have gone the way of Halifax Town, Workington, Aldershot, Newport County, Southport *et al.*: ex-League teams whose non-league careers have been every bit as inglorious as their former existences. At worst, this previously undistinguished Cheshire club, forced to seek re-election on five occasions throughout its life, might not exist — the eighties' equivalent of Aberdare Athletic, Durham City or New Brighton. 'When I joined the board —

CHAIRMAN BRENDAN ELWOOD OUT AMONG THE SUPPORTERS

DES HINKS

more as a favour than anything else — Stockport had two chances,' said Elwood. 'No hope and Bob Hope!'

It's ten years since John Higgins, a former County marketing manager, approached Elwood to become the club's saviour. The two had met socially through market trader gatherings in Sheffield, and it was to prove the best piece of business Higgins ever did for County. He knew Elwood was passionate about his football, though exclusively from a playing and watching perspective. He also knew Elwood had the money to allow him to indulge his fancy and might — just might — be persuaded to cross the Pennines and replenish club coffers with his cash.

County's team at the time contained such illustrious names as Frank Worthington and Asa Hartford, plus the dependable Bob Colville, Bill Williams and Andy Thorpe. Despite that calibre of player, County still languished at the wrong end of the table, though this time erstwhile European Cup Winners' Cup quarter-finalists Newport were destined to drop through the fourth-division trapdoor.

Like many of their contemporaries, the club was crippled by debt. Years of attempting to exist on paltry gates (the visit of Wolverhampton Wanderers in 1987 attracted just 2,233) with little or no commercial back-up had pushed them to the brink of oblivion. 'I remember John's first words to me,' remembered Elwood: ' "Don't laugh, just listen." What he told me was a sorry tale: "We need £25,000 to pay the wages bill and I want you to come over and join the Board." '

At this point it was a case of *déjà vu* for Elwood. He'd already declined the offer to become a director of another football club, in this case Sheffield United. The Blades, like Higgins, had recognised that the Ulster-born property developer could help wake a red-and-white-striped sleeping giant, suspecting they might be on to a winner. After all, Elwood made no secret of his support for the club: they were, and still are one, of the first teams whose results he looks for.

> Reg Brearley offered me a seat on the Board and later, when Paul Woolhouse bought the controlling interest, he approached me with a similar offer. On both occasions I turned them down. It was a great honour to be asked, but I knew I'd made the right decision. I lived and worked in Sheffield and I was the type of fellow who liked to go out to the pub with the lads. Because of those facts, I knew I could do without the hassle that would have gone with the territory of becoming a director, the vice-chairman or even the chairman. I didn't want people approaching me all the time asking why we'd signed such and such a player and why we weren't buying someone else instead. With Stockport, I knew I wouldn't feel like I was living in a goldfish bowl all the time.

However, becoming a director of County had plenty of other drawbacks and few perks. The taxman, for instance, doesn't have any trouble distancing himself from the emotive nature involved in keeping football's minnows afloat. 'I joined the Board more to see what it was like than anything else,' recollected Elwood. Meetings soon became an eye-opener and it didn't take a Wall Street banker to realise the club's plight. 'Ninety per cent of the time they were trying to find where the money was coming from to pay the wages.'

THE MANAGEMENT: THE TEAM OF JONES AND SAINTY AT THE START OF THE CAMPAIGN

Within six months the situation had become catastrophic. The Inland Revenue was pushing for £250,000, the club had debts of £0.5 million, and it was losing £7,000 a week. 'It was disastrous. It was an Accrington Stanley scenario.' Twenty years of playing on a Friday night had contributed to the problem: 'Stockport had lost two generations of supporters.'

Despite the predicament, Elwood was about to break every lesson learned in business. He had no particular fondness for County, as he had for Sheffield United and as he had for his first love, Belfast Celtic. 'Celtic disbanded in 1949 and that's when I first came over to England as a six year-old,' said Elwood. He hadn't even seen a Stockport match before taking up Higgins's invitation and candidly confesses to a memory blank when asked to name his first-ever game. 'It was probably an evening fixture, other than that I can't tell you.'

Elwood still doesn't know what possessed him to become an Edgeley Park director and then later to take an even bigger step into the unknown by accepting the chairmanship.

They asked me at a time when 78 per cent of the shares were unissued and I just decided there and then to take the club over. I didn't need it but, as Danny Bergara, of all people, used to say: 'God moves in mysterious ways.' I just thought what a shame it would be if the receiver had to come in and close the place down. Having agreed to take over meant paying off debts of £5 million and starting to rebuild the club. At first it was an experience. There was no bar, no licence, no sponsors. The players brought in a few cans of beer and sold them for a £1 each. Any profit went into their end-of-season kitty.

From such unpromising beginnings the club has flourished practically beyond recognition, culminating in the historic 1996–97 campaign. However, there have been setbacks along the way for Elwood and his board, both on and off the pitch.

In 1991, under the Bergara regime, County gained promotion from the old fourth division. They also went to Wembley and in 1992 and 1993 finished runners-up in the Autoglass Trophy. Another Wembley appearance followed in the second-division play-offs, but that again proved fruitless.

However, it wasn't failure that cost Uruguayan-born Bergara his post, but an ugly incident at what was supposed to be a happy club social evening. The matter was only resolved earlier this year in the civil courts, but it paved the way for the dawning of the Dave Jones era which would end so abruptly in June 1997 with his departure to Premier League Southampton. Perhaps not surprisingly, Elwood declines to elaborate on his fall-out with the man he brought to drag the club out of the doldrums, but even he probably acknowledges, however begrudgingly, that Bergara — removed from his job at Rotherham in 1997 after failing to pull off a similar rescue package — helped lay the foundations for all the most recent glory.

Bergara has gone — so too as his successor Jones — but Elwood remains to carry through his current five-year plan.

> People laugh at my five-year plans, but what we want to do here can't be achieved overnight. Initially we got out of the fourth division in three years, leaving two years of the plan remaining. That wasn't long enough to implement the next phase, so we ripped up the first plan and started

another. Our goal then was to get in the first division. That took us four of the five years, so now we're into our third plan even though we've only been here nine or ten years.

Elwood won't be dissuaded from his vision of Premier League soccer for Stockport, and can see no reason why County can't pull in crowds of 25,000 by the next millennium. Firstly though, the infrastructure has to be put into place.

> You've got to create an environment and a stadium that can sustain a team in the first division, let alone the Premier League. With what we've got now we'd do well to hold on to our newly acquired status. If we can carry on with the current development, though, then as far as I'm concerned the sky's the limit. And at Edgeley Park there just so happens to be an opportunity to expand.

The magnificent 5,000-seater Cheadle End Stand is a perfect example of what can be done with vision and plenty of money. It's not so long since the same section of the ground was covered by a low-level wooden structure that looked like an elongated potting shed. Had County failed to find a team to match the ground improvements, then the Cheadle End Stand could have been the most expensive windbreak in the North-West. If Elwood gets his way and his enthusiasm doesn't run out, then the rest of Edgeley Park, County's home since 1902, will eventually be modernised along the same lines.

> There is the potential to redevelop Edgeley Park to incorporate a 20,000-seater stadium with sports and leisure facilities attached. At the moment I am prepared to put in the money to acquire the land needed. And it is a feasible proposition. It can

be done: just look at Wimbledon. Barnsley have done it too, and they're no bigger a club than us. It may have sounded stupid a couple of years ago, but not now.

We still have to be careful not to become one of those teams that go up and come straight back down again. The main thing is to stay in the first division and then make progress. What I don't want to find is that it starts to become too difficult. I've had £1 million invested in Stockport over the years and I've probably lost another £1 million in interest. Stockport County has been a labour of love, but it has been a costly one both in terms of time and finance. As I've said, I haven't received a penny interest. Maybe when it's time for me to go, someone will come along and pay me back what I'm owed. I would certainly be happy with that, providing

the person involved demonstrates to me he has the ability and resources to continue what we started.

After the departures of Jones and his right-hand man John Sainty to the Dell, nothing can be certain. Elwood, though, isn't currently looking for buyers for his stake. Instead, he's seeking further co-operation with the local council and the possibility of acquiring three pockets of land that would see the continued growth of Edgeley Park.

It's taken a long time to get the confidence of the council. We've had to prove ourselves, and we've been proving ourselves over a number of years, but they're now conscious of the benefits this club is providing for the town and the people and they

CAUGHT IN THE CELEBRATIONS: ELWOOD IN STOCKPORT TOWN CENTRE AS FANS COME OUT TO CHEER

DES HINKS

have an obligation to ensure that this success continues. They've agreed to sell us or lease the Booth Street Depot: we don't mind which. It's not in the right position for its present use and, in principle, they've agreed to move. They have an obligation to obtain the market value for it, but they can also take into account environmental and community considerations.

Then there's the British Rail site. It's available and not wanted by British Rail, and it's landlocked and doesn't have a great commercial value. To us, though, it does have a useful marriage value. We would pay BR a reasonable price for it, which

and Manchester City play on the same afternoon. I'm convinced twenty per cent must have come from the borough of Stockport.

No club has made greater strides to interest the next generation of soccer devotees than County. Elwood estimates thirty per cent of the average attendance is made up of what he describes as 'young people'. 'A lot of our support in the past was never replaced or simply died off.' Many youngsters have been attracted after taking advantage of free tickets issued through local primary schools, and it's

FOCUS ON ELWOOD IN THE *STOCKPORT EXPRESS* PROMOTION SPECIAL

would only leave the rehousing of the local Labour Club. Again, in principle, they've agreed to being relocated, and we're certainly happy enough to provide better or alternative accommodation for them. Providing those three parcels can be obtained, then the redevelopment of Edgeley Park can progress.

Stockport has a population of 300,000 and can support a Premier League team. Last season, 87,000 people watched Manchester United

the club's intention to invite every primary school in Stockport to a game free of charge for the coming '97–'98 season. The youth policy is also making great strides on the pitch.

When Danny Bergara was here he didn't believe in a youth policy. However, when Dave Jones took over, I set about changing things. I told him I was happy to pay for the coaches, the managers and the pitches to get a youth scheme off and running. We're still behind the likes of Crewe and Wrexham, but we're catching up fast: we've got teams right down to under-9s level and, if it wasn't for Stockport's youth side, Manchester United wouldn't have been able to complete the grand slam like they did: we handed them the title after beating their nearest challengers, City and Liverpool, in the closing weeks of the season. Our Centre of Excellence is attracting youngsters who are choosing to come to County rather than go to Man. United or Liverpool.

Elwood would also like to give the apprentices and the YTS trainees an academic as well as a soccer education. With that in mind, he talked of purchasing Stockport College when it closes in 1999.

It would be a North-West football academy with all the necessary facilities under one roof. There's so much we can do providing, as I've said before, it doesn't become too difficult.

The loss of his managerial team was a body blow, but who is to say Jones's successor Gary Megson — aided by ex-Chester boss Harry McNally and Manchester United star Michael Phelan — won't make an even better fist of the job. And, whenever he gets moments of self-doubt, Elwood should cast his mind back to the night of April 28th when the dream became reality. 'It's the greatest feeling I've had in my life,' he said at the time, 'outside the obvious, like becoming a father. Never has the euphoria lasted this long. At no time did I think we'd cracked it. The pressure got to me in the end.'

All the emotion and tension came flooding out. He raced half the length of the pitch, defying mud and driving rain to join the impromptu on-pitch party: *Only one Brendan Elwood*, sang the fans.

It's moments like that that make it all worthwhile. You keep in the background and just get on with your work. You don't ask for thanks, but you know when the supporters chant your name like they did that night, the effort was worth it. No one can fail to be humble and modest and touched by a show of appreciation like that. It's sixty years since County were last in the old Division 2, so let's enjoy it.

DES HINKS

THE SQUAD AT THE START OF THE SEASON.

BACK ROW, LEFT TO RIGHT: ALUN ARMSTRONG, JIM GANNON, MATT BOUND, RICHARD WILLIAMS, PAUL JONES, NEIL EDWARDS, RICHARD LANDON, TONY DINNING, ADIE MIKE.

MIDDLE ROW: RODGER WYLDE (PHYSIO), JEFF ECKHARDT, PAUL JONES, LEA JONES, DAMON SEARLE, TOM BENNETT, JOHN JEFFERS, SEAN CONNELLY, JOE JAKUB (COACH).

FRONT ROW: ANDY MUTCH, KIERON DURKAN, CHRIS MARSDEN, DAVE JONES (MANAGER), MIKE FLYNN, PAUL WARE, LEE TODD.

2 August

● CREWE CUT ● CHERRY PICKERS ● BRISTOL FASHION

GARETH SOUTHGATE MAY have missed *that* penalty and England may have lost out to Germany once more, but the 1996–97 season was one of the most eagerly anticipated campaigns for many a year, with the arrival of soccer's Foreign Legion and the BSkyB brass thrusting the national game even more into the spotlight. Everyone was still buzzing from Euro '96: the sensational victory by El Tel's stars over Holland and the near-miss against the eventual champions suggested good times ahead for England and the sport. The feel-good factor permeated right down to the second division and Stockport County, as even they had taken their

pick from the continental assortment of players on offer, bringing to England winger Luis Miguel Cavaco.

OK, so the previous season hadn't been much to crow about, the team finishing ninth after pushing for a play-off place for most of the season. But there was a genuine mood of optimism about Edgeley Park as the opening match at Crewe Alexandra approached, with much of the enthusiasm based on the pre-season results where County had impressed against teams from Belenenses to Birmingham.

So, the strains of the Euro '96 anthem 'Football's Coming Home' could still be heard as Dave Jones's team kicked off their preparations at St

SOAKING UP THE RAYS: THE TEAM ENJOY SOME PRE-SEASON RELAXATION IN PORTUGAL.

DES HINKS

Helens Town on July 20th. Few of the Hatters' fans who witnessed a 4–0 victory with goals from Matthew Bound, Kieron Durkan, Chris Marsden and Richard Landon could then imagine the journey of adventure that was about to take place. Three days later, Conference side Morecambe went the same way as the Saints, thanks to Paul Ware and Alun Armstrong hitting the target at Christie Park.

Already a significant incident had taken place, although it wasn't until much later in the season that the full impact hit home. 'Keeper Neil Edwards had few critics among the supporters, and indeed had picked up the Player of the Year award for the previous season. So, there were one or two raised eyebrows when Jones moved in to sign namesake Paul, given a free transfer by Mark McGhee at Wolves. The arrival of the one-time Shropshire Schools centre-half obviously meant Edwards faced serious competition for the number one slot, and his cause wasn't helped by an elbow injury sustained at St Helens. The 6'3" Jones took over against Morecambe, went on the pre-season tour of Portugal and came back as undisputed man in possession.

> I knew I would have to work really hard to get an opportunity in the team. As it turned out, Neil's injury meant I got the chance a lot earlier than I expected. To be honest, I didn't know too much about Stockport, but my old pal Andy Mutch got in touch and really sold the club to me. When I visited the club, it became clear there was a buzz about the place and it didn't take me long to make up my mind to sign.

Next stop after Lancashire was Lisbon for a three-match tour of Portugal. This was a sharp contrast indeed to pre-season life under Danny Bergara, whose idea of burning off the excess summer poundage was to take the squad to an army assault course! A ten-hour delay at Gatwick Airport didn't get the trip off on the correct note, but once in the land of Eusebio and Benfica, the mood changed.

'It turned out to be the finest preparation any side could hope for,' said manager Jones at the time. 'The training facilities were excellent, our opponents were of high standard and the hotel staff and management looked after us like royalty.' It was certainly a warm-up tour in every sense of the word. Training started at 8 am because

STOCKPORT EXPRESS

NEW 'KEEPER PAUL JONES

CAPTAIN FLYNN AGAINST PORTUGUESE SIDE BELENENSES

of the heat and ended — following a midday siesta by the pool — late in the afternoon. 'We were just far enough away from the bars to resist temptation,' grinned skipper Mike Flynn. 'Even Toddy managed to resist it.'

The opening match, on paper, promised to be the toughest. Belenenses were three-times Portuguese Cup winners and the only team apart from the big three of Benfica, Sporting Lisbon and FC Porto to have won the league title. As it turned out, County won the game in the 40,000-seater Estadio Restella Stadium with a goal in the second period from ex-Manchester City striker Adie Mike.

Game number two took the club to Torres Verda, forty miles north of the capital for a fixture with VSCU Toriense, and those spectators who had partaken of too much local brew were mightily confused by County's latest line-up. Goalkeeper Faquinhas was just one of six local trialists who wore Stockport colours, none of which was the future signing Cavaco. It was hardly surprising, then, that the hosts won 2–1 with a consolation from Jeff Eckhardt, later to join Cardiff City. Eckhardt found the net in the final game against VFC Alverca but, like an effort from Armstrong, it was disallowed. The contest was decided by a 14th-minute goal from Rui Vicoria.

Another ten-hour delay marked the return home, giving County little time off before the visit of Birmingham City and their £1-million skipper Steve Bruce. It didn't make any difference and a strong Blues outfit were despatched 4–0. County were 3–0 up at the break through Armstrong, Andy Mutch and Mike Flynn, with Geordie boy Armstrong adding the fourth in the second period. 'Birmingham were

STEVE SOUTHART

STEVE SOUTHART

TOM BENNETT (ABOVE),
ANDY MUTCH
(ABOVE RIGHT) AND
SEAN CONNELLY (RIGHT)

STEVE SOUTHART

STOCKPORT EXPRESS

GOAL MACHINES
ANDY MUTCH (LEFT)
AND ALUN
ARMSTRONG
(BELOW)

STOCKPORT EXPRESS

STEVE SOUTHART

PORTUGUESE STAR CAVACO:
INTRODUCED INTO THE ENGLISH WAY OF LIFE

Tranmere fared little better than their first-division colleagues. Flynn and John Jeffers joined in the act as County left Prenton Park 3–2 victors. 'I just hoped I haven't peaked too early because I don't normally score twice before Christmas,' quipped Flynn. 'It was clear Tranmere didn't want to lose,' recalled Jones. 'They brought in new signing Ivan Bennetti, but we worked hard and revealed the perfect attitude on the night.' With the shadow first team defeating Grove United and Woodley United 2–1 and 5–1 respectively, the scene was set perfectly for the big kick-off at Gresty Road, Crewe.

What a let-down it proved to be. Things began badly when *Stockport Express* sports editor Matt Horn arrived at the Crewe Alexandra ground without his famous hat. As for the action, it was almost non-existent. County didn't create any chances, let alone miss any. Dario Gradi's talented crop of youngsters eventually made them pay with a header from Fran Tierney sixty seconds from the end, after some sloppy defending down the visitors' left, up to which point the Cheshire rivals had been on course for their first goalless draw in 55 games. 'To be honest I don't think either side deserved to win,' explained Jones as County slipped to their first opening day defeat since a 2–0 reverse against Swansea in 1987. 'A draw would have been the fairest result, but they stole it in the end and that's something we've done many times in the past. We didn't play well, and things will even themselves out as the season progresses.' 'It was a bad game for us to start with,' added Espley. 'Had we begun with an easy match at home, things might have turned out differently, but that defeat at Crewe knocked our confidence.'

awful and thought they only had to turn up to win,' smiled Dave Espley, editor of County's highly rated fanzine, *The Tea Party*. 'We took them apart.'

Armstrong, the former Newcastle cast-off with a growing reputation, made it three goals in two games as

Before the next match — a first-round first-leg Coca-Cola Cup tie with John Duncan's Chesterfield — there was plenty of activity behind the scenes with the arrivals of Cavaco from Estoril and Brett Angell on loan from Sunderland, plus the departure for £30,000 of Jeff Eckhardt to Ninian Park. Twenty-year-old Marcus Hallows also came from Bolton on the recommendation of youth team boss Joe Jakub. 'Jeff was offered a three-year deal, so we could not stand in his way,' said Jones.

A twelve-month contract was offered to newly-wed Cavaco, with Jones musing:

> We know he has ability, it is just a question of seeing if he can adapt. The language will certainly be no problem as he has worked hard on his English and speaks it well. Under the old system, Luis would have cost us around about £200,000, but because of the Bosman affair we got him on what is technically a free transfer.

Cavaco, 23, was soon introduced to the English way of life: being taken for a curry by marketing manager Steve Bellis! 'All I can say is that I prefer Chinese food better,' he opined later.

On prodigal son Angell, the boss announced: 'I made no secret of my intention to find another striker and the forwards now must battle it out amongst themselves.' Angell was substitute against the Derbyshire visitors, who included ex-Edgeley Park favourite Chris Beaumont, who left after seven years' service for £25,000. With Andy Mutch scoring in each half, the return at Saltergate was looking like a formality until Bootle referee George Cain took it upon himself to throw the tie back in the melting pot, dismissing centre-half Matt Bound.

MATT BOUND: THE 1995–96 PLAYER OF THE YEAR TAKES AN EARLY BATH AGAINST CHESTERFIELD.

The resulting penalty whistled past Paul Jones.

'Matt won the ball and the referee made his decision from forty yards away,' stormed Jones. 'He did so ignoring his assistant referee who was 25 yards nearer and didn't give it.' Bound, who had undergone a hernia operation in the summer, also pleaded his innocence. 'When I challenged Kevin Davies I was pretty sure I got the ball

fairly. I swung a leg and made contact with the ball, but the referee claimed it was a goal-scoring opportunity and I had to go off. You can't print what I said in response but it wasn't "OK, pal, I'll see you later." '

The first Nationwide League home game of the season against Notts County yielded the first point, but still no goal. Bound, however, got his hand on a piece of silverware before the match with the Magpies. The ex-Southampton defender was voted 1995–96 Player of the Year by the computer wizards who put County on the Internet. Another award went to the uncomplaining Edwards, who made a welcome appearance at half-time to collect a special honour from Lancashire Dairies. The 'Superlife Award' had been created to give recognition to community members who had made great efforts to improve the life of others, and the 25-year-old Welshman fitted the bill, having undertaken more community duties the previous season than any of his colleagues, while also running his own soccer schools. 'It's always nice to be acknowledged this way but at the end of the day I would swap any awards for a first-team shirt,' said the ex-Leeds United starlet. 'I was unlucky with the injury, but all credit to Jonesy: he has done brilliant for us. It's up to me to maintain my form for when my next chance arrives.' Edwards, however, wasn't to start a first-team game until February 4th!

A midweek game against Bournemouth attracted one of the lowest league games of the season to Edgeley Park, and the 3,446 who came expecting 'Cherry' pickings against Mel Machin's team suffered another frustrating ninety minutes. The only side to score were Bournemouth, thanks to a spectacular overhead kick.

JOHN JEFFERS:
EXQUISITE GOAL AGAINST BRISTOL ROVERS

With their latest shut-out, County had equalled an unwanted record of three goalless league games to start a season, matching the all-time lows of 1969 and 1986. In comparison, the Reserves had no trouble beating the opposition keeper. Their opening Pontin's League fixture with Mansfield yielded nine goals, five of them from County. Cavaco marked his debut with a 30th-minute equaliser after the Stags took an unexpected 2–0 lead. Hallows and Richard Landon each bagged a double in an eventful ninety minutes.

The senior side couldn't emulate the nap hand, but they at least managed one in the final game of August. The trip to Bristol Rovers on the last day of the month was a historic one, marking Rovers' return to the city after a ten-year exile at Twerton Park, Bath. However, it was to the Memorial Ground, home of Bristol Rugby Union club, rather than to Rovers' former base at Eastville that County journeyed.

Already under pressure to find a winning formula, Jones responded by axing Armstrong, Chris Marsden, John Jeffers and Kieron Durkan. Replacing them were Mutch and three players making their first full appearances of the term: Cavaco, Jim Gannon and Paul Ware. The contest was memorable for many things, including a set of goals that appeared to be higher than those at the other end of the pitch, some suspect temporary dressing rooms, endless renditions of 'Football's Coming Home', and an exquisite equaliser from JJ. Jeffers replaced

ANDY MUTCH SCORES AGAINST CHESTERFIELD . . .

. . . AND CELEBRATES.

Bound at half-time as Jones shuffled his hand, and seventeen minutes from the end the former Port Vale winger delivered the goods. His superb curling shot cancelled out the Pirates' early first-half opener from Lee Archer and he went close to nicking an away win in the final frantic moments.

Left-back Lee Todd also might have snatched the winner after replacing the tiring Cavaco. Todd had been forced to sit out the opening month after losing his place to Welsh Under-21 international Damon Searle, which prompted speculation in the media that Todd was on his way to Rochdale. 'Nonsense,' retorted Jones, 'Toddy is very much part of the first-team set-up and besides, Rochdale couldn't afford him.' Twelve months later, Todd is adapting to life in the Premier League spotlight rather than life at Spotland.

'JJ knew he had not been playing well,' said Flynn of the Bristol outing. 'But he hadn't expected to be dropped

STEVE SOUTHART

ARMSTRONG LOSES AN AERIAL BATTLE VERSUS CREWE.

so soon. When he was brought on, he was determined to make amends. He finished up scoring a great goal and in the end we were a little disappointed not to get all three.'

Photographic evidence later proved Paul Jones's claim that the Memorial Ground posts were indeed higher than the regulation eight feet. However, as the manager pointed out: 'The big fella might be right, but don't forget JJ scored with a shot into the top corner in the same goal.'

So ended a month of under-achievement. County finished in 22nd spot with a league record of:

P	W	D	L	F	A	Pts
4	0	2	2	1	3	2

In the words of assistant manager John Sainty:

> We didn't make the start we had wished for, especially after our well-documented pre-season results. Maybe we got a little complacent thinking that things would happen for us without working for them. That, though, is a very dangerous attitude in football. If you don't work hard you get smacked in the face, as we found out to our cost. At least we turned the corner against Bristol Rovers, but things still weren't the way we wanted them.

Elsewhere, Danny Bergara — released by Sheffield Wednesday during the close season — had gone to Darlington as assistant manager. That move didn't work out and he resigned at the end of the month following disagreements with the third-division club's management.

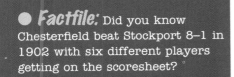

3 September

MATT BOUND'S SPOT OF bother at Edgeley Park in the first leg of the Coca-Cola Cup meant he had to sit out the return at Saltergate on September 3rd. Like Neil Edwards's unfortunate injury in the very first pre-season game, this one incident was to haunt him for the rest of the campaign. Bound's place went to Jim Gannon, who had played his first match of the season at Bristol wearing the number seven shirt. While Gannon became a permanent fixture in the side — and in fact turned County's season round later in the month — Bound managed only more full game.

It had been over twenty years since this writer's last trip to Saltergate, requiring me to ask directions to the ground. I do remember the last visit had been part of a Derbyshire day out, including a sightseeing tour of the splendid Hardwick Hall just down the road. Later I watched the Spireites play Millwall whose team included a lively left-winger by the name of Gordon Hill! The ground looked to have changed little, if at all, since the 1970s, though it wasn't quite as mediaeval as Hardwick Hall. No one, however, could

STEVE SOUTHART

JIM GANNON: CLAIMED THE NUMBER 6 SHIRT FOR HIS OWN.

● *Factfile:* Did you know Chesterfield beat Stockport 8–1 in 1902 with six different players getting on the scoresheet?

have predicted that this game was to feature two of the most unlikely cup giant-killers of recent years as the season unfolded.

County looked lively and more creative than in recent outings. As so often happens, though, they failed to

STEVE SOUTHART

'MAZZA': TEMPERAMENTAL START TO THE SEASON

'It was a good goal,' agreed Ware, now readjusting to life in the Vauxhall Conference with Hednesford United. 'But the one I got at Carlisle the previous season gave me greater satisfaction.' 'In the first half we discovered some of our pre-season form and were all over them,' confirmed Mike Flynn. 'We were unlucky not to go in at least a couple of goals ahead at half-time. It was a real kick in the teeth when Chesterfield took the lead. On another day our heads might have dropped, but the team believe in their ability and we battled on to get our reward.'

The following Saturday, County hit the road again for their third successive away game. Watford were among the fancied teams for promotion, although the managerial combination of Kenny Jackett and Graham Taylor hadn't got the Hornets buzzing as much as they'd hoped. Fearing long delays on the M6 or M1, myself, Matt Horn and Paul Rooney from GMR set off bright and early. For once, there was no news of any queues and we arrived at Vicarage Road for County's first visit since 13th January 1978 well before the turnstiles were open. The ground is first-division standard, probably even Premier-League quality. Presumably though, the allotment behind the stadium is where they get their home-grown players from!

With time to kill before kick-off, we upheld journalistic tradition by adjourning to the local hostelry. The beer wasn't too bad and the natives quizzingly friendly, but the pre-match entertainment wasn't to our liking. September 7th was the date of the NatWest Trophy final and Lancashire were, at the time, getting well turned over by Essex. A few scoops and a healthy pre-match meal of chips set us

convert a bagful of early opportunities and Chesterfield eventually took the lead through Steve Gaughan to bring the tie level on aggregate. Dave Jones was later to claim he felt his team were always likely to prevail, but not everyone sitting in one of the most cramped press boxes in the league shared his optimism. The doubters needn't have fretted. Paul Ware drove in a second-half thirty-yard grass-trimmer and Andy Mutch settled the issue late on to give County a 4–2 aggregate success.

up for the action. The game, however, was flat as the beer and as soggy as the chips. Sean Connelly, Paul Ware and Tom Bennett were all booked, and another dubious penalty was awarded against Paul Jones. Converted by Tommy Mooney, it provided Watford with a 1–0 victory — the same result as eighteen years earlier.

'The ball was played in and clipped off my chest,' said Flynn, playing his 150th league game for the club. 'But Jonesy had already come out for it and he collided with Devon White. It was a complete accident and White would never have got near the ball.' Dave Jones's response was:

> We didn't look like scoring and we didn't create any chances. The players have got to produce better and roll up their sleeves. I can't blame the fans for moaning, they are entitled to, especially when they see such a contrast from one game to the next. It's baffling for everyone when we play well one game and then dip the next. There is enough talent at the club to overcome the present situation, but the players are not playing to the best of their ability.

The return trip from Watford was only made more palatable by news of Lancashire's amazing Glenn Chapple-inspired recovery at Lords to confirm the Red Rose County as one-day cup kings.

With a home game against Wrexham four days away, County, in cricketing parlance, were on a sticky wicket. The players watched a re-run of the Watford game on video — it was X-rated stuff! Just about the only player looking forward to the Welshmen's visit was ex-Racecourse favourite Kieron Durkan. 'I spent eight years at Wrexham and, though I was surprised by Stockport's interest, I had no regrets at moving. As it happens, my last appearances for Wrexham were both against County.'

Durkan began the game on the bench but was introduced into the fray as County lurched from bad to rock bottom. Brian Flynn's team finished 2–0 victors, pushing the home side down to 23rd place. Man of the Match Peter Ward, a fine servant for County but happy enough to help his new side to victory, admitted: 'On paper County look a very good side and I don't know why things are going wrong for them.' Chris Marsden completed a black night for the Hatters by getting himself red-carded; 'Mazza' had arrived the previous season with a reputation as a fine player but one whose temper often let him down, and in these first eight games of the season the ex-Huddersfield, Notts County and Wolves player seemed content to kick the opposition more than the ball.

The abuse from the fans on September 10th told its own story. Said the chairman:

> That night there were the first soundings of 'Elwood out'. It came from a small section of the supporters and, to their credit, a larger section shouted them down. But there was no question: we were under pressure. In retrospect, Wrexham did us the biggest favour they could possibly have done. They hammered us good style and it really brought it home to use that pre-season counted for nothing. From that night no one hammered us again.

> The results were a shock to the system. The players knew they were good players, but they had to do the business. We'd built a team of first-division players on first-division wages, but we were at the bottom of the second division. Our wage bill was far above the income coming in. If it had all gone pear-shaped, I'd have been left with a £1-million-to-

STEVE SOUTHART

THE CENTRE-HALF PAIRING THAT
KICKED OFF THE SEASON: MIKE
FLYNN (ABOVE) AND MATT BOUND

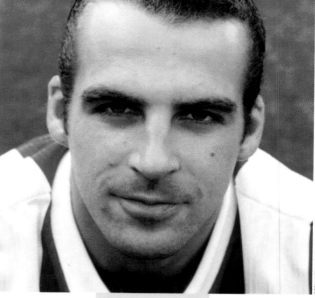

STOCKPORT EXPRESS

STOCKPORT COUNTY FC
THE FRIENDLY FOOTBALL CLUB

DES HINKS

STEVE SOUTHART

FURTHER CELEBRATIONS, THIS TIME AGAINST SHEFFIELD UNITED AT BRAMALL LANE AS THE BLADES ARE EMPHATICALLY OUSTED FROM THE COCA-COLA CUP: JUBILANT ALUN ARMSTRONG (ABOVE AND RIGHT) AND LEE TODD (TOP RIGHT)

STEVE SOUTHART

£1.5-million deficit which I, as owner of the club, would have had to pick up. Before the season, Dave said he wanted better players but fewer of them. As we all know, the road to hell is filled with good intentions. As things stood, we still had 24 professionals on our books.

There was much soul-searching following the Wrexham debacle with theories being put forward for the decline. Said Flynn:

> We need to be more direct. It's OK keeping the ball but we are not going anywhere. Against Wrexham we were on the attack and it broke down. Within seconds they went up the other end and scored. When it's the other way round, it takes us five minutes to create an attack. It's not fair blaming the forwards because they are not getting any service.

As Matt Horn wrote: 'The failure to find the opposing net is no longer a statistical freak, it's an embarrassment.' Whatever the reason, the knives were out for Dave Jones. Dave Espley confirmed:

> I heard a rumour that Jones was on his way out if we lost the next match. Up to that point he hadn't really proved himself as a manager. He had the butt-end of a season when Bergara left and one full season when we under-achieved. People were talking about us going down. I never thought that and I expected us to pull away. I even though promotion was a possibility, though I reckoned we'd have to go through the play-offs again.

A cup of tea, it is said, is the best drink of the day. It certainly was on September 11th when Jones called an emergency meeting with his seven senior professionals, which he described to the press as 'a chat over a cup of tea', making it clear that it was not going to be a slanging match. 'We talked for two hours, discussed what we thought was going wrong and then set about rectifying it,' announced Jones prior to the next game with Plymouth. The manager also had talks with Elwood, giving rise to speculation that his job was on the line. 'I've never jumped on a manager before, but suddenly we have a mini-crisis on our hands and it's imperative we start producing some results. Everything has become a bit too cosy. Dave and myself had a good heart-to-heart,' the chairman confirmed. 'There's no secret about that. We tried to analyse everything that had gone wrong and we came to the same conclusions.'

Part of the solution was to gamble on Brett Angell. Still not match-sharp, he started the make-or-break game with Plymouth. Jones's other major gambit was to revert to the full-back pairing of Connelly and Lee Todd. Before sending out his troops, beleaguered Jones issued a rallying call: 'We have spent a lot of time talking about our problems but now it is time to act. We have got to find men prepared to roll up their sleeves and battle to get out of a hole we have dug for ourselves.' Damon Searle, the summer signing from Cardiff, was axed to find himself out in the wilderness for the remainder of the season.

Newly promoted Argyle, under Neil Warnock, later to take Oldham Athletic into Division 2, arrived riding high, including a 2–0 win at Watford and a 4–4 draw with Wrexham. Leading scorer Adrian Littlejohn, with three, boasted two more goals than the whole of County's line-up put together.

Goal-shy Stockport started with a record of finding the net just once in the previous 540 minutes, but within

57 seconds Jim Gannon had doubled that total. Ten minutes later from a second set-piece, the big Irishman made it 2–0 while Marsden thumped another effort against the woodwork. Gannon, however, quickly turned from hero to villain by giving away yet another contentious penalty, which was converted by Michael Evans. This time, though, the award wasn't costly and Alun Armstrong swooped after 51 minutes to loft the ball over Bruce Grobbelaar for a match-clinching third. At the conclusion of a 3–1 triumph, Armstrong admitted:

how hard we had worked when everyone came off looking shattered at the end. But how could the referee give a penalty when he was forty yards away? Surely, had it been a penalty, I would have been sent off or booked.' Jones added his own thoughts:

> We owed it to the fans and we owed it to ourselves. The chairman had a go at me in the week and told me what he expected. Hopefully we've given him what he wants. We've set the standards now we've got to keep them up.

THE PAPERS FINALLY HAD SOMETHING POSITIVE TO SAY ABOUT COUNTY'S SEASON.

just champion!

Jones joy as County get off mark at last

Stockport County 3 Plymouth 1

CRISIS what crisis? Stockport played like champs rather than chumps to give everyone at Edgeley Park a much-needed fillip.

"We owed it to the fans and we owed it to ourselves," said manager Dave Jones, arguably the happiest man on the ground.

Not far behind in the relief stakes was striker Alun Armstrong. His first goal of the season sealed County's opening victory of a campaign in danger of disintegrating with only half-a-dozen games gone.

"It's a weight off my shoulders" admitted Armstrong. "I was feeling the pressure but I knew if I got the chances I would score.

"Bruce (Grobbelaar) made it easy for me by coming off his line but I was just relieved to get the opportunities. We played them off the park but that's what we've got to do in every game."

Plymouth boss Neil Warnock agreed with Armstrong's verdict when he confessed: "We did well to keep it at three."

And after Jim Gannon struck twice in the opening 10 minutes and Chris Marsden also hit the woodwork a cricket score looked on the cards.

"You could tell how hard we had worked when everyone came off looking shattered at the end," said Gannon, also guilty of giving away a penalty that briefly let Plymouth back into the match.

"How could the referee see when he was 40 yards away," argued the Irish defender. "If it had been a foul surely I should have been booked or sent off."

Unlike the spot kick at Watford that cost County three points, this latest contentious award wasn't as expensive.

It would have been rough justice had it done so but perhaps it's the first sign of a welcome upturn in County's fortunes.

Gannon lifted the pressure with his

By Trevor Baxter

opening goal in 57 seconds and from another set piece move added a second ten minutes later.

It was hard to believe that this was the side that had managed to find the net just once in the previous 540 minutes.

Armstrong and Brett Angell, starting in place of the axed Andy Mutch, were a handful for Argyle's shaky back line.

Both deserve to get on the score sheet and Armstrong managed it, brushing aside a defenders challenge to cleverly loft the ball over Grobbelaar.

"The chairman had a go at me in the week and told me what he expected," added Jones. "Hopefully we've got him what he wanted. We've set the standards now we've got to keep them up."

STOCKPORT: Jones 7, Connelly 8, Todd 8, Bennett 7, Flynn 8, GANNON 9, Durkan 7, Marsden 8, Angel 7, Armstrong 8, Jeffers 7.

FORM GUIDE

■ GANNON FIRE . . . County's Jim Gannon beats Bruce Grobbelaar

MANCHESTER EVENING NEWS

> That goal was a weight off my shoulder. I was feeling the pressure but I knew if I got the chances I would score. Bruce made it easy for me by coming off his line, but I was just relieved to get the opportunities. We played them off the park, but that's what we've got to do in every game.

Joyful Gannon was another happy-but-tired County star. 'You could tell

Prophetic words indeed. A corner had been turned. The Plymouth match was the pivotal point of a season that was about to take off into a totally new plane.

County's reward for their cup success over Chesterfield was a meeting with Sheffield United. Two years earlier,

they'd been cut to ribbons by the Blades in the first leg of the corresponding stage, Kevin Francis scoring the goal, and the tie finishing 6–1 on aggregate. This time, however, there was to be a different outcome.

The links between the two clubs are strong ones. Apart from being Elwood's 'other team', Gannon, Marsden and Angell had had spells at Bramall Lane, Connelly actually hails from the Steel City, and assistant marketing manager Chris Jolley was once a Junior Blade!

County began as they had started against Plymouth and, thanks to Flynn and midfielder Tom Bennett, they were 2–0 up. Scotsman Bennett had been arguably one of the players not to fulfil his potential during the torrid start to the campaign. This was his first goal after three needless yellow cards. With a steadier eye in front of goal, County might have scored

more, but instead Dutchman Michel Vonk, a constant menace from set-pieces, pulled one back to give United hope of turning the tables on their own midden. Even so, manager Howard Kendall was forced to concede the first-division aristocrats had been savaged by the second-division alley cats.

Before County could complete the job, they had to journey to York for a league fixture. If you're a fan, there are far worse places to visit for a football match than the historic city, though it is debatable whether the average punter is interested in strolling around the Roman walls or visiting the Minster. In any case, the fixture provided an opportunity for a weekend outing for the writer's wife and border collie, although only the former attended the game — along with 3,061 others.

10-OUT-OF-10 MAN-OF-THE MATCH ALUN ARMSTRONG FINDS THE NET AT BRAMALL LANE.

DES HINKS

STEVE SOUTHART

MEMORY LANE: THE SCORERS GANNON, ANGELL, BENNETT AND TWO-GOAL ARMSTRONG

Mid-table York were preparing to welcome Everton in the Coca-Cola Cup, having drawn at Goodison Park in midweek, so they were hoping to beat County at Bootham Crescent for the first time since the 1988–89 campaign. And when former Oldham midfielder Neil Tolson registered a goal against the run of play, they looked a good bet. With the visitors in need of inspiration, Brett Angell provided it with his first goal since arriving on loan from Roker Park. And, like your local bus, having waited ages for one they come along in twos. A double inside three minutes gave the sub-editors their first chance to write the headline 'Angell Delight'.

The dream topping would have been a hat-trick, but somehow he contrived to make a hash of a late opening. The main criterion, however, was maximum points and a 2–1 success. That made it three wins in row for County. Crisis: what crisis?

What came next was, for me, one of County's best displays of the season. The victory at Middlesbrough was outstanding, so too the result at the Dell, but rarely did they overwhelm a team like they did Sheffield United. For those privileged to witness the game (even Signal Cheshire, but not Piccadilly, chose to send a reporter across the Pennines), County merited the

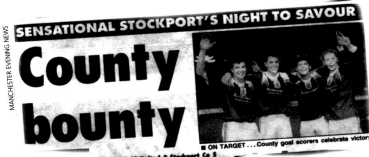

MANCHESTER EVENING NEWS

SENSATIONAL STOCKPORT'S NIGHT TO SAVOUR

County bounty

■ ON TARGET . . . County goal scorers celebrate victory

Sheffield United 2 Stockport Co 5

BOTH sets of fans left Bramall Lane shaking their heads in disbelief, after one of the greatest nights in County's history. Recent upsets over Ipswich and QPR, plus last son's epic FA Cup duels with Everton rank along ... five-star display. ...gallant failure against Manchester

standing ovation they received from both sets of supporters. Mind you, there weren't many Sheffield supporters left. A good number had set off for the exits by the time Bennett made it 3–0 after only 33 minutes.

The match finished 5–2 — 7–3 on aggregate — with Armstrong (2), Gannon and Angell grabbing the other goals. Armstrong produced a stunning display, notwithstanding his goals. In the *Manchester Evening News* the following night I felt justified in awarding him the perfect 10 out of 10. 'If Alun keeps playing like that, the big clubs will all be watching him,' said Flynn.

Elwood was ecstatic. 'When did you last hear County fans on an away ground against a team from a higher division, singing "We want six"? This is the best County performance I've ever seen,' he drooled. 'Quite unbelievable.' Jones refused to go overboard. 'This makes up for the hammering they gave us two years ago. But we've got to maintain this high standard, starting with Gillingham on Saturday.'

He needn't have worried. The Kent side showed little ball control and even less brawl control. Captain Andy Hassenthaler was sent off and five of his team-mates were yellow-carded as the home side notched a 2–1 win. Armstrong, plus an own-goal from Mark Morris, helped the club up to sixteenth position at the end of the month. The record read:

P	W	D	L	F	A	Pts
9	3	2	2	8	9	11

Way out in front at this stage were Dave Webb's Brentford; Crewe and Watford were tucked in behind, while Rotherham were the strongest team in the division because they were propping up the rest!

4 October

● *LIONS TAMED* ● *BARNES-STORMER* ● *WILD ROVERS*

ACCORDING TO THE HARDY souls who ventured south of the Thames on the night of October 2nd, the performance against Millwall matched — possibly surpassed — the display at Sheffield United. It certainly reaffirmed County's pre-season belief that they had the makings of one of the best teams in the division. The Lions, under Jimmy Nicholl, were also fancied to gain promotion and had made a far better start than their North-West visitors. They played their part in a rip-roaring ninety minutes, but had to concede — as did their motormouth celebrity fan Danny Baker — that this was County's night: a single goal out of seven separated the sides, but County should have won with room to spare.

'The win at Millwall really brought it home to me that we had a good team,' said *Tea Party* editor Dave Espley. 'We had five minutes of madness that almost cost us two points, but really we deserved that victory.' Indeed, had Kieron Durkan's 35-yard piledriver crossed the line rather than bouncing down off the bar, it might have finished 6- or 7–1. Durkan, now finding his form after an indifferent start to the term, had struck first in the 24th minute, courtesy of Brett Angell's cross. Northern Ireland international Anton Rogan squared the issue shortly afterwards and, though Alun Armstrong crashed one against a post, the main drama began to unfold after the interval.

On the hour Armstrong restored County's advantage from Chris Marsden's assist and, ninety seconds later, it was 3–1, thanks to reliable Jim Gannon. Then came Durkan's near-miss, and Millwall made the most of their reprieve with Rogan and substitute Paul Hartley obtaining parity for the Londoners.

The New Den — and the old Den for that matter — are and were intimidating places even when empty. The fear factor increases tenfold with 7,000 natives bellowing their allegiance to the cause with a famous comeback win in sight. To their laudable credit, County never wavered. Lee Todd attempted a Beckham-esque shot from near halfway and finally, in the dying embers, Armstrong applied the *coup de grâce* to Tom Bennett's approach play. It brought Armstrong's tally to six goals in as many games and also brought him to the attention of an interested spectator: Graeme Souness, then manager of Southampton.

That night Armstrong completely overshadowed another Kevin Keegan discard, Darren Huckerby, who, having graduated with some style to Premier League escapologists Coventry City, was then on loan at Millwall. 'People ask me whether I worry when I don't score,' says Armstrong. 'If the side is winning and creating chances I'm not too bothered. But it was a lot worse at the start of the season when we were drawing and losing as well as not making scoring opportunities.'

STEVE SOUTHART

CHRIS MARSDEN — 'MAZZA':
FEROCIOUS IN MIDFIELD

STEVE SOUTHART

WHO'S WHO? A SECOND LOOK NEEDED TO TELL THE
DIFFERENCE BETWEEN KIERON DURKAN (LEFT) AND
SEAN CONNELLY (RIGHT)

Two incidents before and after the game showed the good and ugly side of soccer fans. They could have happened at any ground, not just Millwall. With GMR man Paul Rooney unable to make the trip, Clubcall's Des Hinks, the utility man of the local press corps — Paul Madeley with a microphone, if you like —was asked to cover the game. Attempting to locate the New Den, he enquired directions from a local, who just happened to be a skinhead of gargantuan proportions. Although he may have looked like a one-man fist-fight waiting to kick off, instead he shepherded apprehensive Des, carrying his BBC gear, through the back streets, enabling him to broadcast on cue. However, the nutter that boarded the team coach after the match to try to assault Mike Flynn was no Mr Nice Guy. With a little persuasion from John Sainty, the idiot was removed.

The success at Millwall completed six straight victories for the Jones boys: what better record to take to old foes Burnley?

There are many understandable bitter rivalries in football: United–City, Rangers–Celtic, Liverpool–Everton, Arsenal–Spurs. But Burnley–Stockport? I'm convinced only the most blue-nosed County fan knows where the antagonism originated from, but make no mistake: games between the two are real grudge encounters. To shed light on the dispute I sought the counsel of Dave Espley again. It transpires the feuding is a modern-day phenomenon, according to Dave.

We played quite a few times in the 1980s having not met in the league at least for nearly fifty years. After one such visit to Turf Moor, Steve Bellis wrote an article in the local free sheet about how shabbily he'd been treated at the ground. Seemingly, a Burnley fan living in Stockport obtained a copy and it ended up being reproduced in the Burnley fanzine. I think there are a lot of other elements, but that was part of the reason why there is no love lost between the clubs.

Matches have rarely been dull or pretty. Chris Pearce and David Frain were sent off at Turf Moor in 1991, Chris Beaumont and Michael Wallace walked at Wembley three years later in the second-division play-off final, and I recollect an incident involving Ted McMinn at Edgeley Park when he claimed he'd been struck with something thrown from the crowd. It was against this backdrop of unpleasantness that the two teams squared up to each other on October 5th.

Burnley started on the back of three defeats and with £400,000-signing Paul Barnes without a goal in eight starts. It isn't difficult to predict what happened next: Burnley won 5–2 and Barnes scored all five! 'If you gave me the room he had I would have scored five,' stormed Dave Jones who later claimed, with some justification, that County created more chances. But it's goals that are entered in the record books.

The game was a nightmare for the defence, in particular Jim Gannon and Lee Todd who blundered their way through the debacle. 'It was only in the car driving back home we realised Barnes had got the lot,' sighed Espley. 'He was given a standing ovation when he came off before the end so we thought he'd probably got a hat-trick. But five!' Buoyant Burnley were 2–0 up at the interval and, though Brett Angell reduced the deficit after the break, County committed soccer suicide again. Barnes went on to bag three more with Andy Mutch finding the target for the first time in over a month. 'Stockport have generally been a lucky side for me,' grinned Heath, who marked his Burnley debut with a goal against the Hatters. 'It's a pity we can't play them every week.' Red-faced Mike Flynn grimaced at the memory:

> Thankfully it was just a one-off. It was really strange because at the start of the season we weren't letting in many goals but we couldn't score. At that time the situation had been reversed. Some strikers always seems to score against certain teams and Paul Barnes usually manages it against us.

Flynn had arrived at Edgeley Park for £150,000 from Preston and it was his old club who provided the opposition a week later. He confessed:

> I'll always have a soft spot for North End. They rescued my career when I was languishing in the reserves at Norwich. It was a good chance to move North again and I didn't have any hesitation. Along with Oldham, I always look for Preston's result.

> ● *Factfile:* Jim Gannon made his 250th league appearance for Stockport against 1995-96 third-division champions Preston.

Despite the defeat at Burnley, the Lilywhites attracted a crowd of 8,505, the best of the season up to that stage, and the majority left for home happy after Brett Angell pounced in a 1–0 win, his goal one of the quickest of the day. However, John Jeffers produced just as vital a touch with a goal-line clearance in the last minute. Joked Jones:

JJ had a random drugs test after the match and I hope it doesn't prove positive — I don't know what he was doing back there on his own line at that stage of the match!

I thought for the first half hour we had the jitters. Preston made things difficult but a clean sheet and a win is nice after the defeat at Burnley. Kizza [Kieron Durkan] and Alun had good chances just before half-time and had they gone in we could have relaxed a bit more.

For the attractive fixture against pace-setters Luton Town on October 15th, 3,000 County 'fans' deserted from the previous Saturday, though a good proportion had travelled down the M61 to swell the final figure. The stay-aways missed a treat with the other Hatters dominating the opening 45 minutes and County regaining the initiative in the second half. The game, the first between the sides at Edgeley Park since 1970, ended 1–1, with Angell earning a point with his sixth goal of the season. Ex-Burnleyite Steve Davies headed the opener.

Afterwards the press conference turned into a mutual appreciation society. 'Stockport are the best team we've played so far,' said Town boss Lennie Lawrence. 'Luton posed us more problems than any other side,' retorted Dave Jones. 'For the first half-hour I didn't think we were going to score, but in the end it was an entertaining game.' Lawrence was later to win the October Manager of the Month award, ahead of Jones, largely because of the savaging at Burnley.

While Luton were one of the division's upwardly-mobile squads, Wycombe Wanderers were among those in the drop zone. Ex-Crystal Palace manager Alan Smith had paid the price with his job for the poor start, and Neil Smillie was given the reins as caretaker coach. Rich pickings beckoned for the improving visitors to Adams Park on October 19th, a fixture that provided me with the perfect opportunity to tick off another ground on the trail of the '92 club'. I'd visited Wycombe's former home at sloping Loakes Park during my days as the *North Western Evening Mail*'s Barrow AFC correspondent, and it has to be said Adams Park was a great improvement, apart from the location, which is at the end of the only road through the local industrial estate. The neat stadium itself was beyond criticism, though the press seating arrangements appeared rather perverse: while I had been allocated a ticket on one side of the ground, Matt Horn and Clubcall's Des Hinks were seated directly opposite.

Named in Wycombe's line up was John Williams, whose claim to fame — apart from being an ex-postman with a tidy turn of speed (handy when it comes to running away from the neighbourhood Rottweiler) — was that he scored the first hat-trick at Adams Park since Wanderers' elevation to the Football League. No prizes for guessing the team on the receiving end: Stockport County, during their 4–1 defeat during 1995–96! However, there was no repeat of that result in a bizarre contest, played in constant drizzle.

County should have been 2–0 up inside ninety seconds with Andy Mutch, deputising for Armstrong, the culprit. Brett Angell finally breached the defence with his seventh goal in eight outings after seven minutes. Rather than the floodgates opening,

FLYNN DELIGHTS AS THE WHISTLE IS BLOWN ON PREMIER-LEAGUE BLACKBURN.

STOCKPORT EXPRESS

the only deluge was the number of corners County were forced to concede, with the final tally being something like 17–7 in the Buckinghamshire side's favour, but they couldn't break through. 'I don't think I've been in a game where we've defended so many corners,' was the boss's verdict.

It was left to Angell to show them how it should be done, while there was still time for Mutch to qualify for 'miss of the season'. Somehow he scooped a shot over the crossbar from directly on the goal-line. He later claimed he would have been offside, but the match officials would have allowed it to stand. Mutch was to lose his place next match, not because of his howler, but because Armstrong was fit again.

After getting the result at Wycombe, County could focus their attention on the next phase of the Coca-Cola Cup. For destroying Sheffield United, County deserved a home draw, but instead they were paired with Blackburn Rovers at Ewood Park. This time there wouldn't be two legs to decide the winner: this was where the real competition began, and many of the 4,253 County fans who flocked to the stadium that Jack built believed it was going to be County's night. Stockport fans, however, were somewhat taken aback when their team ran out of the tunnel. Because of a clash of colours, County had had to ditch both the home and away strips in favour of a Romania-style yellow and blue.

Rovers may have been a Premier League outfit, but their feared SAS strikeforce of Alan Shearer and Chris Sutton had long been broken up, a fact reflected in their lowly league position. All the ingredients were there for a cup shock, and in a week when the so-called minnows swallowed up the

■ FLASHPOINT . . . Blackburn's Tim Sherwood heads County's winner

MANCHESTER EVENING NEWS

County hit the jackpot

Blackburn Rovers 0 Stockport County 1

WHATEVER happens to County from now on in the Coca-Cola Cup, they can bask in the glory of last night's third-round victory over their moneybags neighbours.

True, the decider which plunged the Premiership whipping boys and their manager Ray Harford into deeper trouble was a bizarre own goal, but there was no denying County's right to go through.

As 4,000 fans whooped their way home to Stockport, some disenchanted Rovers' followers staged a fitful demonstration outside the VIP entrance.

Meanwhile, County manager David Jones was paying a glowing tribute to his troops.

"I'm not bothered that it was an own goal . . . don't forget it came from a long throw in by Mike Flynn which is all part of our set piece play.

"Then we had a purple patch of about 20 minutes in the second half when we could have had another goal or two."

In grim contrast, Harford had to fend off barbed questions about his future. His reply: "I'm not here to

By Mike Conrad

talk about me — let's talk about the game."

It was in the 22nd minute that Tim Sherwood, the Rovers' skipper, was credited with the goal which counted for County.

Flynn hurled the ball in with one of his prodigious throws and Tim Flowers, trying to knuckle it away, instead hit Sherwood on the back of the head.

The keeper could do nothing as the ball rebounded into the far corner of the net.

But there was no fluke in the way County kept grip on the game for a famous victory.

COUNTY: Jones 8, Connelly 7, FLYNN 9, Gannon 8, Todd 8, Durkan 8, Bennett 8, Marsden 8, Cavaco 7 (sub Searle 81 mins), Armstrong 6, Angell 8. Subs: Mutch and Edwards (Not used).

competition's bigger fishes, County didn't let Rovers wriggle off the hook. The only goal of the game after 23 minutes wouldn't have won any Goal-of-the-Season competitions, but none of the County contingent were complaining. Mike Flynn hurled one of his trademark long throws into the penalty area, Tim Flowers punched the ball at the near post and hit Tim Sherwood on the back of the head. The rebound looped back over the stranded Flowers, much to the joy of the away supporters.

County might have doubled or trebled their lead during a purple patch in the second half while Paul Jones completed several timely saves. Despite the best endeavours of both teams, there were no further goals and County were into the fourth round and the last sixteen for only the second time in the club's history. Dave Jones praised his team:

STOCKPORT EXPRESS

I couldn't throw enough bouquets at the lads because they were superb. I think overall we deserved the result. Our plans had gone well. We'd kept another clean sheet and we were in the next round. You couldn't ask for anything better. I'm not bothered that it was an own-goal. Don't forget it came from a long throw, which was all part of our set-piece play.

There was a word of praise for the fans: 'They made so much noise they gave me a headache,' added Jones.

Chairman Brendan Elwood speculated about the future: 'The big bucks will come if we get in the first division. There's a near-£2-million gold mine waiting there and promotion is the long-term aim.'

While County fans celebrated, the disenchanted Rovers fans staged a fitful demonstration outside the VIP entrance. This defeat did more than raise County's profile: it signalled the end of Ray Harford's solo reign at Ewood Park. 'I'm not here to talk about me, let's talk about the game' was his stern warning to the media.

County had been on the receiving end of a few dodgy penalty awards in the opening months of the season, but none were quite so controversial as that given by Steve Baines in County's 1–1 draw at Walsall in their next match. Baines, an ex-professional footballer, whose clubs numbered, among others, Walsall, adjudged Angell had held down Adrian Viveash. None of the Saddlers' players appealed, none of the home fans complained about the challenge and Mr Baines was in a minority of one. Kevin Wilson made the most of the gift and County trailed at half-time. Mr Baines had chances to even things up in the second period, but a blatant handball and a foul on Jim Gannon went unpunished.

TONY DINNING: ELEVENTH-HOUR GOAL

Walsall were a lively enough side and should perhaps have taken maximum points, especially when Kyle Lightbourne's header looked to have cross the line. Again, Mr Baines declined to intervene leaving Kieron Durkan to convert a Jeffers centre in the last seconds. It was the first time County hadn't won at the compact Bescot Stadium, but a point was gratefully accepted. On leaving the ground, a 'friend' was good enough to phone to inform me Man. United had just been beaten 6–3 at Southampton. And they weren't even wearing grey shirts!

County finally got their own penalty in the last game of the month — a third meeting with Chesterfield — and promptly missed it! Tom Bennett was the culprit as Billy Mercer saved well.

The night might have been a bad one for Bennett, but not for Tony Dinning. He came into the team as replacement for Jim Gannon who broke his wrist at Walsall and celebrated with another eleventh-hour goal. Chris Marsden played in the corner, Durkan flicked on and Dinning headed into an unguarded net for his only goal of the campaign. After several unfortunate goals in the wrong net the season before, Dinning had acquired the nickname 'Dinnin*OG*'. 'Tony has waited a long time for his chance,' said Jones. 'He's got the shirt, now it's up to the others to take it off him.'

County were now up to tenth position, with a record reading:

P	W	D	L	F	A	Pts
16	7	4	5	20	19	25

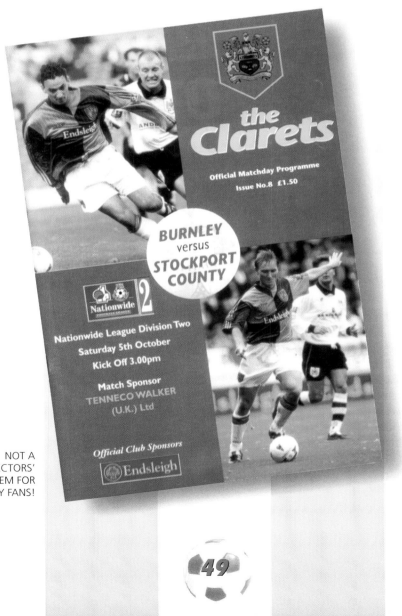

NOT A COLLECTORS' ITEM FOR COUNTY FANS!

STEVE SOUTHART

LIQUID REFRESHMENT: TOM BENNETT
(BELOW) TAKES A WELL-EARNED
BREATHER AND LEE TODD (RIGHT) IS
ON THE SOFT STUFF FOR A CHANGE.

STEVE SOUTHART

5 November

BRISTOL CITY ARRIVED AT Edgeley Park on November 2nd as the division's top scorers and, more significantly, unbeaten on the Stockport ground since 1913! They also came with a new player, utility man Clayton Blackmore, on a month's loan from Middlesbrough. Now Blackmore — dubbed 'Sunbed' in Old Trafford fanzines due to his year-round tan — was never the most skilful player to have pulled on a United jersey, but this Red Devils devotee will always have a soft spot for him. It was Blackmore's long-range free kick at Montpellier that took United into the European Cup Winners' Cup semi-finals, and it was his last-gasp goal-line clearance in the final against Barcelona that prevented the game going into extra time. So, even when I heard he'd been at the centre of a 'hand-of-God' goal, I still forgave him his sin. Even Dave Jones wasn't too bitter. 'We are not making an issue out of it. These things happen from time to time but it made our task that bit harder. The keeper is positive though that Blackmore handled and so was the rest of the defence.'

Blackmore's handiwork separated the sides until seven minutes from the end when a Flynn howitzer was the catalyst that enabled Tom Bennett to ensure County received their just desserts. A pulsating game also included a Sean Connelly strike that clattered back off an upright and a couple of stunning saves by Paul Jones.

STEVE SOUTHART

LUIS CAVACO STUNG THE BEES AT BRENTFORD WITH HIS FIRST GOAL FOR STOCKPORT.

STEVE SOUTHART

SEAN CONNELLY: THE WAIT GOES ON FOR HIS FIRST GOAL.

had been followed by fourteen winless journeys.

The afternoon was to take on a familiar look, but, after falling two goals adrift with only thirteen minutes remaining, a 2–2 draw was the best County dared hope for. Scott Canham and Nicky Forster netted for the hosts, Brett Angell and a jubilant Luis Cavaco replied for the Cheshire set. Super-sub Cavaco's first since his transfer from Estoril was well worth the wait, bypassing David McGhee and rifling home a sweet left-footer beyond the reach of Kevin Dearden. Angell's goal was his ninth of his loan stint and another timely nudge to Dave Jones to make his move a permanent one. Said Jones:

> We've got to learn to defend harder away from home. Naturally, we're pleased we fought back to draw, but I gave them a really hard time for putting themselves in that position in the first place. We always felt that once Luis scored we'd have a job catching him! At the moment we reckon he is more effective coming on as substitute, but once he gets a little stronger and more streetwise towards the English game you'll see a lot more of him.

Despite setting himself a bench-mark for the rest of the season, Cavaco was marking time on the bench for the opening venture into the 1996–97 FA Cup campaign. The giant-killers became Goliath for the arrival of Don-caster Rovers on November 16th, and momentarily the slayers were in dan-ger of being the slain. Colin Cramb put Kerry Dixon's third-division outfit in front after half-time when Lee Todd and John Jeffers suddenly forgot which way they were meant to be kicking. The chance still wasn't a formality, but Cramb displayed admirable composure

A trip to Brentford made it a tough start to the month for County. The Bees had slipped from top spot but were neatly tucked in behind new leaders Millwall. Griffin Park hasn't been a happy hunting ground for the Hatters and they weren't too upset when Crewe's play-off final victory back in May kept the Londoners in Division 2. A 4–1 triumph on their inaugural visit nearly forty years earlier

to run and slip the ball beyond Paul Jones.

It transpired the goal acted as a wake-up call to County. Within four minutes the tie was back in the balance. Mike Flynn had switched on Stockport town-centre Christmas lights during the week, but now he was pulling the plug on Donny's celebrations with a header from Marsden's corner. The winner was fit to grace the final itself with Andy Mutch sweeping home Kieron Durkan's cross for his first goal since September 3rd. Even then, Doncaster refused to surrender and Paul Jones twice stretched his 6'3" frame to the limit to thwart a replay at Belle Vue.

The game marked the first appearance of the season of Richard Landon who had recently declined a loan move to the Yorkshire club. 'It would be great if we didn't always leave ourselves so much to do,' acknowledged Paul Jones. 'But we've developed this never-say-die attitude and once again that came to our rescue.' Namesake Dave had been well aware how Doncaster would perform. 'We know how we've raised our game when we've played teams in higher leagues,' he said. 'The goal gave us the kick up the backside we needed. But full credit to Doncaster for having a go.'

Among the 4,211 spectators were three Edgeley Park veterans who had

SURVIVORS: THE TEAM THAT ENDURED ONE OF THE LONGEST MATCHES IN BRITISH FOOTBALL

STOCKPORT EXPRESS

played in one of the longest matches in British football: Colin Gleave, Ken Shaw and Arthur Burrows were members of the County team who had lined up against Doncaster in 1946, a game that went on for 203 minutes before bad light and exhaustion ended proceedings!

If the breaks weren't going County's way at the start of the season, there were few complaints after a game with Blackpool on November 19th which marked Lee Todd's 200th for the club in the league. Tom Bennett stole a victory that made it ten matches unbeaten, albeit with a classy finish. 'Pool, however, had good cause to lament 'We was robbed' against a County defence that was anything but rock-like. Three times they saw 'goals' chalked off and then had Micky Mellon red-carded for swearing. 'I'd like to know who was offside for the first that was wiped out,' said Tangerines red-faced boss Gary Megson. 'The second was disallowed for handball when our player headed in and the referee blew up too early to cancel the third.'

Jones knew his team had been fortunate. 'We've played better and lost,' he conceded. 'Sometimes, though, you have to battle and scrap it out to get results.' The match also marked the last game of Brett Angell's three-month loan period. Reported to be on £2,000 a week at Sunderland, a drop in wages would have to be agreed before a lasting deal could be struck. The much-travelled Angell clearly wanted to stay, and indicated as much in the programme for the Blackpool fixture: 'I'm thoroughly enjoying my time here and I can only hope the two clubs reach agreement. The support you have given me since my return has been incredible.'

In the next couple of days his wish was granted. Back in October 1988,

Angell had become the club's then record signing, Asa Hartford paying out £32,000 to bring the promising young striker from Derby. It was expected Dave Jones would have to do the same to bring him back to County. (Angell left for Southend after collecting the fourth division's Golden Boot award for 23 goals in 43 outings.) Instead, the amount being floated in the media was £120,000. If the final amount was correct, the figure represented a shrewd piece of business as Sunderland had paid £600,000 for him from Everton, who in turn had acquired him from Southend.

Now County are by no stretch of the imagination among the wealthiest clubs in the game. But it makes you think when Shrewsbury Town supremo Fred Davies — no, not the former snooker player — goes on record as saying 'Stockport are a team with a fair deal of financial clout. I can only imagine what it's like to be in David Jones's position.'

Angell immediately began repaying County's faith with a seventh-minute goal and Chris Marsden got his first of the season in a five-goal thriller at Shrewsbury. Unfortunately, Town replied with three, including a wonder-strike from Paul Evans to end County's unbeaten run. The normally phlegmatic Jones went into orbit: 'If you allow players to cross balls for fun you're going to get punished. When we got it back to 2–2 we should have kept it tight and we didn't. We let them off the hook.'

Angell, now on a two-and-a-half-year contract, insisted the forthcoming match against West Ham in the Coca-Cola Cup hadn't detracted from the team's display. 'If we want to achieve promotion we should be picking up three points at places like Shrewsbury.

Hopefully defeats like these are minor hiccups.' Angell also elaborated on his reasons for renewing his County ties. 'The club are ambitious and so am I. I feel I have come back to do the job I started six years ago. And that's to try and get us up.'

Angell wasn't the only one putting pen to paper. Alun Armstrong, Lee Todd, Sean Connelly and Mike Flynn all signed extensions to existing contracts. Flynn's deal tied him to County until 1999 and he wrote at the time:

> It wasn't a difficult decision because I enjoy playing here and I believe we are on the verge of success. Having said that, I was influenced by the decisions of others. When I saw the club were going to sign Brett and that players like Sean, Alun and Toddy were all going to sign I had to share that commitment.

Armstrong, reputed to be a target for Premier-League sides, received a one-year extension; full-backs Todd and Connelly signed until 1999.

Apart from the result, the trip to Shrewsbury was an enjoyable one. Like York, the city is agreeable and the locals friendly — with the exception of one character that GMR's Paul Rooney had the misfortune to meet. The terror of the tea bar made West Ham's notorious Inter-City 125 gang appear like choirboys in comparison on the occasion of County's next excursion into the Coca-Cola Cup. Rooney reveals all.

> I was waiting for the hut to open because I'd arrived too early as usual. I asked one of the stewards how long before it would be before it would open up. At that moment, the girl who was due to serve walked past. Jokingly I said: 'About time too, we're all freezing.' Without stopping, she turned round and told me to F-off. I was a bit taken aback, but then forgot

THE MUCH-TRAVELLED BRETT ANGELL: A BARGAIN BUY FOR HIS OLD CLUB

STOCKPORT EXPRESS

> all about it until later when the company secretary came to apologise and told me she'd been given her cards. I didn't mean to get her into trouble, but it's not on to swear at the man from the BBC!

As soon as the draw for the fourth round had been made, it revived happy memories for long-standing County die-hards and assistant manager John Sainty. 'I played in the same team as their manager Harry Redknapp at Bournemouth and I'd played against him when he was at

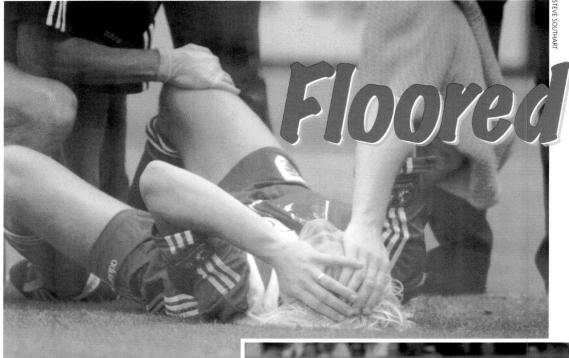

STEVE SOUTHART

Floored

THE AGONY: ARMSTRONG WRITHES IN PAIN AS HE RECEIVES ATTENTION FROM PHYSIO AND EX-SHEFFIELD WEDNESDAY STAR RODGER WYLDE.

STEVE SOUTHART

STEVE SOUTHART

Again!

DOWN AGAIN:
THIS TIME
AGAINST
BURNLEY, WYLDE
HELPS A DAZED-
LOOKING
ARMSTRONG TO
HIS FEET.

STEVE SOUTHART

STOCKPORT EXPRESS

CAVACO 'HAMMERS' HOME AT THE FIRST LEG AT UPTON PARK.

West Ham and I was at Spurs.' Sainty attracted a few quizzical looks when he explained: 'We had West Ham watched earlier in the same season but for no reason whatsoever.'

Stockport and West Ham had met 24 years earlier in the previous round, when over 13,000 saw Brian Doyle's upstarts dump the Hammers out of the old League Cup with goals from Mal Russell and Tommy Sword (penalty). Bermudan international Clyde Best replied for a visitors' team that included Bobby Moore, Trevor Brooking and Billy Bonds.

Would history repeat itself? For the first twenty minutes, it didn't seem so. Florian Raducioiu, United's £2.4-million Romanian star, gave them an early advantage, while Todd kicked another effort from Iain Dowie off the line.

Eventually, realisation began to dawn on County that their Cup bubble didn't have to burst. And when Dave Jones sent on Luis Cavaco for the second half, the tide began to turn. With compatriots Paulo Futre and Hugo Porfirio watching in the stands, County's own Portuguese man-of-war went to work. Having dispossessed Julian Dicks, normally not one of the most sensible things to do, Cavaco weaved his way past three defenders before striking a stinging equaliser beyond Ludek Miklosko. (If you had watched Granada Soccer Night for the briefest of highlights you would have heard the commentator award the goal to Tony Dinning!) Cavaco almost made a replay unnecessary, but Miklosko denied him another moment of glory.

However, the toast at Upton Park that night, in *vinho verde* rather than claret, was Luis Cavaco. 'To be honest, I thought we should have finished them off,' said Jones. 'Still, the chairman will be happy enough with a replay. I can't praise the boys highly enough and our supporters gave us a real boost.'

Opposite number Harry Redknapp, whose managership was already in jeopardy, was less content:

> We might still be in the competition where a lot of big teams have gone out. But how can I be satisfied with a draw at home to Stockport? Now I've got to look to the replay and pick a committed side who would be prepared to go up there and roll up their sleeves to get the result we need. Edgeley Park is a difficult place to win at.

Prophetic words indeed. The job was unfinished, but County went into the

hat for the quarter-finals for the first time since the tournament's inception in 1960, receiving the ideal pairing with either Oxford or Southampton.

Just over a month after leaving the Saddlers blazing due to a late point-stealer, County lined up against Walsall once more in the last game of the month. This time there was a marked improvement in the display and, after

MANCHESTER EVENING NEWS

ONE MAGIC MOMENT FROM SUPER-SUB HALTS LUCKY LONDONERS
Hammers foiled

West Ham 1 Stockport 1

AN inspired half-time substitution helped Stockport to a well-deserved draw at Upton Park.

Dave Jones brought on Louis Cavaco for the second half and the Portuguese striker scored after only three minutes with a superb solo effort to level the match.

"I'm very pleased with Louis," said Jones. "He's only been in the country for a few months but he's already started to settle in."

Cavaco took the ball off the feet of Julian Dicks 30 yards from the West Ham penalty area, made a dazzling run past three defenders and launched a blistering shot to beat Miklosko.

It was just reward for a fine Stockport performance. As early as the eighth minute, Durkan broke through on the edge of the box to deliver a stinging shot that had the West Ham keeper at full stretch.

Despite the positive start by the visitors, it was West Ham who scored with their first attack of the game, through Radciokis.

Stockport dug in and slowly dragged themselves back into the match. Gannon was only inches wide with a header inside the six yard box just before half time then manager Jones made the change that proved so decisive.

Cavaco followed up his equaliser with a swirling shot, five minutes later, that almost gave Stockport the lead.

Gannon came close again as the visitors finished strongly, prompting Jones to say after the match: "We could have won it.

"To be honest, I think we could have finished them off. Still, the chairman will be

happy with a replay I can't praise the boys highly enough. They battled well after going a goal down and I always felt we would get back into it."

Jones thanked the fans who had travelled down to London. "The support was tremendous, it really gave us a boost," he said. "Now we've got home advantage and that gives us every chance."

A disappointed Harry Redknapp admitted he didn't relish the replay at Edgeley Park. "It's a very difficult place to win," the West Ham manager conceded.

GOALS: West Ham - Radciokis 11 mins. Stockport - Cavaco 48 mins.

COUNTY: Jones 7, Connelly 7, Todd 7, Bennett 7, Flynn 6, Gannon 7, Durkan 6 (sub Dicking 80 mins), Marsden 8, Angell 7, Armstrong 7, Jeffers 8 (sub Cavaco 45 mins 8). Subs: Edwards (not used).

Brett Angell outwits Hammer Steve Potts

Special Angell

Stockport 2 Walsall 0

STOCKPORT County embark on the month that could make or break their season in the highest possible spirits.

After the midweek heroics at West Ham it would have been easy for them to rest on their laurels.

Instead they rode their luck early on to dominate a match and set themselves up for a testing programme of six league fixtures and games in three separate cup competitions.

"It's upwards and onwards," said star striker Brett Angell after claiming two more goals that take his tally to 12 in 16 outings.

"Our aim is to get in the first division next season and had we managed to turn more of our draws into three points we would have been right up there by now," added Angell.

"My move to Edgeley Park has been perfect for me and I hope things continue to go as well as they have been doing."

Angell despatched his first goal after 35 minutes with a right foot shot from the edge of the area after being faced with a one on one against keeper James Walker.

His second six minutes after half time came via a delightful cross from winger Kieron Durkan. "All I had to do was put my head to it and I couldn't really miss," added the former Sunderland striker, quickly repaying his £120,000 transfer fee.

After going 2-0 up it was just a question of how many more

Brett's double keeps County on course for title challenge

By Trevor Baxter

County might score. Twice they hit the woodwork and another chance was kicked off the line as the game progressed to its expected conclusion.

Angell might have completed a hat-trick late on but was just the wrong side of an upright with a smart shot on the turn.

"We needed that first half to get the West Ham game out of our system," said boss Dave Jones.

"But after half-time I thought we were in control and in charge. We could have had a few more goals but I'll settle for the three points."

There were plenty of plus points for Jones to enjoy. The flowing move that led to Tom Bennett hitting the woodwork, a couple of sensational saves by

Paul Jones and the form of Portuguese winger Louis Cavaco.

"He's got pace, ability and frightens defenders to death," said Jones.

Word is that 20-year-old midfielder Kiko from first division OS Belenenses is even better.

Cavaco's compatriot was at Edgeley Park to watch the game and to join the hundreds of other Continental assortments plying their trade in the English game.

And with such a heavy fixture list ahead Stockport need the strongest squad available if they're to stay in the chase for honours.

FORM GUIDE **COUNTY:** Jones 8, Connelly 7, Todd 7, Bennett 7, Flynn 7, Gannon 7, Durkan 7 (sub 77 mins Searle 7), Marsden 8, ANGELL 9, Armstrong 6, Cavaco 8.

GOAL ... Brett Angell celebrates his second strike

MANCHESTER EVENING NEWS

BY NOVEMBER, THE PRESS HAVE BEGUN TO TALK ABOUT COUNTY'S TITLE POSSIBILITIES!

riding their luck in the game's infancy, County took charge. 'It's upwards and onwards,' said Angell after a double helping of joy. 'Our aim is to get in the first division next season and, had we managed to turn more of our draws into three points, we would have been right up there.' Angell swooped in the 35th and 51st minutes as County went on to hit the woodwork twice and had another chance kicked off the line.

'We needed the first half to get the West Ham match out of our system,' said Jones. 'We could have had more goals but I'll settle for three points.' The only worry concerned his striking partner Alun Armstrong. 'The last fifteen minutes were just agony. It's a matter of playing and resting but I don't want to miss any games.'

County completed the month still in tenth place as Millwall led the division. The Hatters record was:

P	W	D	L	F	A	Pts
21	9	6	6	28	25	33

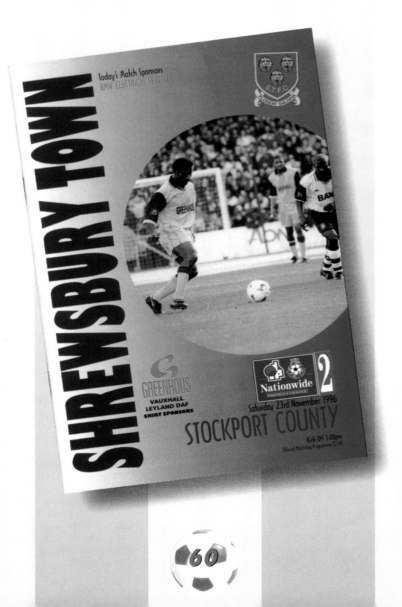

6 December

STEVE SOUTHART

IF IT HADN'T SUNK IN YET, THE month of December rammed home the message that the season was going to be extraordinary: promotion became a real talked-about possibility, while there was the added enjoyment of three flourishing cup runs. Just how much credit for County's amazing U-turn in fortune over the years could be accredited to David Jones's predecessor Danny Bergara remained opened to conjecture. It was no secret some of the senior players found the Bergara era almost intolerable and, had he not gone in March 1995, there could have been something of an exodus. 'A lot of people have criticised Bergara, but to me he was brilliant,' said *Tea Party* editor Dave Espley. The fact was that, for the game against Bergara's new club Rotherham at Millmoor on December 3rd, there were six players Bergara had brought to Edgeley Park.

There was little vitriol from either camp in the pre-match build-up, given the acrimonious manner in which Bergara had exited. Pointedly, however, in his programme notes Bergara made no mention of Jones, chairman Brendan Elwood or the players:

> I would like to welcome all Stockport supporters who gave me such great backing in my Edgeley Park days. I had some tremendous times and If I'm not careful I could get involved in too much of a sentimental situation.

'KIZZA' DEATH: DEADLY DURKAN SENT MILLERS SPINNING TO DEFEAT.

DAVE ESPLEY'S
AWARD-WINNING FANZINE

As it turned out, the game was won by one of the Jones boys, Kieron Durkan. His 25-yard free kick deflected off the Millers' wall over the head of Steve Cherry. Rotherham had scored only eight times in ten league outings, so chances of an equaliser were remote. But on a bitterly cold night, when the frost even penetrated the M&S thermals, United came out after a half-time roasting all stoked up. John McGlashan, now at Dundee, nearly levelled and Rotherham forced five

corners in the blink of an eye. The danger passed, though, and a 1–0 win, one of twelve occasions on which County prevailed by the same margin during the season, sent them to within four points of the leaders.

County had again failed to obtain home advantage for their next FA Cup engagement, but there weren't too many long faces when the draw matched them with Mansfield Town. True, the Stags had won both previous cup clashes, but the present-day Field Mill side were struggling in the wrong half of Division 3.

Prior to kick-off, the greatest danger to County's chances appeared to come from the weather, as the fog swirling around this area of Nottinghamshire cast a doubt on whether proceedings would commence. From the back of the main stand and from the television gantry there seemed little hope, but at pitch level the view was less obscured and County's eighth cup-tie of the season got under way on time.

Within minutes came the first attack — unfortunately, between rival fans in the away section! The culprits were quickly frog-marched away without any halt in play. Mansfield, as Doncaster did in the previous round, belied their lowly status and posed plenty of problems for an overworked County defence. Stalemate, then, was the situation approaching half-time — much to the chagrin of the home faithful, who, although few in number, made plenty of din at the appropriate moment.

There wasn't much hullabaloo two minutes into injury time, however, when County broke through in a highly unlikely manner. A corner was County's consolation after a penalty claim was declined, and from the flag-kick the ball pinged around the six-yard area and finished up nestling in the net. With the fog even thicker than before, it was impossible to determine which player applied the vital touch. Bets were taken on Mike Flynn and Mansfield's Tony Ford with the latter's name being given out to the national news agency, Press Association, to alert the necessary media outlets. It transpired, however, that Brian 'Killer' Kilcline, an FA Cup winner with Coventry in 1987, had failed to escape a Scott Eustace clearance and done the damage.

If the first goal had been against the run of play, so too the second. Jim Gannon had just cleared off the line when Durkan made it 2–0. Alun Armstrong claimed the assist and 'Kizza' finished with the help of a post for his second goal inside a week. A similar pattern followed when Mansfield were unlucky to have a valid penalty appeal refused and a shot that bounced into play off the woodwork before Durkan rounded off the scoring with a crisply struck shot. The Republic of Ireland Under-21 international revealed:

> I set myself a target of ten goals for the season and I'm halfway there. But I thought they might not count. At one stage, a few of the Mansfield lads were asking the referee to abandon the game when the fog closed in.
>
> I made my debut here for Wrexham as a 17-year-old and that was a far less happy occasion. We lost 3–0 and one of the goals — not one of mine — was featured on the *Own Goals and Gaffs* video!

Lady luck deserted County once more when the draw for the Auto Windscreen Shield took place: a trip to Doncaster on December 16th. Only 988 (fool)hardy souls saw the game, including two County stalwarts who

Richard Harnwell's Season	
Best home league game	*Millwall and Burnley*
Best home cup game	*The West Ham game had everything: proper English weather (rain and mud—TB), live TV and a 2–1 win.*
Best away league game	*Millwall again. A great stadium in a horrible area and a match that had everything.*
Best away cup game	*I never thought I would see County score five goals away at a first-division club as we did at Sheffield; the atmosphere at Blackburn was incredible; the results at West Ham and Southampton superb; and we went out on a high beating Middlesbrough. It would be impossible to pick just one from that list.*
Best player(s)	*Paul Jones and Mike Flynn*
Worst away league and cup games	*Burnley and Carlisle*
Worst teams	*Millwall and York*
Worst grounds	*Doncaster and Luton. Because we won promotion I now have to do every game this season as well!*

STEVE SOUTHART

YOUTH AND EXPERIENCE: RISING
STAR ALUN ARMSTRONG IN
ACTION AGAINST BURNLEY
(ABOVE), AND MR DEPENDABLE JIM
GANNON (RIGHT)

STOCKPORT EXPRESS

MIDFIELD GENERALS TOM BENNETT (ABOVE)
AND CHRIS MARSDEN (ABOVE RIGHT).
WINGER KIERON DURKAN (RIGHT).

had pledged to watch every match home and away. I've already introduced Dave Espley earlier in the book; now it's the turn of Richard Harnwell to take a bow. Richard is the club historian and the commentator for the club videos. Like Espley, he never imagined they would embark on such an incredible journey. This is their tale, starting with Harnwell:

> I first went to County during the fourth-division championship-winning season of 1966–67. I became devoted, even if meant having the piss taken at school by Manchester City and United fans. (We wouldn't do that Richard, honestly—*TB*). Despite all the lows and occasional highs, I remained loyal. The proud feeling I experienced as I stood to sing the

National Anthem the first time we went to Wembley was incredible; it was all I could do to hold back the tears.

My wife Nicola has had to put up with my obsession over the years, but her loyalty was pushed to the limit when I told her of my intention to watch every match last season. Sixty-seven games later I'm knackered and understand what the players went through. Not only have they got to travel as I did but they had to graft their backsides off for at least ninety minutes as well.

To fulfil his dream Richard travelled a total of 9,986 miles for the 67 league and cup games from his Radcliffe home. In April alone he clocked up 2,056 miles, and in that period County scored just eight goals from eleven games (the Luton game included). His longest journeys were: Plymouth, 598 miles round trip; Bournemouth 548 miles; Gillingham 510 miles; Southampton 492 miles; West Ham 460 miles, and Millwall 440 miles. Every one was a midweek fixture. Working at thirteen pence per mile and not taking into account wear and tear on the car, the cost came to £1,198.32. With tickets, programmes and other miscellaneous items, Richard reckons his total outlay was £1,869.83. And his verdict: 'It was worth every penny!'

So, what were his highs and lows? Richard gave us the Stockport fan's viewpoint (opposite).

County's promotion coincided with Espley's 25th silver jubilee as a Hatters fan:

> My dad used to follow them and I think his dad before him. I decided last summer to do every game expecting it to be a final total of about the low 50s. In the end, it could have been 72 had we ended up at

KIKO: ONE TO WATCH IN THE FUTURE

COCA-COLA CUP, 4TH ROUND REPLAY: WEST HAM'S IAIN DOWIE HEADS INTO HIS OWN NET.

Wembley in the Coca-Cola, Auto Windscreen Shield and play-off finals. Thankfully my wife was happy enough to let me get away with it. On Saturdays at least she always took the kids to her mums.

Espley, who built up *The Tea Party* to become Fanzine of the Year in 1994–95 and third the following year, could have reduced his overheads by £420 had a £5 bet come up. Instead, he had to settle for £36.25 when a less risky £5 each-wayer paid up once promotion was attained.

Then there was Peter Collins. He began the season aged 64 and finished up at Luton celebrating his 98th birthday!

Peter is the membership secretary for the Hyde & District Hatters, and his real age is 47. The tale began on the opening home game of last season

when, Peter having aged 18 years overnight, a request to announce his 65th birthday failed to come to fruition. Stung into action, *Tea Party* contributor Graham Privett decided to write to every away team where County were playing and ask them to announce Peter's birthday. A year was added for every trip, which is why at Luton Peter had reached a sprightly two short of his century.

Not every club obliged with the dedication. Most did, however, including Crewe on Stockport's second visit to Gresty Road when the announcer tried to get him on the pitch to congratulate him on his 89th birthday. At Millwall, aged 68, his birthday was printed in the programme; at Blackburn — his 71st birthday — he received two mentions and a slot on the scoreboard.

Of the games where Peter's birthday was announced, County won fourteen, drew six and lost only once . . . at Birmingham City. On the twelve occasions the ruse was rumbled, County won three, drew six and lost seven. Could it be that the Collins birthday phenomenon rather than the goals of Brett Angell or the saves of Paul Jones got County promoted!?

So, it was Espley and Harnwell that trekked to Belle Vue for the opening hurdle of the Autothingy cup. What they didn't see was a classic, but they did come away singing the praises of another Portuguese signing, Kiko Charana. At this stage of the season, Kiko was rated a better prospect than Cavaco and he showed why with a vintage display. Ten minutes after replacing John Jeffers, he produced a right-foot shot which Andy Gray could only divert into his own net, though the marksman claimed it for himself. Sixty seconds later, following a good run by Sean Connelly, Kiko's goal attempt was bundled over the line by Cavaco.

'I'm not yet fully fit and I have got some hard training to do,' said the boy from Belenenses. Sadly, in his limited

BRETT ANGELL'S GLORIOUS 27TH-MINUTE HEADER SINKS THE HAMMERS.

STOCKPORT EXPRESS

BRETT ANGELL CLOSES IN ON GOAL AGAIN AS COUNTY ARE WITHIN MINUTES OF A FAMOUS WIN.

appearances during the rest of the term, Kiko didn't sparkle as brightly again. 'He is one for the future,' said Dave Jones. 'We are trying to ease him into our game and it's hard for him to take it all in.'

Another player who made less of an impact on his debut that night, but might prove a sounder investment, is Canadian international Martin Nash It was Kiko, though, who was named as substitute for the game with Peterborough on the penultimate Saturday

shopping day before Christmas. Instead of Santa, however, Posh played Scrooge. All good things must end, and County failed to score for the first time in 24 matches and thus didn't equal the club record. According to Jones:

> That was the type of game we were losing last season so it was important to pick up a point. We had eighty per cent of the ball but didn't do anything with it. Our crosses weren't good enough and they had chances to nick it.

STOCKPORT EXPRESS

GIANT-KILLERS! AFTER-MATCH CELEBRATIONS;
GOAL-SCORING HERO BRETT ANGELL (RIGHT)

STOCKPORT EXPRESS

Even so, the *Stockport Express* sports editor noted: 'Posh keeper Bart Griemink dealt with a couple of centres more like Bart Simpson!'

Kiko eventually replaced Alun Armstrong (eleven matches without a goal), while leading the Peterborough line was Ken Charley, later to make such a devastating impact after signing for County.

Angell delight

Night of glory for Stockport journeyman

By PETER FERGUSON

Turning point: Iain Dowie (above) rises unchallenged to head the Ham ball replicate the full impact of his mistake

IT'S THE PROUDEST NIGHT IN STOCKPORT'S HISTORY

County's muddy marvels

By Peter Gardner

Stockport Co 2 West Ham 1

STOCKPORT'S muddy marvels re-wrote the record books on their most glorious night.

County left Premiership rivals battered, bruised, humiliated and hammered as they reached their first ever quarter final of a major knock out competition.

And who will be brave enough to bet against them continuing the triumphant march towards Wembley when Southampton arrive at an intimidating Edgeley Park early next month?

Proud boss Dave Jones insisted today: 'They won't relish coming here on a cold January night and there's no reason why we can't go through to the semi finals.'

Match winning hero Brett Angell, the striker rescued from Premiership oblivion with Sunderland in a £125,000 deal last month warned: 'The Saints are next on our hit list. I fancy our chances and if we can beat West Ham, there's no reason to fear them.

But then County fear no-one. Ask Sheffield United. Ask Blackburn. Both were beaten on the way, with the fourth round elimination of Rovers even leading to the departure of manager Ray Harford.

Said Jones: 'This result rates alongside them and I thought the way the boys battled, they really deserved it. In the second half West Ham threw everything at us and we couldn't get out of our half, but we never dropped our guard.'

County superbly dragged themselves through the ploughed-up pitch, coming from behind to snatch stunning victory in a breath-taking replay where every player was a hero.

Yet West Ham, held at Upton Park thanks to a Luis Cavaco equaliser, threatened to swamp Stockport in an opening stint that saw Julian Dicks powerfully head them into the lead following a right flanking Ilj Dumitrescu corner after 22 minutes.

It was the first of three goals in a scar

■ HERE WE GO . . . hero Brett Angell storms in to head Stockport's winner last night picture Andy Yates

---

However, he failed to make an impact on Jones's replacement Gary Megson, who allowed him to leave for Barnet.

Despite a substantial outlay on the pitch, the surface still resembled Blackpool beach, a worrying prospect for County as the Coca-Cola Cup relay with West Ham drew nearer. Most lower-division sides taking on top-flight opposition would have been glad of a glue-pot to play on. Not County: they played the ball around with the best of them and weren't looking for any advantage from the elements.

Come the big night and the heavens opened, but the raindrops were to became tears of joy for most of the assembled crowd of 11,000. A goal down to a Julian Dicks header after 23 minutes, Stockport stormed back to win 2–1 with Iain Dowie heading a bizarre own-goal and Brett Angell soaring high to convert Tom Bennett's cross. Peter Gardner in the *Manchester Evening News* summed up County's performance:

From the sound handling of Paul Jones through the commanding grip of Flynn and Jim Gannon at the back, the midfield motivation of Tom Bennett and Chris Marsden to the unselfish work of Armstrong and Angell up front it was Stockport at their best.

Chairman Brendan Elwood again had pound signs in front of his eyes.

We have made £350,000 from the knockout competitions this season. We'll more than double our money by reaching the semi-finals. With commercial spin-offs and more television revenue, we are aiming for the magical £1 million. This club is now geared for higher-grade football and what has happened recently tells me we are a first-class organisation. We have broken our wage structure several times already this season to bring in quality players and that is exceptional for our current standing with average gates of 4,500.

Angell, delighted to show he could still knock in the goals at the highest level, beamed: 'Southampton are next on our hit-list. I fancy our chances, because if we can beat West Ham there's no reason to fear them.'

After the cup endeavours, County managed to fit in two Nationwide League games before the big freeze wiped out a mass of fixtures. Gigg Lane, however, was passed fit on December 21st and the champions elect, Bury, met the eventual runners-up. The game, with Tony Dinning coming in for the suspended Tom Bennett, ended in a goalless draw, but there were of incidents to keep both sets of supporters happy. Angell headed straight at Dean Kiely from a clear opening while Paul Butler crashed a header against the bar. Said Bury boss Stan Ternent:

> At least we did what Sheffield United, Blackburn and West Ham all failed to do this season: we held them and stopped them scoring. If we had played any other side we would have won and the same applies to Stockport. And on that performance both sides will be there or thereabouts.

Explained Jones: 'We would have settled for a clean sheet and a draw at the start because Bury have been banging in the goals all over the place.' The draw extended the Shakers' resolutely firm home record to fourteen games without defeat: the platform on which they erected their trophy-winning campaign.

Amazingly, the Racecourse, Wrexham, was deemed fit to play on Boxing Day, despite practical wipe-out elsewhere. And though the surface wasn't perfect, it attracted few complaints from either camp. Stockport had played 26 matches since losing 2–0 against the Welshmen in September and now they were about to exact

revenge. The game began disastrously, however, with Steve Watkin after seven minutes and Steve Morris after sixteen putting Wrexham 2–0 ahead. Alun Armstrong, with his first goal since October 2nd, dragged County back into contention in a pulsating opening 45 minutes that almost made you forget the cold.

The second period was every bit as frenetic as the first. Had there not been so many epic cup wins to choose from, this would have rated among the matches of the season. With almost an hour gone, County tied the scores with Jim Gannon sneaking in at the back post. It didn't take them long to find a winner. Luis Cavaco, kicked from pillar to post all afternoon, was brought down once more, but this time the offence occurred inside the box and Tony Dinning, filling in in midfield for the suspended Tom Bennett, converted the spot-kick.

Still the pace didn't slacken, and a full-scale brawl almost erupted when Gannon accused Mark McGregor of diving to get a penalty. Both players were cautioned, a goal-kick was awarded and County survived another five tense minutes to become the first side to win at the Racecourse that season. The victory also guaranteed that Dave Jones was recognised with a long overdue Manager of the Month award.

It took County to fifth spot — their loftiest position so far, with a record of:

P	W	D	L	F	A	Pts
25	11	8	6	32	27	41

7 Captain Fantastic: Mike Flynn

THE £150,000 INVESTED BY Danny Bergara on Mike Flynn rates among the best pieces of business County's former manager ever completed. For Bergara, the transfer of Flynn from Preston North End was an expensive one, as he rarely paid half that fee for any of his signings, and it remained a club record until the £200,000 acquisition of Ian Gray from Rochdale.

Flynn made his debut on 27th March 1993, coming on as a substitute for Alan Finley in a 4–3 victory at Plymouth Argyle. Since then the Oldham-born defender, who spent a brief and unproductive twelve months at Norwich City, has chalked up nearly 200 appearances for County and has become one of the club's finest-ever centre-halves. He's also been known to contribute the occasional vital goal and can throw the ball almost as far as other players can kick it. His dependable, motivational and inspirational qualities made him a natural to be named as club skipper.

No one embodied County's never-say-die attitude better last season than Mike Flynn, and he thoroughly deserved the headlines that accompanied his Man-of-the-Match roles: 'Captain Marvel', 'Captain Courageous', 'Captain Fantastic' — choose any one, they all fit the bill. Trevor Francis was impressed enough to offer a derisory £500,000 as deadline day approached last March to try and

tempt him to Birmingham City, and at the time of writing the father of two has been linked with Southampton. County fans would be sorry to see him leave now — or in the future.

'You only notice how good Flynnie is when he's having a bad game,' says club historian Richard Harnwell. 'You take him for granted because he's so consistent, so when he does make a mistake it stands out.' Flynn's performances were also recognised by his fellow professionals, being voted into the PFA second-division team of the season for 1996–97. The subsequent medal sits proudly on top of his television. He said modestly:

STEVE SOUTHART

> I didn't really expect to get in — it was a very strong division last season with a lot of very good players, so I'm obviously very honoured. Over the years County should have had more recognition than it has but for some reason we didn't. But last season with the high-profile cup games, me and Mazza have picked up the awards. Jonesy should have been in it and I also think Sean Connelly and Toddy should as well.

However, after the first few games of the season, there seemed little chance of recognition for himself or the team. Flynn recalled:

> There was definitely a mood of optimism pre-season. We'd missed the play-offs by one point the season before, but knew we had the quality in the team to go straight up. Looking back, though, I think the lads got carried away by the start we made. We beat a virtually full-strength Birmingham side 4–0 and it could have been more. Trevor Francis complained about the length of the grass at Edgeley Park, but I suppose he had to moan about something. If you've just spent £5 million on players and your team gets beaten by Stockport, the directors are going to want to know why.
>
> At Tranmere we played the eleven who would more than likely start the season and got a great 3–2 result. Those two games showed the difference between Dave [Jones] and Danny Bergara. Danny wouldn't have risked being beaten by sides like Birmingham and Tranmere. But Dave wouldn't be led by anyone: he is very much his own man. I understand when he went to Southampton the first thing he did was cancel a trip to

an army camp and give the players an extra week off.

It was a massive blow, then, to Flynn and his team-mates when they lost the opening game at Crewe and continued to slide.

> When I was at Preston and we'd suffered a couple of pre-season defeats, it spurred us on to make sure the same thing didn't happen when the league kicked off. After beating first-division sides like Birmingham and Tranmere, perhaps we thought the second division would be easy. You could sense the relief when we got our first point at Bristol Rovers. We beat Chesterfield in the Coca-Cola, but though we'd stopped the rot we weren't out of the woods yet. We were still playing well below par, and it was as puzzling to us as it was to the fans why we'd blown hot and cold in such a short space of time.

The first signs of unrest on the terraces came after the 2–0 home defeat by Wrexham. The catcalls didn't fall on deaf ears.

> We were all aware of the shouts of 'Jones out'. To us it was unfair, but we understood the fans had paid their money and wanted to see a winning team. People were not doing what they had pre-season. Mazza went round kicking people and Tom Bennett hadn't shown what he is capable of.

You may have gathered by now that Flynn is a big fan of Dave Jones. However, he feels the Jones ethic of 'Be your own man' was responsible for the decline.

> Under Danny the playing system was much more rigid. He told you what he expected you to do in certain parts of the field and not step over into someone else's territory. Under Dave he always instilled this thing of being your own man — almost a free spirit, if you want. He encouraged us to do things off the cuff, and we knew we weren't likely to get a rollicking for trying something different.
>
> It's OK doing things off the cuff when things are going well, but when they're not it's time for a rethink. And that's what we did after the Wrexham game. However, instead of ranting and raving after that game he gave us the Wednesday off and told us to go away and think about our own performances. Then on the Thursday he called the senior players together for an informal chat over the now-famous cup of tea. There was me, Paul Jones, Mazza, Benno, Andy Mutch and Jim Gannon. Most of us had been at clubs involved in relegation battles before and we all put forward suggestions as to how we could turn things round. One of the areas where we thought we needed to improve was set-pieces. It seemed to do the trick, because in the next game against Plymouth I flicked on Mazza's corner and Jim Gannon scored!

STEVE SOUTHART

JUBILANT AFTER THE 5–2 ROUT AT BRAMALL LANE

Had County lost that match with Plymouth there was speculation that Jones could have lost his job, and that wasn't a prospect the players relished.

> We enjoyed the style of play the gaffer introduced and if someone new came in he might try to alter it. But he told us he'd been to see the chairman, Brendan Elwood, and his position was fine. I don't know if it was kidology on his part or if his neck really was one the chopping block, but his words reassured us. A lot of the players he had brought to the club and didn't want him to leave.

The victory over Plymouth flicked a switch. 'We definitely turned a corner that day,' said Flynn. Before the Plymouth

STEVE SOUTHART

NO ONE EMBODIED COUNTY'S NEVER-SAY-DIE
ATTITUDE BETTER THAN MIKE FLYNN.

that good, the club decided not to have a bet. Even before the Plymouth game, they didn't put any money on us. Perhaps they thought we were too much of a long shot.

I'm not a betting man really, but I remember Andy Preece doing a similar thing when we played Burnley in the Autoglass final. He was on a bonus of £1,500 to £2,000 if we won, so, just in case we lost [which County did], he had a bet on Burnley to cover himself. I just think that puts too much pressure on yourself: but each to their own!

After the Plymouth victory, the revival continued with the 7–3 aggregate win over Sheffield United. Said the captain:

Those wins didn't flatter us: after the first leg at Edgeley you could see their players thinking they'd done the job in holding us to a one-goal lead. They probably regret feeling that way now. But we knew how badly you can let yourself down by being over-confident.

The 4–3 triumph at Millwall that followed was a night to remember, especially for Flynn. 'I nearly got chinned by one of their fans,' he laughed, 'although it wasn't so funny at the time.' Things were going well until Lee Todd executed one of his trademark back-passes, using his knee, a move that is quite within the rules, although plenty of soccer-watchers — and, on this occasion, the officials — are unsure. Explained Flynn:

We were 3–1 up and the match was in the bag, when Toddy does this back-pass and the linesman starts flagging — he was flagging so hard I thought he was going to fall over. The referee stopped the game and, for a reason best known to himself, gave Millwall a throw. That decision unsettled us and really got their crowd going. It also resulted in them pulling a goal back. I'd been having a banter with

game, there were extremely generous odds on County achieving promotion, but the club's decision not to take advantage was to backfire as Flynn explained.

We had been promised a £150,000 bonus as a squad to win promotion. To insure against having to pay out, a club might have a bet at the start of the season. If the club is promoted, they would receive money back from the winning bet which could be used to pay the bonus. If the club didn't get promoted, the lost stake money would be much less than £150,000. Because the pre-season odds weren't

one of their fans who kept calling us 'northern scum' — that sort of thing. When it was 2–3 he called out: 'You don't look so happy now, number five!' The whole crowd were fired up and baying for blood. Next minute their sub comes on and with his first touch equalises. The loudmouth in the crowd is at it again: 'Blown it number five — northern ****ers!'

At this stage, we'd have settled for a point, but Alun Armstrong gets the winner in the last minute. Now it was my turn to have a go back and I reminded him of the score. Then the final whistle goes, this bloke's on the pitch and I'm off down the tunnel as quickly as possible.

The lads loved it and were giving me stick in the dressing room, but I thought no more of it and went for a drink in the players' bar. Later, we all got back on the coach waiting to go home. I was sat there and I heard this voice: 'Where's that number five?' It was this geezer again. I just slid down in my seat and hid behind the fanzine I was reading, but next minute he's on the coach looking for me. I'd suddenly forgot about the match.

Thankfully, John Sainty came out of the directors' room at that moment and escorted him off the bus — much to my relief. I'm glad we won't be playing Millwall again this season. I just hope we don't get them in the cup.

The defeat by Burnley in the next match was a shock to the system and, for once, Dave Jones lost his cool.

He read the riot act. Not so much at the forwards but at the defence. It was a freak result, but it just happened to be against our arch-rivals. No one was more upset than the players by that result. They know what it means to beat Burnley. Thankfully, it was just a minor blip.

Burnley were a useful side, but they weren't among those I fancied to go up, especially by automatic promotion.

Luton, on the other hand, I thought would do well. When we played them at our place I knew we were in for a hard game just by looking at the names on the team-sheet. Up to that point they were the hardest team we'd played.

The trip to Blackburn for the third round of the Coca-Cola Cup provided County with an even sterner task

OK, so they'd sold Shearer and both Chris Sutton and Graham Le Saux were missing, but they were a quality Premier-League side. I'd played at Ewood Park while I was with Oldham, but since then the ground had changed out of all recognition. The gaffer told us to go out and believe in ourselves. And, if they had an off-night, there was no reason why we couldn't win.

In the end, the 1–0 victory didn't reflect how well we played. At the start of the season, our aim had been promotion and the Auto Windscreen Shield final again. We expected to go a few rounds in the League Cup or the FA Cup, maybe causing an upset like we had against QPR, but after beating Blackburn everyone was on such a high. We suddenly thought: if we can beat them we can beat most teams. We couldn't wait for the next game: nobody wanted to miss out.

It was disappointing to hear we'd drawn West Ham away, but we still felt confident. The last time I'd played at Upton Park was for Norwich Reserves before a handful of spectators. This was just a bit different.

County were second best for the first half and West Ham deserved to be a goal up. Flynn described the scorer, Florin Raducioiu, as

. . . the quickest player I've ever faced: he was greased lightening. At half-time Dave went over the old ground about believing in our own ability, etc. We came out for the second half, Luis Cavaco scored a

STEVE SOUTHART

'Confident are we?' Bishop sneered. I just had a feeling we would win the replay.

And that's the way it turned out, with Flynn's long throw initially instrumental in Dowie, to quote Flynn, 'rising like a salmon', heading in the first of two County goals.

My long throw is something that's always been with me. I've never really worked at it. I used to throw the javelin for Oldham Schools, so maybe that had something to do with it. But I think it's a great asset to the team. It gives us a lot of options and can be more accurate than a free-kick or a corner. It means extra responsibility for me, but I'm a fit lad and it gives me a great satisfaction if it comes off.

A combination of the cup runs and the bad weather meant County faced a backlog of matches. The prospect worried Flynn.

It's OK having games in hand, but you've got to make the most of them. In the past we've been in good positions but haven't taken advantage. This season it was different, because both ourselves and Bury went straight up having had games in hand on the rest.

However, Flynn is adamant the effort used up in the 2–1 replay win at Southampton cost County the second-division title.

Southampton was a great night, but the next match was a tough one at home against Brentford. It was asking a lot for us to come back and play a good side like that. We'd not recovered from the Dell and had hard games before. Brentford took advantage and beat us.

The two games against Graeme Souness's team provided Flynn with a chance to renew old acquaintances.

cracker and we went from strength to strength. At the end we were sorry not to have finished it off without the need of a replay.

After the game I was stood with John Keeley [the ex-Brighton keeper who had a brief spell at Edgeley Park] in the players' bar. Next to us were Iain Dowie and Ian Bishop and we were all watching the draw for the quarter-finals. When they read it out, I turned to John and said: 'Not bad — Southampton in the next round. Bishop and Dowie couldn't believe it.

He'd been on tour to Brazil with Matt Le Tissier when both were members of an England Under-20s squad, and due to a strike by the Brazilian national side the England team were forced to play three local teams. 'As such they didn't award caps but at least I can say I played for England!' But while Le Tissier used the trip as a launchpad to a glittering career in the Premier League and full international honours, Flynn got left behind — until now.

When I went to Brazil I was in Oldham's first team and things were looking good. When I came back, I broke a bone in my foot and was out of action for over three months. After getting over the injury, the club sold me to Norwich. Suddenly, from being a regular first-teamer at Boundary Park and playing for England, I was in the Reserves at Carrow Road. I signed a four-year contract with Norwich, but lasted only a year. Dave Stringer was manager at the time and admitted things hadn't worked out, saying that if they got their money back they'd let me go. Eventually, Preston came in for me and I moved back to the North-West.

Now Flynn, against some of the country's top strikers, showed he was quite comfortable playing at the highest level.

We could hear Souness having a right go at the Southampton lads after they lost to us. They were due to get a bonus and a trip abroad if they'd won, but all that was knocked on the head. Life couldn't have been better for us: there was so much media attention and the lads loved it. Before the Middlesbrough game, we were even talking about County playing in Europe — that's how confident we were.

'Boro proved one side too many in the Coca-Cola Cup, but only after two frenetic games.

Juninho didn't play in the first leg at Edgeley Park and that was a bonus to us, but we still didn't do ourselves justice. The pitch didn't help. Two years earlier Danny Bergara would loved to have played Middlesbrough on a pitch like that, but it was a measure of how far we'd progressed that a glue-pot surface only hindered us. Even losing 2–0, we still felt upbeat about playing them at the Riverside. I met Brian Moore before the game and he asked me what I thought the score might be. I said 1–0 to us. Later, he came up to me again and said: 'You were right, so it would have been better if you'd said 2–0!'

In the end I guess it wasn't meant to be, but we didn't disgrace ourselves. We'd kept a clean sheet against a side that had beaten Liverpool and Newcastle in the same competition and I'm convinced if Ben Roberts had been in goal for the second leg instead of Mark Schwarzer we would have done them. Roberts didn't look confident against Chesterfield in the FA Cup, while Schwarzer was a giant who didn't miss anything.

Still, Flynn had a treasure trove of memories to take with him from Teesside.

After the match, Ravanelli came up and asked if we could swap shirts. I wasn't going to turn him down. Then Nigel Pearson, their captain, wanted to swap armbands, so I got myself another souvenir.

Flynn's eye-catching displays alerted Trevor Francis who tabled a bid for the six-foot defender as the end-of-season deadline approached.

Every transfer I'd been part of in the past had come right out of the blue, but this was different. It had been splashed over the papers and speculation was rife, so it was difficult to ignore. On deadline day, every time the phone rang I half expected it to be the gaffer saying the clubs had agreed

SUCH WAS STOCKPORT'S SEASON: FLYNN FINDS HIMSELF IN THE UNUSUAL BUT WELCOME POSITION OF BEING INTERVIEWED BY ROB PALMER FROM SKY SPORTS.

terms. But as the 5 pm threshold got nearer, I knew I was staying put.

At the time I was asked whether I was disappointed the move didn't come off. The answer is: no. I was delighted to be at a club that was doing well and in with a chance of picking up some silverware.

Defeat by Carlisle in the Auto Windscreen Shield kiboshed one avenue to a trophy, not that Flynn and the team shed too many tears.

Of course, we tried our best to win but losing wasn't such a big blow. It would have meant re-arranging another league game, playing an extra match and playing three times a week for the remainder of the season.

In the final run-in, it showed we weren't always at our best, but at least we kept sneaking the results that mattered. There were hiccups at Gillingham and Preston, but we still had it in our own hands when we went to Chesterfield.

There was nothing special in the build-up to that game, like the cup matches earlier in the season. We arrived at the ground at normal time and the gaffer did his best to keep our minds on the game and told us not to talk about promotion. But what was the only word mentioned on the coach? Promotion, of course. The lads were already working out which sides they wanted to play against in the first division. I hoped Oldham wouldn't get relegated so we could meet them. Mazza wanted to play Huddersfield and Sheffield United, while Benno and Paul Jones looked forward to a match with Wolves.

Like us, Chesterfield had played in some big games and they could still go up. However, I think we wanted the game more badly. They were due to go to the Dominican Republic for a break and their minds, I think, were partly on that. Brett gave us the ideal start after five minutes and then it was just a case of making sure they didn't score for the next 85 minutes. I remember the referee played on and on and on. Jonesy made a great save and I kept saying, 'Blow your whistle, man.' Finally he did. The scenes at the end were wild. The chairman was dancing on the pitch like he didn't have a care in the world and I suppose it was great for him after the money he'd invested in the club. There was the customary champagne in the dressing room when we got back. I don't remember much of it getting drunk: it just got sprayed around, as is usual on these occasions.

On the way back to Stockport, every car was blue and white. It was just before the general election when we won promotion and I remember someone had altered the posters you see advertising the local candidate. Someone had put my picture over the top and underneath it read: 'Vote for Flynn'.

When we eventually got back to Edgeley Park, there were loads of people waiting to meet us. From there, most of the lads went up to the Fingerpost where we stayed until 3.30 or 4 am. I stayed at a friend's house that night and there was more booze when we got back. I was on such a high. I remember saying to my wife, Joanne, 'If we win, you won't see me for a few days.'

In fact, the celebrations went on all week. It was hardly the best preparation for the Luton game, but it was fantastic to go there with our goal achieved. The championship would have been the icing on the cake. Luton tried so hard and I'll never forget this lad who nutmegged Mazza. As he went past, he shouted, 'Nuts!' Mazza just looked at him and replied,

'Bothered? We're promoted!' The lad's face just dropped. When one of us made a mistake the rest of the team just laughed at him: I think most of us were still drunk. We did well to get a draw.

On the coach coming home, we had a crate of Bollinger waiting, as a friend of the gaffer's at the *News of the World* sent him a bottle every time we won a cup match. I've never drunk so much champagne in my life.

So much for the past: what about the future? Flynn admits he would find it hard to resist a big-money move to a Premier-League club if the offer was right.

You've always got to think about the future. Everyone knows a footballer's career is a short one, and not everyone goes into management or gets a job in the media like Andy Gray. I mentioned John Keeley earlier on. I remember someone coming up to him and saying: 'You must have earned a few bob — you're all right.' Keeley was working as a plumber's mate at the time!

A lot of players have earned good money and have got nothing left, so I make sure I plough as much as I can into a pension so when I call it a day I don't have to scramble immediately to take the first job that comes up. I want to be able to provide a similar standard of living for my wife and kids.

Flynn, who lives in the 'posh' part of Oldham in a pleasant detached house, has already started to make provisions.

I've just started a security firm and a plant-hire business in Stockport. Because of the success County has enjoyed, people hopefully want to be associated with your name.

Flynn's name will certainly always be associated with Stockport County. It perhaps only remains to be seen how long for!

STEVE SOUTHART

STEVE SOUTHART

STEVE SOUTHART

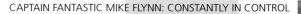

CAPTAIN FANTASTIC MIKE FLYNN: CONSTANTLY IN CONTROL

STEVE SOUTHART

The **Alexandra** Football Special

MAIN CLUB SPONSORS

BOLDON JAMES

CREWE ALEX v STOCKPORT COUNTY

Nationwide FOOTBALL LEAGUE

DIVISION TWO

SATURDAY, 17th AUGUST, 199

Kick-off 3.00 p.m.

Price £1.50

Season 1996/97
Issue No. 1

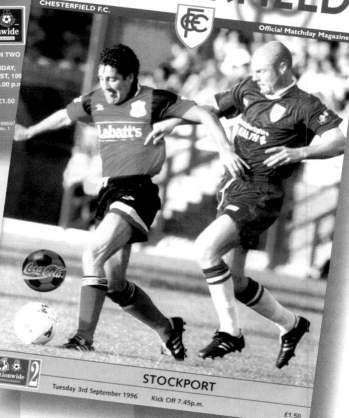

CHESTERFIELD

CHESTERFIELD F.C.

Official Matchday Magazine

Nationwide 2

STOCKPORT

Tuesday 3rd September 1996   Kick Off 7.45p.m.

£1.50

BRISTOL CITY v STOCKPORT COUNTY

NATIONWIDE LEAGUE DIVISION TWO
FRIDAY 7TH FEBRUARY 1997
KICK-OFF 7.45PM

PLAYER PROFILE • keith welch

CITY LIFE • the doc
prescribes
'keeper-blockers

MATCH SPON £1.50

A&S
DECO

Rotherham United F.C.

Nationwide
Division 2

Vs STOCKPORT COUNTY

Tuesday 3rd December 1996, KO 7.45pm

Club Sponsor
Parkgate
• RETAIL • WORLD •

AUTO-WINDSCREENS SHIELD WINNERS 1996

Today's Match Sponsors:

STOCKPORT EXPRESS

IN THE THICK OF IT:
KIKO (ABOVE) AND
ARMSTRONG (LEFT)

STEVE SOUTHART

8 January

BY THE START OF THE NEW Year, County had already completed 35 league and cup games, but as it transpired they were just over halfway through their programme with only four months of the season remaining. At the time, though, it seemed a good thing when the Arctic weather laid to rest much of the Nationwide League schedule and forced the big boys to turn up the under-soil heating to regulo six! However, as the giant-killing cup runs continued, the enforced lay-off left County with a massive fixture jam. Those advocates of a winter break certainly had excellent substance for their arguments, as Ice Station Edgeley remained as frozen as the Russian tundra.

It turned out that the 0–0 draw with Peterborough on December 14th was County's last home league game for nearly five weeks, with the fixtures against Watford (December 28th) and York City (New Year's Day) at Hardcastle Road being postponed. At least it allowed for a proper New Year's Eve celebration for once.

County's rather flattering FA Cup victory at Mansfield gave them a third-round tie against Stoke City — once more away from home. The groan that followed came not only from the club, but also from this cheesed-off scribe, as, from a purely mercenary point of view, these away ties were depriving me of income. A good cup run —

primarily at home — meant the newspapers would order extra match reports plus the chances to peddle preview and follow-up material, but ties at Belle Vue, Field Mill and now the Victoria Ground were not in my money-making patch. Required instead was a draw plus a win for County in the replay. Instead, they won 2–0 and came out of the hat for Round 4 — away at Birmingham! More of that later.

The Stoke match never had a prayer of taking place on the traditional third-round day of the first Saturday of January, and it was January 15th before conditions improved sufficiently. As a result, chairman Brendan Elwood missed the match, having previously booked a golf break in Dubai.

County showed plenty of initiative in being as prepared as possible for when the thaw came moving to the luxury surroundings of Mottram Hall near to leafy, mega-wealthy Prestbury to shed the festive excesses from their system. The venue had been used by Germany during their triumphant Euro '96 campaign, and it didn't seem to do *them* any harm. Sammy McIlroy generously set up a friendly with his Vauxhall Conference championship-chasing Macclesfield side. Witton Albion also acted as sparring partners. 'We desperately needed the game against Macc,' confirmed Dave Jones. 'They gave us a really hard workout, and the pitch at Mottram Hall was

STEVE SOUTHART

DURKAN: THIRD FA CUP GOAL OF THE SEASON

blanket of freezing fog covered the Victoria Ground. Even after referee D'Urso gave the green light, there was a fifteen-minute delay due to congestion at the turnstiles. That was the signal for one of Paul Rooney's season's recollections:

As it was the only game on involving a team from the GMR area, we decided to do full commentary. I'd arranged for Kevin Francis to do the summarising because of his old County connections and because his team were due to play the eventual winners. As the original kick-off time approached, I began to do the broadcast, only for Matt Horn to pass me a note to say the match wouldn't start until 8 pm. I duly explained what was happening and intended handing back to the presenter Jimmy Wagg in the studio.

At that moment, I heard a frantic voice in my headphones. It was a YTS lad helping Jimmy out. 'You can't hand back yet, Jimmy's gone to move his car and I don't know what to do!' Kevin could hear what was happening and struggled to stop himself laughing. Anyway, I spent the next ten minutes asking him all kinds of questions, and I think the next one was going to be: 'Well, Kev what did you have for tea tonight?' when suddenly the YTS lad shouted: 'You can hand back, we've found Jimmy!'

frost-free. Before then, we hadn't trained on grass for nearly twenty days.'

The combination worked a treat and County claimed the scalp of opponents that are just below Burnley on Stockport fans' hate list. Like Jones, Potters chief Lou Macari had won a divisional Manager of the Month award in December, his side boasting a 100% success rate from five games. However, up to an hour before kick-off, the game remained in doubt as a

Finally, much to the relief of Paul and the players, the game started and County slipped into a familiar gear. However, overdrive was not needed against a surprisingly passionless Stoke City side. Kieron Durkan pounced for his third FA Cup goal of the season after 26 minutes to give the visitors the lead and an injury-time second from Alun Armstrong rubber-stamped the outcome following a couple of, by now, customary saves from Paul Jones. Matt Horn in the

Stockport Express wrote after this latest County scalp the headline 'Shockport!', which must have been one of the most-used headlines in the national papers that season.

● **Factfile:** Kieron Durkan netted six times for County in '95–'96 and not one of them was scored at Edgeley Park.

The victory left County as the only team in English football still involved in four domestic competitions. 'We've won nothing yet,' warned Dave Jones. 'We have to keep our feet firmly on the ground and continue to work hard as we have always done all season. We have always maintained our priority is promotion.'

Mike Flynn was less reticent about predicting the future. 'Where will it all end?' he was asked. 'Hopefully in the first division and three Wembley cup finals,' he replied. Before the long-overdue return to league action, Jones attempted to explain the reasons for the rise and rise of his sensational side.

> The players are prepared to work extremely hard. They don't want to stop even when you tell them it's time to pack up. I like their attitude and application: at some clubs when players have a cold they stay at home, but not our lot. They want to come in and carry on working. That's the sort of approach any manager must applaud and I certainly do.

On the difficulty of progressing on four different fronts, Jones added: 'Nobody but ourselves has got us into this position and we wouldn't have it any other way. We are just happy to be involved and having to play all these games.'

Most of the superlatives had already been used by the time Millwall came to town on January 18th. So, what do you say when the former second-division leaders have just been vanquished 5–1. Cue Matt Horn again: 'Imagine winning the lottery on a Saturday night three hours after you've won the pools. Imagine being a Stockport County fan.' This was one of those matches you didn't want to end — unless you were a Millwall fan. Ninety minutes seemed like nine and the scoreline could certainly have been 10–1.

ANDY MUTCH FOUND THE NET AFTER ONLY TWELVE MINUTES AGAINST MILLWALL.

STEVE SOUTHART

the tea party

stockport county fanzine

price £1

issue 64

Auto Windshields "not a Mickey Mouse trophy" say organisers

the tea party

stockport county fanzine

price £1

issue 65

Tension mounts as season nears climax

Oh, f...

...f...

...f...

...four more points should just about be enough

We're the famous Stockport County

Issue 27 March 1997

ANOTHER BUMPER 48 PAGES

Issue 23: Novemb

and we're going to ...

I.. O.. COUNTY

inside Brett Angell latest

Edgeley Park ticket hike

plus County v West Ham .. a full history

I.. O.. COUNTY

STEVE SOUTHART

ALUN ARMSTRONG: WEMBLEY IS HIS 'LUCKY GROUND'!

With Southampton due at Edgeley Park in midweek, the game attracted new faces to the press box. Clive Tyldesley, representing the *Sunday Telegraph*, and Pat Gibson of the *Times* left mightily impressed. So too was Lions boss Jimmy Nicholl, who was soon to lose his job at the New Den: 'Stockport are capable of anything,' said Nicholl. 'They are well organised, no nonsense at the back, comfortable on the ball and away you go. No one is going to relish coming here to play.'

County had made the breakthrough within eleven minutes. Flynn's long throw was the can-opener to tear apart the Millwall rearguard and Andy Mutch, deputising for the injured Brett Angell, obliged with a delightful finish. Back-to-back contentious decisions then spiced up the plot. Lee Todd was adamant a header from Damian Webber hadn't crossed the line, but his protests brought only a yellow card, and an equalising goal. Wigan official Terry Lunt then had the visitors spitting feathers by awarding a penalty for deliberate handball against Marc Bircham, and he also sent off the teenager whose shirt bore the imprint of the ball on his stomach.

Armstrong accepted the spot-kick and Millwall fell into disarray. Flynn scored number three before the break, while Luis Cavaco drilled in a second-half brace. With 39 minutes remaining after Cavaco's second, more goals seemed inevitable, but 5–1 it stayed. Ray Wilkins, when he finally hangs up his boots, won't look back with fondness on his trips to Edgeley Park. He was a member of the 1994 QPR team beaten 2–1 by County in the FA Cup, and on this latest occasion, recently arrived from Hibernian, the 40-year-old former England international was booked for a petulant foul.

The stars were certainly all out five days later as the Coca-Cola Cup quarter-final with Southampton went ahead at the second time of asking. The initial postponement proved a blessing in disguise as Sky TV opted to cover the game live, so swelling club coffers by a further £100,000. To ensure this tie, and the previous one against Millwall, took place, County had invested £4,000 in ground covers — a small price to pay for more national exposure.

Of course, there were no spare seats in the press box as the media scented another possible overthrowing of a Premier-League outfit. They almost got one as well until Egil Ostenstad, a £900,000 Graeme Souness signing from Norwegian club Viking Stavanger, struck five minutes from time to earn the Saints a second bite at the Dell a week later. However, at this point even the most optimistic County fans must have thought their team had blown it. And only Flynn's timely intervention foiled Matt Le Tissier at the death, a goal-line clearance that just landed him the individual match honours. His reward: a mountain bike! 'I wish the sponsors had eleven mountain bikes to give them because all my players were outstanding,' said Dave Jones. 'I could feel their fans behind me sucking the ball in,' smiled Flynn.

Flynn, Alun Armstrong and Paul Jones had all been under the microscope of the scouts in recent months, but Chairman Elwood had no intention of selling. 'If a major club came along today and offered me £2 million for Armstrong, I would turn them down. No one will be leaving while we are still involved in the FA Cup and Coca-Cola Cup.'

Armstrong had his team-mates in fits when he announced:

> If we do reach Wembley I'll be a happy man. It's my lucky ground. Mind you, I've only played there once before — for Durham Under-18s. We won 6–1 and I scored four: I've still got the match ball. At the time, one of the Wembley ground staff told me the last person to score four there was Gary Lineker! That's just what you

THEY THINK IT'S ALL OVER - NOT BY A LONG CHALK!

County heroes

By PAUL HINCE
CHIEF SPORTS WRITER

STOCKPORT 2 SOUTHAMPTON 2

want to hear when you're fifteen, and I haven't looked back since.

If Armstrong ever leaves Edgeley Park, then Newcastle will benefit to the tune of 50% of the fee — a sell-on clause insisted upon by Kevin Keegan when he let the player go.

'We have to be happy getting a second bite after being a goal down with five minutes left,' said Southampton manager Graeme Souness. 'But we must not think we've done the hard bit.' Those were sentiments echoed by Brett Angell, who had replaced the unlucky Mutch in the starting line-up.

> They would be wrong to believe the job was done at our place and that they need merely to go through the formalities. Graeme Souness is sure to stress that to his players, despite the fact the advantage has tilted their

way by being at home. You only have to look at our record to find evidence that we are happy wanderers.

However, on the night, just as they had done in both games against West Ham, County were to find themselves playing catch-up. Neil Maddison's ball caught County napping and Ostenstad out-paced Lee Todd before beating Paul Jones with a low shot from twelve yards. Todd didn't dwell on his misfortune for too long. From his free-kick Angell cleverly chested the ball down into the path of Armstrong whose delicate curling shot eluded the recalled Dave Beasant.

Joy turned to delirium just sixty seconds later as Stockport struck a second time. Chris Marsden was the instigator as Cavaco flung himself at the midfield organiser's centre to tuck in a header off the woodwork. It wouldn't have been sound judgement, however, to try to defend the advantage and County weren't about to try. For all their attacking forays, though, County were repeatedly forced back. Jones conjured up one superlative save to deny Alan Neilson while from the subsequent corner Ulrich Van Gobbel headed against the bar.

The semi-finals beckoned, but could County hold out? No. Eyal Berkovic, left on the sidelines at the start, dribbled into the area and Ostenstad turned to shoot beyond Jones with the ball taking an eternity to cross the line to make it 2–2. So, a last-four showdown with Ravanelli, Juninho and co. had to be put on hold. 'We'll have gained their respect following this performance,' added Angell. 'That's why they'll feel the tie isn't over yet.'

The Southampton tie certainly wasn't finished, but County's FA Cup hopes finally ran aground against Birmingham City, a team they'd beaten only four times in 27 previous encounters. To rub salt in the wound, Edgeley Park legend Kevin Francis netted the clinching goal, a rare high spot for the 6'7" Brum-born marksman after an unhappy transfer to the West Midlands club. A 3–1 final scoreline flattered Trevor Francis's team, though it gave them a measure of revenge for their pre-season hiding.

All the same, had Alun Armstrong's first-half header been a fraction lower before Birmingham had scored, who knows what might have happened. But Paul Furlong, Paul Devlin and Francis did find the target to virtually seal their place in the last sixteen. However, referee Paul Jones turned down a definite penalty after Brett Angell pounced for a consolation, Ian Bennett stopped four that should have been goals and County's lot was up, despite a final corner tally of 14–3 in their favour.

'We were going to lose eventually,' said Dave Jones, fuming at the performance of his namesake, the Loughborough official. 'It will be interesting to see how the team react. I can't knock the lads for the performance, just the individual mistakes that cost us the game.' The game was an instantly forgettable one for captain Mike Flynn. Not only did he help to give a goal away but he discovered someone who could throw the ball further in ex-Swansea midfielder Andrew Legg.

If Southampton thought County were finally showing signs of cracking on January 29th, they discovered otherwise. Despite trailing to a vintage Matt Le Tissier goal, Jones's Dell-boys achieved another sensational result by

STOCKPORT COUNTY FC

THE FRIENDLY FOOTBALL CLUB

DAILY STAR

GUARDIAN ANGELL: Stockport's Brett Angell celebrates his equaliser on the way to their win over Saints

ONE STEP TO WEMBLEY AS COUNTY SUB MAKES SURE

MANCHESTER EVENING NEWS

■ ON TARGET.... Stockport's Brett Angell celebrates the first goal (left) and substitute Andy Mutch makes sure with the second

Mutch too much

By PAT SHEEHAN

SORRY SAINTS

By JAMES DOBSON

County are Mutch too good as their Wembley march goes on

SOUNESS KICKED UP THE MUTCH

Cup king Andy piles on agony for Saints

SunSport's No1 FOR LATE-NIGHT SOCCER ACTION

Magical Mutch

Saints sunk by sub as Stockport do it again

By KEIR RADNEDGE

DAILY MAIL

DAILY MAIL

SOCCER SPECIAL

Super Stockport

Saints go crashing as Mutch crowns fightback

By NICK TOWNSEND

Perfect timing: Southampton's van Gobbel moves across to challenge Angell at The Dell last night

Southampton	1	Stockport	2

SEMI-FINAL LINE-UP

Stockport v Middlesbrough

Leicester v Wimbledon

THE SUN

Cup heroes (left to right) John Jeffers, Andy Mutch and Brett Angell celebrate their stunning Cup win

SOUTHAMPTON BECOME THE THIRD BIG-NAME SCALP TO BE DESPATCHED BY COUNTY. BY THIS TIME THE CHESHIRE CLUB HAVE BECOME A FAMILIAR SIGHT IN THE NATIONAL PRESS.

BRETT ANGELL PUTS COUNTY LEVEL
IN THEIR COCA-COLA CUP QUARTER-FINAL REPLAY AT THE DELL.

reducing the Saints to sinners. Goals from Brett Angell and Andy Mutch capped a brilliant comeback victory and sent the Hatters into a semi-final with 'Boro. Mutch, the striker Jones bought for the price of a pint, had the champagne corks popping with the easiest goal of his career.

'They always said my first touch was a good one,' grinned the ex-England 'B' striker, who tapped in from inches after 83 minutes to help home Alun Armstrong's initial effort. 'It might have looked simple, but I've missed worse than that.' (We know, Andy — remember Wycombe?) 'We were laughing on the bench before I went on that if I scored the winner I could have a ride in the boss's new Ford Probe. I might just see if he keeps to the bargain.'

County's win slashed their odds of lifting the trophy from 25–1 to 8–1, with Middlesbrough, then the new favourites, at 6–4. 'I don't think the whole team has cost more than £400,000 to assemble,' Jones revealed to the incredulous press corps. 'And I bought Mutchy for a pint. I'm proud of everyone. It's not as though we came here and hung on, we took the game to them.'

Perhaps the only Southampton fan pleased to see County go through was Mrs Graeme Souness, formerly Bramhall-born Karen Levy, voted Miss Stockport in 1979. Now, Souness has never been one of my favourite foot-ballers, and it didn't help that he once tried to give Ray Wilkins a face-lift without the aid of anaesthetic during a match between United and Liverpool at Old Trafford, but on this night he went up in my estimation. 'Stockport were the better team and deserved to win,' he praised. 'We froze on the night and that's a strange thing to say when you're a Premiership team entertaining a second-division club. Apart from two brief spells, Stockport outplayed and outfought us.' Those sentiments were echoed by all those privileged to see the victory.

Sadly, in my case there had to be a cloud to the silver lining. I returned to my car, having parked it in a church-yard backing on to the Dell, to find my passenger-side window put through. It meant a draughty ride to my sister-in-law's at Bracknell and a bill for £120 to have the damage repaired. I contemplated asking Brendan Elwood for a

DAVE JONES RECEIVES MANAGER OF THE MONTH AWARD FOR JANUARY FROM THE MAYOR OF STOCKPORT.

sub from County's ever-expanding bank balance, but instead settled on an increase in phone rental for next month's Coca-Cola Cup semi-final with 'Boro. Southampton were also out of pocket: next day the Stock Market reported a drop of 7.5 pence per share!

The solitary league success over Millwall took County up one place to fourth with a record of:

P	W	D	L	F	A	Pts
26	12	8	6	37	28	44

9 February

● TURFED OUT ● BURYED! ● BOYS FROM BRAZIL

THE CELEBRATIONS AFTER THE Southampton game continued long into the night and also into the early hours as County made the return trip by coach from the south coast. The cup run had brought unforeseen riches, but not enough to enable the chairman to charter a plane for the night.

Victory at the Dell had once more thrust the players and management team into the spotlight. Now, County were renowned for getting rid of managers — 25 of them since the Second World War — and it was known locally that Dave Jones hadn't been operating a contract. Now the knowledge was in the wider public domain, and before the game with Brentford on February 1st speculation began as to when and if Jones would sign on the dotted line. He explained:

> I haven't got a contract and have never had one. The chairman spoke to me a couple of weeks ago, but we haven't sat down and negotiated anything. I think he might want to now! I've always said I want players at this club who are ambitious and I'm no different.

Southampton, for one, had been alerted by the increasing success Jones was bringing to Edgeley Park, and despite only one Nationwide League victory, Jones received his second successive Manager of the Month award.

Another County employee attracting rave reviews was goalkeeper Paul Jones. Less than 24 hours after the Southampton game, Bobby Gould put Jones on standby for Wales's friendly with the Republic of Ireland on February 11th. When Wrexham's Andy Marriott dropped out, Jones was included in the squad. 'It shows the team is getting good press,' said the £60,000 bargain buy. 'I was born in Chirk, just across the border, but I probably qualify just because of my name. I've been on standby when at Wolves, but it's great to have got into the full squad.'

In the end, Jones didn't get his opportunity, but was finally rewarded after the season had finished in a friendly against Scotland.

PAUL JONES IN FLYING FORM

Bobby Gould said he would try and give me the last fifteen or twenty minutes, but the game was very tight and he obviously didn't want to lose the match by making unnecessary changes. Mark Crossley did his future chances no harm and in the end it was all a bit of an anti-climax.

With their respective recognition, it was very much a case of keeping up with the Jones's!

The biggest league crowd of the season up to that point, then, gathered to salute their conquering heroes against Brentford. However, as so often happens, it proved a case of 'after the Lord Mayor's show'. Brentford arrived as leaders and a 2–1 win earmarked them as potential champions. Suggested Jones:

> The game came a day too soon. We were tired, not so much physically as mentally. We were half a yard off the pace. We had no tempo. We got home from Southampton at 4 am and Flynnie was up two hours later doing a TV interview. Then I saw him again on television again at night. Maybe we should have stayed away until the interest had died down.

County were still without the injured Chris Marsden, while Andy Mutch got a ride in the gaffer's sponsored car but not a place in the starting line-up. In spite of their fatigue, County snatched a second-half lead from Luis Cavaco — his third goal in a row at Edgeley Park. However, it wasn't enough, as David McGhee headed home Scott Canham's corner and much-travelled Bob Taylor guided home a 76th-minute winner. Mutch nearly instigated another Houdini-style escape act, but this time shot inches wide.

Defeat was County's first at home in fourteen matches since the Wrexham debacle, though Griffin Park chief

Dave Webb insisted: 'Stockport will still be in with a shout at the end of the season.'

The team Dave Jones sent out against Burnley on February 4th for the second round of the Auto Windscreen Shield bore no resemblance to the one hammered 5–2 four months earlier. Jones made sweeping changes, giving season's full debuts to Neil Edwards, Kiko, Adie Mike and Martin Nash, while five-goal Paul Barnes was missing for the Clarets. There was also a spot on the bench for Lee Jones, Dave's sibling. Credit to Burnley that night for reducing admission prices.

Edwards and Nash were to play starring roles in an exciting contest, packed with incident. It took Nash only eighteen minutes to make an impact, half-volleying home Kieron Durkan's cross. Even though he ended up on the subs' bench for the away match at Bristol City, Nash's goal no doubt helped him achieve his dream of playing for his country. Already a Canadian Under-21 international, he made the grade a month later, appearing on the left wing in a World Cup qualifier against El Salvador in Vancouver.

On the evidence of his ninety minutes against Burnley, Nash Jr, who created further opportunities for

● **Factfile:** Martin Nash's brother Steve has just completed a rookie season in the National Basketball Association. Two years older, Steve is a point guard with the Phoenix Suns. Their father, John, played professional soccer in England and South Africa, while Martin spent a season with Tottenham Hotspur's youth squad.

Mutch and Mike, looks to have a bright future.

County held their lead at Turf Moor until the 72nd minute, when Damon Searle handled Nigel Gleghorn's header on the line. Searle, restored to the team for the first time since September 10th, was sent off leaving Edwards to beat away a David Eyres spot-kick to protect the advantage. It was a good effort, given Edwards's record of keeping out penalties and the fact that Eyres had previously missed only two of his last 29. County's ten men hung on to secure a meeting — away of course — against Bury.

The 'stars' came back for the game at Bristol City three days later as County attempted to beat their Ashton Gate bogey: they hadn't won in this part of the world since the First World War and had conceded an average of four goals a game. Over 13,000 Bristolians created a super-charged atmosphere at a ground worthy of higher-grade action. However, the expense of another long trip, coupled with the likelihood of getting snarled up on the motorway, kept the number of visiting fans down to a minimum. They were the ones in good voice, though, as County's 'twelfth man', referee Alan Butler, claimed an assist for the opening goal. The Nottingham policeman couldn't escape from a Sean Connelly shot and deflected the ball into the path of Armstrong.

Seconds later Armstrong was celebrating his eleventh goal of the campaign, and Mr Butler incurred the wrath of the Robins' less-than-chirpy supporters again close to half-time. This time he refused to accede to their request for a penalty when Flynn sparred with Paul Agostino, who still managed to hit the crossbar.

DAMON SEARLE: DISMISSED AGAINST ARCH-RIVALS BURNLEY

County rode their luck just once too often 45 seconds after the resumption, however. Durkan and Todd bungled an attempted clearance, giving Junior Bent the chance to cross for Shaun Goater to equalise. Armstrong should have restored the lead only to rush his attempt when faced with a one-on-one against keeper Stuart Naylor, who later kept out a Tony Dinning block-buster, but Paul Jones also moved smartly to deny Goater a second goal.

In the end, was it a point won or two points dropped? Neither manager was too sure.

'We weren't going to come to a place like Bristol City and get our own way,' said Dave Jones. 'It was a good game between two teams fighting to get out of this league.' Commented Joe Jordan, City's manager: 'I think we had the better chances, but I'm not saying we deserved to win it. We should have had a penalty though.'

Of more concern to Jones were four bookings: Armstrong, Todd, Bennett, and Gannon for dissent, plus Marsden's injury. 'We're hoping it's nothing more serious than a badly bruised bone and a scan should tell us either way.'

Marsden missed his fifth consecutive game when the Hatters went to Bury for the northern quarter-final of the Auto Windscreen Shield, played in torrential rain. With six weeks of the season remaining, the eventual champions were eight points behind the leaders and, surprisingly, given the amount of cup games County had played, Bury still had a match in hand on the Hatters. Neil Edwards came in for Paul Jones while Andy Mutch was promoted to start the match when Armstrong pulled a hamstring in the warm-up.

The Auto Windscreen Shield competition doesn't have the same glamour as other knock-out events, but there was no shortage of thrills and spills in County's run this season. They won a penalty after ten minutes when Chris Lucketti handled and Dinning drilled home from twelve yards. Bury boss Stan Ternent didn't agree with the decision, but referee Uriah Rennie has more good games than bad ones and is gaining an excellent reputation — so much so that the Yorkshire official was promoted to the Premier League for the '97–'98 campaign.

Bury levelled through Paul Butler after 31 minutes, despite the finer endeavours of Edwards, but neither side could prevent extra time and the added tension of the golden goal. The Shakers believed they'd stolen it when Chris Lucketti headed in, but Mr Rennie settled County's indigestion by ruling there had been a push (told you he was a good ref!). With 99 minutes played, up stepped Brett Angell with his own version of the golden shot to keep County on the Wembley trail. 'I'd rather these games went straight to penalties but having scored the important goal, I'll settle for the current system on this occasion,' said Jones following a 2–1 victory.

The home match with Shrewsbury on February 15th came after a spell of five away games in six fixtures. On paper, the Shrews were there to be buried. In reality, County had to call on the AA — Armstrong and Angell — to boot them back into the play-off zone. Peter Whiston appeared to have put a spoke in the promotion wheel with a goal on the hour, but a double from Angell and the third from Armstrong, his last until the penultimate Saturday of the season, saved the day.

However, just how close Angell came to missing out on his badly needed brace will never be known. He looked a prime candidate for being replaced by Andy Mutch, until he connected with Mike Flynn's throw to equalise in 74 minutes. Inside a minute Angell climbed highest to convert Kieron Durkan's centre leaving Armstrong to tidy up the spoils. 'Mutchy was raring to go,' agreed head boy Angell. Then with a grin he added: 'But I don't know who he was coming on for.'

Victory was a relied to Dave Jones. 'Now we can concentrate on beating Middlesbrough. We only ask three things of our players: ability, commitment and attitude. When you've got all three together, you know you're on your way.'

As it worked out, the dual with Middlesbrough had to be put on ice. Or, rather, water. The monsoon-like weather — making it one of the wettest Februarys on record — washed out the midweek first-leg semi-final. Like the rain, the flood of protests about ticket allocation for County's biggest game in their history wouldn't subside. Dave Espley, editor of *The Tea Party*, called the situation

SOUVENIR POSTCARD FOR THE COCA-COLA CUP SEMI-FINALS, 1997 — BUT WHO IS THAT COUNTY PLAYER?

. . . a disgrace. This wasn't the first time they've had a ticketing fiasco. Three basic questions had to be asked. Why were season ticket holders allowed three tickets each? Why was no voucher system used? And why was there no ticket limit when they went on open sale?

It was reported some people had bought ten tickets at a time — claims strongly denied by the club. The *Stockport Express Advertiser* revealed the plight of 77-year-old Stanley Marriott, who'd been a supporter for seventy years but still missed out. One supporter who didn't, as reported in The Tea Party, was Tony Turner, who forked out at least £500 to fly over from Bermuda.

Gary Glendenning, club secretary, attempted to diffuse the anger.

Staff were told to use their discretion and allow no more than three or four tickets per person on open sale. Of the 9,200 tickets allowed for the home crowd, up to 6,000 could have

gone to the 2,000 season ticket holders who were allowed three each. Sponsors also get some, and around 2,000 remained for the public. I am in favour of a voucher system, but time didn't allow us to implement it.

Anyway there was no need for a ticket for the next game: Blackpool away. Rarely in this memorable journey had Stockport fans left for the exits well before the end, but many County fans had already voted with their feet before Andy Mutch popped up with a late consolation.

Even six minutes of injury time couldn't save Dave Jones's side from their first away league reverse since November and a broadside from their boss. 'If you don't put your chances away you don't win matches,' he blasted. 'However, I'm more angry at the two goals we gave away. They were sloppy and this defeat was entirely of our own making. We keep getting into

● **Factfile:** Jock Dodds scored eight times and also missed a penalty when Blackpool trounced County 9–2 in February 1941.

ourselves in a good position in the league and then blowing it.'

It took the Seasiders almost an hour to cash in on County's charity, with Edgeley Park old boy James Quinn shooting them ahead. Chris Marsden, eventually restored to the side, should have equalised almost immediately, but four weeks of inactivity didn't help when it came to beating Steve Banks. Tony Ellis made Mazza's miss even

more costly, side-footing the clinching goal after 73 minutes.

County, as usual, had no time to dwell on what went wrong. The Coca-Cola Cup semi-final beckoned and the press pack were out in force at Mottram Hall on the Monday after the Blackpool game. 'I was surprised by number of people who turned up, but I was pleased the attention was shared among the whole squad,' said Mike Flynn. 'The original postponement might have disappointed some, but it worked in my favour because I was struggling with a thigh injury at the time.'

Another relieved player was Lee Todd. He missed the game at Bloomfield Road because of suspension and also had one other game to sit out. The ban, however, didn't affect Coca-Cola ties, giving Todd a chance to play against the club he supported as a boy. 'I never used to miss a game home or away,' owned up the former Hartlepool player. 'But those memories will have to be put on one side.'

Dave Jones used his pre-match programme jottings to discuss his future at Edgeley Park, again under the microscope. They now make interesting reading. Wrote Jones:

> The whole situation has been blown out of all proportion. I suppose there is bound to be speculation when a manager has not signed a contract.
>
> *But I can assure you I am more than happy at Stockport. I'm not even halfway through a job here.*
>
> Contrary to reports I have not had a bust-up with the chairman. In fact, we have a good working relationship and it is not all about money [Jones's emphasis].

LEE TODD: AN OPPORTUNITY TO PLAY AGAINST THE CLUB HE SUPPORTED AS A BOY

ANGRY BOSS JONES BLASTS REF

MAD AS A HATTER!

FAN FLARE . . . an angry Stockport supporter confronts referee David Elleray as tempers grow

REFFING ELL!

Jones slams blunder

Stockport County 0 Middlesbrough 2
STOCKPORT boss David Jones blasted top referee David Elleray after watching his Wembley dream turn sour.

By PETER PITTON

DAVE JONES'S DISPLEASURE WITH REFEREE DAVID ELLERAY WAS WIDELY REPORTED.

■ BALLOON GOES UP – Akın Armstrong has to contend with Middlesbrough's Phil Stamp and a balloon which drifted onto the pitch

The Middlesbrough match marked County's tenth tie in the competition; 'Boro had played five including victories over Newcastle (3–1) and Liverpool (2–1) in the quarter-finals. They'd also hammered Hereford 10–0 on aggregate in the second round, with European Cup-winner Fabrizio Ravanelli helping himself to four. The majority of their Foreign Legion was on show: Aussie Mark Schwarzer, Dane Mikkel Beck, Italians Ravanelli and Gianluca 'Uncle' Festa, plus Brazilian Emerson, but no Juninho, on international duty with Brazil. The club once known as the 'Bank of England' side had now been assembled at a cost that would have drained the International Monetary Fund.

For 72 minutes, though, County held their own on a pitch that looked as if it had been borrowed from a farmyard and in fact had only been passed fit 45 minutes before kick-off. Then disaster struck. Kieron Durkan failed to move up with his defence, Neil Cox threaded a pass through to beat the offside trap and Beck shot home. Seven minutes later came the goal that ultimately cost County a final place against Leicester City, and it left Jones raging.

Ravanelli clearly fouled Mike Flynn on the halfway line, but the referee didn't want to know. He had his whistle up ready to blow and Flynn took his eye off the ball and mis-kicked. We've had this fellow before, and he always manages to cock things up. I realise this could cost me a fine but I can't keep it bottled up.

The man on the receiving end was Harrow School housemaster David Elleray, who booked seven players including scorer Ravanelli. 'He did the same thing when handling three of our four Wembley appearances,' added Jones. He wasn't the only one livid. A spectator breached security to confront Elleray on the pitch but was escorted away before the club suffered any bad publicity.

'For the first goal, though, we committed suicide,' conceded Jones.' But he also warned Middlesbrough not to fall into the same trap as Sheffield United and Southampton. 'We're down but not quite out. Write us off at your peril.'

Bryan Robson, who had played alongside Jones for England Youth and Under-21s, couldn't hide his delight: 'They went for it and gave us a tough time but we're now in the driving seat. Our fans have waited a long time for this.'

The Middlesbrough game was the final one of the month and defeat at Blackpool dropped County into sixth place. Their record was:

P	W	D	L	F	A	Pts
30	13	9	8	43	34	47

AFTER THE MIDWEEK excitement, but ultimate disappointment, against Middlesbrough, it was back to reality for the first game in March. Bottom-of-the-table Rotherham visited Edgeley Park, meaning a first return since his acrimonious departure for Danny Bergara. The cheers that greeted his appearance suggested the fans hadn't forgotten his contribution to pulling the club up by its bootlaces.

The Millers' lot hadn't improved greatly since the reverse fixture three months earlier, though they were still hard to break down. It took a deflected Kieron Durkan free-kick to beat them at Millmoor and this time the luck was out. There are every conceivable end-of-season awards handed out these days, but none, as far as I'm aware, for the most blatant penalty never given. If this was the case, County would have won with Kevin Pilkington's 'foul' on Kieron Durkan. The winger was clearly tugged over as he lined up a shot, but Pilkington, on loan from Manchester United, was found not guilty. It's rare for both managers to agree on contentious penalty decisions, but this time they did.

'The referee said he never saw it but everyone else in the ground did,' ranted Dave Jones. 'But how did Kizza end up on the floor? Was he blown down by the wind?' Even Bergara admitted: 'It looked a penalty to me.'

The official in question was Trevor Jones from Cumbria. He was rarely so controversial officiating in the Barrow Sunday League that I graced for three years in my time with the redoubtable Hawcoat FC. Indeed, he wrote a referees' column for the local evening paper and the answers to his rules of the game quiz were always (most of the time) correct.

However, when most of the after-match debate centres on only one talking point, you know it's been a bad game. Chances had been few and far between, with Paul Jones making a telling contribution in the opening half-minute and Mike Flynn missing a chance late on. After the energy-sapping game against 'Boro, County looked weary, but Jones was having none of it. 'If people keep telling the players they are tired, they will begin to believe them. I firmly believe it is a mental rather than a physical thing and one we can overcome.'

Despite the theory, the last thing County needed was extra-time when they met Crewe three days later for a place in the Auto Windscreen Shield northern final. So, what happens? 'Golden goal' again, only this time there's no goal, just thirty minutes' more unwanted exercise.

'I considered standing with the home supporters,' admitted Dave Espley of *The Tea Party*, 'because I didn't want to cheer any goals. For once I wanted us to lose to save ourselves for the league.' On the plus-side, the entertainment was of the highest order and in sharp contrast to the

STEVE SOUTHART

ANDY MUTCH: BROKE THE DEADLOCK AGAINST
EVENTUAL CHAMPIONS BURY

sterile league match between the two at Gresty Road. For the record, this was County's eighteenth cup-tie and 49th game of the season. In the majority of those matches, Paul Jones had been a wonderful last line of defence, and on this occasion he proved a hero again, only now as a goal-scorer. After two hours the tie had to be decided on penalties.

Earlier, Danny Murphy, tormentor-in-chief of Brentford during the second-division play-off final, and now at Liverpool, gave smart Alex the lead. Chris Marsden, with only his second of the season, cancelled it out before half-time. It stayed at 1–1 until the spot-kick shoot-out, thanks largely to a breathtaking double save from Jason Kearton to deny Todd and Durkan.

Crewe kicked off penalties in the worst possible way with Shaun Smith blasting over the bar. 'I've only seen Shaun miss penalties twice and they've both been against Stockport,'

said Crewe manager Dario Gradi later. 'That's the last time he takes one against Stockport.' Andy Mutch, Luis Cavaco, Tony Dinning and Tom Bennett all converted, and though Crewe slotted three of their own, the outcome rested on Paul Jones. He had no hesitation in ripping off his gloves and smashing the winning kick out of reach of Kearton to send County into the northern final.

Victory (5–3 on penalties) also avenged a 3–0 shoot-out defeat when the sides met at Edgeley Park in the Associate Members Cup. 'We sorted the penalty-takers out on the night,' revealed Dave Jones. 'I learned my lesson in the Isle of Man trying to pick them beforehand. Jonah wanted to take one and, like most 'keepers, he fancies himself as an outfield player in training.'

Bryan Robson and assistant Viv Anderson undertook a spying mission at Gresty Road and left with much food for thought. 'We want to go as far as possible in all competitions so I was delighted by the eventual result,' enthused the manager. 'Having said that, I wouldn't be over-keen on the golden-goal system or penalties every week.'

Bury arrived at Edgeley Park on March 8th third in the league and with a reputation for no-nonsense defence and a simplistic approach, i.e. get the ball from back to front as quickly as possible. They didn't disappoint. Well organised they certainly were, but attractive to watch? After witnessing this game, you can understand why the Shakers' supporters didn't exactly turn out in their droves last season.

With five men strung across the back and four pressing the space in midfield, Bury's intention was clear. Thankfully, Andy Mutch, deputising

110

for Brett Angell, the subject of a mystery viral complaint that later turned out to be tonsillitis, broke the deadlock and made them rethink their strategy. Despite the lurking presences of Chris Lucketti and Paul Butler, Mutch stole a march to loop Mike Flynn's throw out of Dean Kiely's reach after less than two minutes.

With the exception of a Chris Lucketti long-range drive, tipped over by Jones, County laid siege to Kiely's goal. They had to wait until 33 seconds into the second half to double their tally, but it was well worth the delay. Sean Connelly, Mutch and Alun Armstrong created the opening and John Jeffers, on his 50th league appearance for Stockport, cleverly side-footed home for 2–0.

If Armstrong had scored instead of striking the post moments later County would have won in a canter. Instead, they conceded a goal to Butler from Bury's first corner of the second period and then lived dangerously until the final whistle.

Paul Jones had been the goal-scoring hero at Crewe, and now he was the goal-stopping hero. He blocked a one-on-one with Adrian Randall and then in injury time denied substitute Tony Battersby, on loan from Notts County. 'This was a real six-pointer for us,' said Dave Jones. 'A draw would have suited Bury more than it would us. Paul did well for us, but that's what he's paid for. Besides we should have killed the game off before then.' Mutch was more complimentary about his team-

CONNELLY THE GOAL-SCORING HERO AT THE RIVERSIDE STADIUM — HIS FIRST EVER FOR STOCKPORT

ALLSPORT

STEVE SOUTHART

ALUN ARMSTRONG: A BARGAIN FOR £35,000 FROM NEWCASTLE IN 1994 AND A FIRM FAVOURITE WITH THE FANS

STEVE SOUTHART

DES HINKS

STEVE SOUTHART

STEVE SOUTHART

TWO OF COUNTY'S RAREST SCORERS:
PAUL JONES (ABOVE), WHO RIPPED OFF
HIS GLOVES TO CONTRIBUTE TO
STOCKPORT'S PENALTY VICTORY OVER
CREWE; AND SEAN CONNELLY (LEFT),
WHO SCORED HIS FIRST AND ONLY
GOAL OF THE SEASON AGAINST
MIDDLESBROUGH

STOCKPORT EXPRESS

mate's display. 'He's been a colossus. For me, Paul has made the difference between us being an average-to-good side last season to being a very good one this season.'

As a result of the draw, Bury dropped back to fifth while County were eighth. At this stage Brentford, Luton and Millwall led the division. All three failed to last the course.

One of the problems involved with working for yourself is having to go where there's work and not going where you want to. Over the years, I've lost count of the number of trips, nights out, sporting events or invitations I've missed in order to earn a crust. The main culprit has been snooker: I follow the professional circuit full time and cover other sports when the green baize calendar allows.

Fortunately, one of my free nights coincided with the Middlesbrough game at the Riverside Stadium, and, even though I wasn't there in my capacity as a reporter, I was suitably hooked to see if County could reverse their 1–0 first-leg deficit, and for once my decision was rewarded with a classic night to remember.

I'd been to Ayresome Park a handful of times but the Riverside was another new ground. It was certainly an impressive sight, as was the enormous floating oil tanker/refinement terminal moored alongside the adjacent quay. Now, Middlesbrough isn't one of those places you want to go on holiday, but the stadium is a different matter, despite being located in the middle of wasteland. Still, the locals were friendly and helpful and the food

MARK SCHWARZER (NUMBER 19) LIES INJURED AFTER A CLASH WITH CHRIS MARSDEN. JOHN JEFFERS ACTS AS PEACEMAKER.

DES HINKS

cheap: you could get excellent Juninho burgers, Ravanelli fritters and a mouth-watering hot-dog, whose name escapes me, from a hot food caravan parked close to the ground. If you were a Middles-brough fan you could also already purchase memorabilia emblazoned with: 'Boro Wembley '97'. Talk about confident.

The pre-match hospitality was in full swing, but not if you were with the County party. Chairman Brendan Elwood later complained to the club's chief executive Keith Lamb and oppo-site number Steve Gibson how shabbily the directors' wives had been treated. However, for the fans down below the beer was flowing nicely. Whatever the outcome, they were out to enjoy the evening. So, imagine the euphoria when Sean Connelly, after only six minutes, chose the moment to score his first goal for the club after nearly 150 appearances. Commenta-tors, even the local ones, had to double-check to make sure they didn't credit the goal to a team-mate. Could County possibly add their name to a list con-taining the names of Swindon, QPR and Aston Villa: second-division clubs (then old Division 3) who had made it to Wembley in the League Cup?

They gave it their best shot. Had Juninho missed this game, as he had the first leg, County might have done it, but he was the difference between the teams and threatened to conjure up an equaliser every time he touched the ball. Emerson, in contrast, was extremely ineffective.

With twenty minutes left, County almost levelled on aggregate. A mis-take by Festa gave Cavaco a clear sight of goal, but he went for precision rather than power and debut-boy Schwarzer made the save. County's task was made even more mountain-ous when Tony Dinning was sent off in

DES HINKS

ANDY MUTCH CELEBRATES COUNTY'S GOAL AGAINST THE FORMER PREMIERSHIP CLUB.

the 75th minute. Ravanelli should have joined him for play-acting. Dinning's retaliation merited, at worst, a book-ing, but with Ravanelli writhing in apparent agony, the ref produced red. The incident provoked one of the quotes of the season from Dave Jones. 'He went down as though he'd been shot. I don't think he was even holding the leg that had been kicked!'

If anything, County upped the tempo. Middlesbrough's only thoughts were survival and they showed no inclination to equalise as the seconds ticked away. Seldom can a team have less deserved the standing ovation that greeted Middlesbrough at the end. As one wag suggested: 'The only team to have done a lap of honour after being beaten at home by Stockport.'

COUNTY'S STAR TREK COMES TO A MAGNIFICENT END

■ WHEN THE BOOT COMES IN ... Chris Marsden challenges Mark Schwarzer and has to take cover from a flying tackle from Nigel Preston

Final frontier

Jones' crew go so boldly

By Peter Gardner

BOLD, brave Stockport were today basking in the glory of a night of triumphant failure.

County were so near, yet so far from achieving a modern-day footballing miracle.

Mighty Middlesbrough mopped up the glittering Wembley prize, but Dave Jones and his gallant Second Division players richly and rightly earned the Coca-Cola Cup praise after scaring the pants off the Premiership aristocrats.

They added jittery Boro to a growing list of top-notch scalps on the way to the club's first-ever major semi-final and now they lost by the narrowest of margins.

No-one gave little County a hope in hell after losing the Edgeley Park leg 2-0 to Bryan Robson's £30m foreign legion of superstars.

Yet they almost pulled off mission impossible. Just as they had done in beating Blackburn, West Ham and Southampton along the way to a £1.5m pot of gold.

But no team in the 36-year history of the competition had overturned such a deficit in the second leg away from home. Yet Sean Connelly's stunning strike for his first goal in senior football after just five minutes brought County within touching distance of writing a further chapter to soccer's record books.

And had little Luis Cavaco accepted an even better 70th minute opportunity, the fairy tale might not have ended in unashamed tears.

County took the Riverside Stadium by storm on a night of unbearable Teesside tension that finished with ... sent off and the ... home side hanging on by the skin of their teeth.

Middlesbrough 0 Stockport County 1 (Boro win 2-1 on aggregate)

'The Jones' boys achieved what Newcastle and Liverpool before them had failed to do in the competition by beating Boro on their own ground. And Boro still went on a lap of honour after losing at home to Second Division Stockport!

So sure of victory were Boro they had arrogantly arranged the immediate after-match sale of special Wembley commemorative Coca-Cola Cup final shirts.

How close they came to having egg on their faces... and meaningless goods on their hands.

Credit County for giving their lot in what started as a lost cause and ended with a story of what might have been.

Said Jones: "I couldn't have asked for more. They were absolutely magnificent. I am naturally disappointed because we haven't reached Wembley. But I'm still so proud because this was our final. Had that chance by Luis gone in, they would really have been twitching."

However, it started with County suffering from an early touch of nerves as Emerson, later so ineffective, linked with the ever-dangerous Juninho for Beck's finish to hit the side of a post.

Chris Marsden's careless loss of possession then provided Juninho a platform only for the little Brazilian to shoot over.

But suddenly County found their composure. Heroic skipper Mike Flynn drove in a free-kick, the alert Alun Armstrong turned the ball into the path of Connelly and the trigger finger clicked for a glorious fifth minute finish.

County at times still lived dangerously, but the superb Paul Jones defied Boro with a string of breath-taking saves. Juninho exposed a Flynn error only to again shoot over, but the fateful 70th minute and Cavaco's close-in strike majestically blocked by Mark Schwarzer was the moment Boro booked their first Wembley visit for a major final.

Dinning's 75th minute red card followed retaliation to a shirt tug by Ravanelli, yet the Italian made such a meal of the incident, Jones insisted: "He went down as if he'd been shot. I don't think he was even holding the leg which had been kicked."

FORM GUIDE STOCKPORT: JONES 10, Connelly 9, Todd 8, Bennett 8, Flynn 8, Dinning 6, Cavaco 8, Marsden 8, Mutch 7, Armstrong 6, Jeffers 8. Subs: Angell 6, Gannon ...

■ YOU BEAUTY ... Andy Mutch celebrates Sean Connelly's ...

MANCHESTER EVENING NEWS

So, after eleven matches, 990 minutes or 16½ hours, the Coca-Cola Cup dream was over for another season. 'I couldn't have asked for more from them,' said Jones. 'They were absolutely magnificent. But our priority has always been to get out of the second division and that remains the single-minded intention.'

After the first game against Middlesbrough, County stumbled through their next Nationwide League match with Rotherham. As the season was now coming to the boil, they could ill afford any similar slips when they went to Peterborough following the trip to Teesside. The cup run was history. A Wembley date in the Auto Windscreen Shield would be a bonus: all that mattered now was promotion.

It took the opening 45 minutes at London Road to get the 'Boro match out of their system. When inspiration rather than perspiration was needed to open up Posh, Cavaco provided it, skipping through a forest of legs to strike a shot into the far corner of the net. At 1–0 there was still work to be done, mainly from Paul Jones, as Craig Ramage and Ken Charlery both discovered why the 'keeper had been the recipient of so many rave reviews. The saves proved crucial and Marsden put the result beyond doubt after a game chase by Armstrong and pinpoint centre by Jeffers.

'Stockport have been a credit to the division all season and deserve an automatic promotion spot,' declared Barry Fry, later to see his team relegated. 'They are a very good footballing side.' Jones was just pleased to seal the points. 'We had to grind out our result and I was delighted by the efforts the lads put in.'

It wasn't only the players that needed a rest: the team bus was clocking up the miles. Next stop was Brunton Park for the first leg of the Auto Windscreen Shield northern final with Carlisle. When players and fans were to look back at season 1996–97, this match definitely provided one of the low spots. Carlisle had promotion

> **Factfile:** Ten players have appeared for both County and 'Boro including Oshor Williams, Harry Kirk and one Tom Green!

STEVE SOUTHART

aspirations of their own, and under ex-West Ham and Leeds 'keeper Mervyn Day had become a tough outfit to beat.

When the sun's shining, Cumbria can be as idyllic a place as you can find. When the rain's driving in off the fells, it's no place for sheep, let alone humans. The latter conditions turned Brunton Park into a mushy mess and the quality of the football mirrored the awful weather. Owen Archdeacon eventually punished Todd for losing possession by giving United a 55th-minute advantage. However, the real damage was inflicted deep into injury time. County hadn't looked capable of equalising even when Angell and Durkan replaced Armstrong and Cavaco, but they would have settled for a 1–0 defeat.

It was to get worse. Chris Marsden made the French connection, striking Parisian Stephane Pounewatchy and was sent off. From the free-kick Todd was viewed to have tripped Warren Aspinall and Archdeacon planted the penalty past Paul Jones for number two. 'A couple moments of madness might have cost us a Wembley place,' conceded Mike Flynn. 'I thought we controlled the game without ever looking effective. It's OK enjoying possession, but you also need to create danger in the goalmouth and have a few shots.'

If County didn't get the breaks at Carlisle, there were no complaints following the League match at Notts County, Stockport's fourth away-day in a row. Ex-Manchester United defender Graeme Hogg scored an injury-time own-goal to prompt the headlines: 'Pig sick!' Even the visitors' first might have been an own-goal. Perm anyone from Devon White, Matthew Redmile or possibly Mike Flynn to have got the touch from Kieron Durkan's corner after Hogg needlessly headed behind.

MARCH SAW THE ARRIVAL OF OLD-TIMER GORDON COWANS FROM BRADFORD VIA ASTON VILLA, BARI *ET AL*.

Not in doubt was the final score: 2–1 to the Hatters and their first win at Meadow Lane for 38 years, a victory that helped push Notts County into Division 3 at the end of the season. Ex-Magpie Chris Marsden was more pleased than most as County stole the victory. Flynn summed up the performance: 'Every game is like a cup final at the moment, though we haven't exactly been playing like a cup-final side.' Jones was also spot on with his verdict: 'It wasn't pretty to watch, the

STEVE SOUTHART

ARMSTRONG BATTLING AGAINST CREWE

Competition for places had now began to hot up. With the transfer deadline almost upon him, Jones signed Kevin Cooper from Derby, Gordon Cowans from Bradford and Peterborough's Ken Charley. He also turned down an approach from Birmingham for Mike Flynn and welcomed back Adie Mike from a spell at Doncaster. Cooper replaced John Jeffers for the return with Carlisle and Cowans took a seat on the bench.

Due to the exodus of fans from Carlisle, kick-off was delayed for fifteen minutes. They were rewarded with a fine rearguard action, though just how County failed to score, especially in the opening half, will always remain a mystery. As it became evident, the Twin Towers were receding from view as every minute frustration mounted. Marsden was booked for lashing out at Richard Prokas and Tom Bennett was dismissed for two second-half tackles on the same player.

When County broke through it came in the final minute and was disallowed — not that Carlisle chairman Michael Knighton noticed. Interviewed on the radio later, he extolled the virtues of his side though it was a pity, he said, Carlisle had lost 1–0 on the night. Perhaps he'd been seeing aliens again![*]

And so it came to pass on Tuesday, March 25th, County's cup saga came to an end. They had played 21 ties, winning fifteen and losing only three. There were now twelve more matches to see them into the Promised Land of the first division. 'The game was lost in the last few mad minutes of the first leg,' claimed Jones.

Considering Ken Charley had scored the goal for Peterborough that

pitch was very bobbly and they fought hard. We got away with it.'

With Tony Dinning suspended, the game marked the return of Jim Gannon. Angered by his recent demotion to the subs' bench, Gannon let his feelings known to the management team, but it wasn't the first time the talented but temperamental Irishman had done this over the years. Once re-united with the number six shirt, Gannon kept possession for the remainder of the season.

---

[*] That season, Carlisle chairman Michael Knighton had been subjected to a great deal of ridicule following his revelation that he had seen alien spacecraft over the Cumbrian fells!

STEVE SOUTHART

STEVE SOUTHART

MORE ACTION AGAINST CREWE:
LEE TODD FIGHTS AN AERIAL
BATTLE (ABOVE), AND KEVIN
COOPER SLOTS IN THE VITAL
PENALTY (RIGHT).

cost County promotion in 1992, he received a warm welcome for his debut against Crewe on March 29th. Steve Antrobus, formerly of Shrewsbury, made his first appearance for the Grecians in another do-or-die match. The game did in fact belong to a newcomer — Kevin Cooper. He netted the game's only goal fractionally before half-time from a pass from Tom Bennett, the recipient of a new two-year contract.

'Crewe are known as the aristocrats of the second division and over the last two games with them I think we've matched them in every department,' was Jones's assessment. 'But we won't rest on our laurels and we'll continue to build upon the foundations we've laid.'

Paul Jones, who declined an invitation to join the Welsh squad for the game with Belgium, made his customary intervention to send County into April in fourth place with a record of:

P	W	D	L	F	A	Pts
35	17	10	8	50	36	56

COUNTY'S FIRST MATCH OF the new month fell on April Fool's Day. Striker Alun Armstrong commemorated it by becoming the fourth County player to be sent off in the last three weeks, while Nottingham referee Frazer Stretton gave a performance that defied belief — at least if you were a County fan. It added up to a 0–0 draw at Bournemouth which, at this stage in the term, was a result neither side wanted.

In the days leading up to the Dean Court trip, there had been doubt whether the match would be played — not because of the weather, but due to the Cherries' horrendous financial problems that left the official receiver wanting to close them down. Had Bournemouth's record been expunged, then County would have benefited having lost 1–0 at Edgeley Park over seven months earlier. For the good of soccer in general, however, it was good news when a rescue package was found, and as a result there was a cup-tie atmosphere around Dean Court when the match got under way.

With Chris Marsden suspended, Dave Jones brought in Gordon Cowans, while Armstrong and Andy Mutch worked in tandem up front due to Brett Angell (injured) and Ken Charlery (suspended) both missing. Despite the uncertainty over Bournemouth's future, their past results had been encouraging, especially at home where they hadn't lost since October.

Too many misplaced passes spoilt the game as a spectacle, and it wasn't until Armstrong struck the post after 39 minutes that County fans had

STEVE SOUTHART

ALUN ARMSTRONG'S FRUSTRATION LED TO A DISMISSAL AGAINST BOURNEMOUTH.

something to cheer. With Armstrong it was either feast or famine and, sadly, now he was in the middle of another goal-scoring drought and due to go a twelfth game without finding the target. Against this backdrop of frustration, his temper boiled over, when in the 57th minute he argued about being pulled up for an innocent-looking challenge and was booked. Armstrong continued to claim a miscarriage of justice and was duly red-carded.

His dismissal changed the complexion of the contest and Bournemouth went all out for the winner, but stout defending, including Lee Todd's late goal-line clearance from Matt Holland, kept them at bay. Later, Dave Jones risked official censure by backing Armstrong against Mr Stretton. 'The referee gave us nothing all night — he didn't even give us a foul until the 35th minute. I don't blame the lad. If I'd been on the pitch, I'd have done the same thing. I think we might have blown our chances of winning the fair-play league,' he added, smiling at last.

Prior to the match with Bristol Rovers on April 5th, there had been newspaper speculation that Jones was to replace Joe Royle in the Everton hot seat. Again, Jones scotched the rumours. 'It's nice to be associated with such a big club, but it's all just pie in the sky. My only interest at present is finishing the job in hand.' Also staying put were Matt Bound and Damon Searle, Bound tying himself to a new two-year contract and Searle rejecting a move to Peterborough.

Neither, however, were in the fourteen for the match with Rovers. Also absent was Brett Angell and the suggestion was he wouldn't play again this season because of knee trouble. Charlery came back into the team to

KEVIN COOPER:
ANOTHER VITAL PENALTY CONVERSION

bolster an attack that had scored only once in its last three outings, and it so nearly became one in four until Kevin Cooper scored the only goal from the penalty spot five minutes from time.

Bristol survived quite comfortably until then and could easily have been in front with 'midget gem' Jamie Cureton such a handful. Instead, it was another Jamie — Clapham — who literally handed County the points. The substitute had been on the field only twelve minutes when Luis Cavaco left him right up the junction. Clapham could only handle Cavaco's intended spooned cross to concede the penalty. There was no doubts he handled, though Rovers felt aggrieved play hadn't already been stopped to allow skipper Andy Tillson to receive treatment.

Cooper took responsibility and stroked the ball beyond Andy Collett, though careless County did their best to share the spoils. However, thanks to Paul Jones, the 1–0 scoreline stayed intact when he produced one of his finest saves of the season to tip over Cureton's deflection of a Justin Skinner shot. 'I thought he should have held it,' grinned Dave Jones who, for once, didn't add the rider: 'Well, that's what he gets paid for.'

Those fans at Crewe who had witnessed Jonah's penalty, half-expected him to come up and take this latest award. Cooper, however, refused to be swayed. 'I didn't mind taking it, even though there was a bit of pressure on it. I knew which way I was going to place it and besides there weren't too many volunteers.' Super Cooper was also delighted that the same day Derby had humbled Man. United at Old Trafford (he and a few million others, no doubt). 'They won't want me back if they keep getting results like that. I've been at Derby since I was a schoolboy, but I was delighted to come to Stockport.' (Cooper eventually made a permanent move to Edgeley Park with the 1997–98 season already a game old.)

As the team travelled down to Plymouth three days later, Mike Flynn spelt out the promotion goal: 'If we can get four points from every two games we should be OK. 'The game with Bristol wasn't a classic but we got the points and that's all that mattered.'

Those supporters not exactly enamoured by the performances of Ken Charlery during the end of season run-

KEN CHARLERY: 'I OWE THE FANS A LOT'

in should know he almost missed the journey to Devon. The team agreed to meet at Hilton Park services near Birmingham, but waited half an hour without any sign of Charlery. Keen to avoid the M6 bottleneck, they rang him on his mobile. While they were sitting on the southbound services, Charlery was on the northbound side! 'Ken gave us a few laughs and quickly became one of the lads,' says Flynn. Charlery himself kept smiling through the lean spell.

STEVE SOUTHART

ANDY MUTCH SETTLES THE SCORE AGAINST BURNLEY IN APRIL WITH AN ELEVENTH-HOUR WINNER AFTER COMING ON AS SUB SEVEN MINUTES BEFORE THE END.

STEVE SOUTHART

STOCKPORT COUNTY FC
1883
THE FRIENDLY FOOTBALL CLUB

■ BEAUTY ... County's Luis Cavaco is mobbed after scoring their second goal

BOSS JONES SALUTES COUNTY REPLAY ACE

DAVE'S DELL BOYS

Elwood warns

STOCKPORT County chairman Brendan ... today slipped ... his late ... signs on ... Edgeley Park start ... has taken some to ...

Bruce ... from the big ...

By Paul Hince

PROUD Stockport manager Dave Jones today paid tribute to his 11 heroes who went within five minutes of a Coca-Cola Cup semi-final place last night.

County were leading Southampton 2-1 with five minutes to play in the home quarter-final but a scrambled equaliser from Norwegian Egil Ostenstad earned the Premiership side a replay at the Dell next Wednesday.

"My boys were brilliant," said Jones. "I was proud of every last one ...

Mutch to cheer

County Plea to Fans

Stockport 1 Burnley 0

PATIENCE is a virtue Stockport fans are urged to acquire as the second division promotion race heads for a photo-finish.

Manager Dave Jones and skipper Mike Flynn both appealed for the Edgeley Park faithful to make their support constructive rather than destructive in the remaining three home games.

"The fans expect us to win and win by scoring three or four goals," says Flynn. "At this stage of the season the main priority is just to get the three points."

"Away from home we can express ourselves a bit more. But we are all aware of how much is at stake."

"I'm sure the gaffer would settle for us winning every game until the end of the season 1-0."

Flynn's form has been instrumental in helping County keep six successive Nationwide League clean sheets.

By Trevor Baxter

■ JOY ... for County's Andy Mutch after his last minute goal

... strong's replacement hooked the ball into the net after a mistake by keeper Russell.

"I heard some people having a moan and groan that I hadn't brought on Andy sooner," said Jones. "But if they think they can do better, let them apply for the job."

To say Mutch's goal didn't go down a storm with the Burnley fans would be an understatement ...

... lot of stick before he went on," added Flynn. "Besides it was a big game and perhaps he let his emotions get the better of him."

It remains to be seen whether the club take any internal action against Mutch. However with Watford and leading scorer Brett Angell out for a fortnight, it might be diplomatic to mete out any punishment at a later date.

FORM GUIDE STOCKPORT: Jones 7, Connelly 7, Todd 8, Bennett 8, Flynn 8, Gannon 6, Cavaco 5

JONES IS COUNTY SAVER AS SHAKERS ARE DENIED

Paul's a pearler!

Stockport 2 Bury 1

ANDY Mutch was vying for Stockport's man of the match honours until Paul Jones produced the save that earned County a vital promotion victory.

"Paul's save didn't surprise me because he's been making them all season," said Mutch whose own display counterbalanced the absence of leading scorer Brett Angell.

"He's been a colossus. For me Paul made the difference between us being an average to good side last season to being a very good one this season."

Jones, the penalty hero at Crewe in midweek, twice denied Bury a share of the spoils after Paul Butler struck back following goals early in each half from Mutch and John Jeffers.

He blocked a one-on-one attempt from Adrian Randall after 74 minutes that ... stifle rather than ...

By Trevor Baxter

wrecked the best laid plans of manager Stan Ternant whose starting formation aimed to stifle rather than score.

"Bury are a hard, physical side and it's a fantastic victory for us," added the veteran striker whose touch set up Armstrong to cross for what proved to be the winning goal.

"A draw would have suited Bury more ...

■ DENIED ... Bury goalkeeper Dean Kiely snatches the ball from Alun Armstrong

"At times we played some great one-touch stuff. And I don't care who you play, eventually if it's executed properly you will find space and create chances in the box."

"Paul did well for us but he's paid for. It should work that far because we should get the game off."

Angell, Armstrong, and Louis Cavaco are ... the Coca-Cola Cup re ...

Saturday suffering from a mystery infection.

"We were a little bit thin for us today but the players that came their jobs well" added Jones.

... STOCKPORT ...

Sub Mutch too hot to handle!

Stockport ... 1 Burnley 0

SUPER sub Andy Mutch struck a late winner to give Stockport a valuable promotion victory.

Mutch had been on the field just three minutes when he netted his sixth-minute goal. It was his tenth of the campaign.

Mutch's jubilation was understandable given County's earlier threatening occasionally on the break, until Mutch volleyed in.

The Clarets gave little away while the start of the season, saw them collect only two points from their first five games. Now ...

By Trevor Baxter

Sadly, new boy Ken Charlery doesn't look the answer to the goal drought. He put himself about with enthusiasm after the break but missed a goal to bring back his confidence.

Thankfully for the home team Burnley's prolific scorer Paul Barnes suffered an off day too.

Kevin Cooper, the match winner against Crewe and Bristol ... good save from keeper Russell after 22 minutes while Charlery should have opened his account three minutes from half time.

After the break, Charlery had ...

■ ANDY MUTCH ... hit winner

A FLYING START SETTLES NERVES

County turn screw

Stockport ... Wycombe ...

STOCKPORT boldly attempted to turn the promotion screw today.

Just after it minutes goes from a flying start ending his own advanced confidence on the legal midfielder ... his target ...

Armstrong's pace after just four minutes ...

By Peter Gardner

The referee had taken ... to pay the advantage and after Jeffers had ... to play in front of a good ...

Paul Wycombe enjoyed a ...

... delighted to come to ... port when the opportunity ...

... spent most of my time ... reserves so it's been ... to play in front of a good ... for a change.

... of the crowd could ... bear to watch as Cooper ... to take what proved a ... winning penalty, five ... from the final whistle.

... need not have worried ... the 22-year-old winger ... a man-of-the-match ... display with an ice-cool finish.

"I didn't mind taking it, even though there was a bit of pressure on it.

"I know which way I was ...

THREE WYCOMBE PLAYERS BOOKED

DERBY'S shock win at Old Trafford did nothing ... Manchester United's Premier League hopes – ... it could earn Kevin Cooper a permanent place at Edgeley Park.

'Superman' is on loan from the ... Ball Ground until the end of the ... on and appears keen to stay ... upwardly mobile County.

... on hearing the news filtering back ... across town, Cooper grinned: "They ... want me back if they keep getting ... is like that.

... ve been at Derby since ... a schoolboy but I ...

Super Cooper!

Loan star is a last-gasp goal hero for County

By Trevor Baxter

going to place it and besides, there weren't too many other volunteers."

Rovers disputed the penalty award on two counts, although their claim that Jamie Clapham had not handled deliberately smacked of desperation.

They were more justified to argue should already have been halted due to an injury to skipper Andy Tillson.

However, there was no denying County a vital promotion victory and as manager Dave Jones said later: "We got our just desserts.

"The fans were getting frus-

trated because they want to see us scoring bagfuls of goals.

"But that's not going to happen at this time of the season. And I'll be happy to see us win every game until the end of the season 1-0."

It almost ended up 1-0, but Paul Jones pulled off another amazing injury-time save from his repertoire to deny Jamie Cureton and keep County on course for automatic promotion.

FORM GUIDE STOCKPORT: Jones 8, Connelly 7, Todd 8, Bennett 7, Flynn 8 Gannon 8, Durkan 6 (sub 61 mins Cavaco 7), Cowans, Charlery 6, Armstrong 6 (sub 71 Mutch), COOPER 8.

■ SPOT ON ... Kevin Cooper celebrates his penalty goal

ALL MANCHESTER EVENING NEWS

125

The reception I got from the fans on my home debut was tremendous considering what had gone on in the past. I owe them a lot and I'll be doing my best to repay them in the first division. I felt sorry at leaving Peterborough but in the past I'd always put the club before my own interests. This time I decided to look after number one.

The Plymouth game won't linger long in the memory, though it was interesting to note how the fortunes of the respective clubs had changed since September 10th: while County were now going hell for leather for promotion, Argyle were still in danger of relegation. Home Park had previously been a happy hunting ground with three back-to-back victories and nine goals in the process, and in fact their last trip was also Danny Bergara's final one in charge before his ignominious dismissal.

This time the match finished scoreless, though Armstrong again found the woodwork and had another attempt kicked off the whitewash by Jason Rowbotham. Plymouth weren't without their moments and Todd was alert to boot Mick Heathcote's effort from under the crossbar. Adrian Littlejohn was easily the home side's most dangerous forward, but the stalemate remained, leaving County with a point and an unbeaten seven-match league run.

With goal-scoring still a worry, Dave Jones happily announced Angell could yet have a part to play in the final run-in. 'He's had a cartilage operation and came through just fine. Brett even managed to walk out of hospital.' In the old days, such surgery would require two or three months' R&R.

The game with Burnley on April 12th started a run of five fixtures in eleven days. County politely asked for an extension to the season, but League spokesman Chris Hull gave them the answer: 'There will be no extension for Stockport County or anyone else. The season will be concluded on week ending May 3rd and 4th.' So, it was onwards and upwards, but only after a pulsating ninety minutes against the old foe from Turf Moor.

On police advice, kick-off was brought forward to 1 pm, but not everyone noted the switch, and one national journalist arrived for a 3 pm start with the game already drawing to a conclusion.

Had Paul Barnes conjured up the same finishing prowess he displayed in the reverse fixture, Burnley might have celebrated a double, but he failed to make another deposit in his Nationwide goal account and, as one wag suggested: 'Paul Jones has got more clean sheets than the Holiday Inn.'

For the third consecutive home game one goal was all it took for County to win the day, and what a sweet way to avenge last October's mauling. Only seven minutes remained when Andy Mutch replaced groggy Alun Armstrong who staggered off, looking as though he'd gone twelve rounds with Evander Holyfield. That was sufficient time for Mutchy to send most of Edgeley Park into raptures. Mutch struck when Wayne Russell, deputising for the injured Marlon Beresford, dropped a Jim Gannon cross. As the ball broke loose, all hell broke loose as well when Mutch found the back of the Burnley net. His instincts took him over to a section of Burnley fans who had been giving him stick while warming up. His over-exuberant celebrations went down like a lead balloon and might have sparked a major incident.

126

Calm was eventually restored after several visiting fans complained to the stewards but no further action was taken. Even the police were happy to let the incident pass without speaking to the player concerned. Said Flynn:

Andy was a bit naughty, but he'd taken a lot of stick before he went on. Besides, it was a big game and perhaps he let the emotions get the better of him. The fans expected us to win by scoring three or four goals a game and at that stage in the season our main priority was just to get the three points. The gaffer was happy for us to win every game 1–0 if that's what it took to get us up.

Even placid Jones let rip after the end of the game. 'I heard some people having a moan and groan that I hadn't brought Andy on earlier. If they think they can do better, let them apply for the job.' However, defeats for leaders Bury at Blackpool and for second-placed Luton at Walsall soon restored Jones's normally sunny countenance.

Flynn and Chris Marsden had good reason to feel smug in the next 48 hours. They were named in the second-division team of the season, voted for by their fellow professionals. It was the second time Mazza had been selected. 'I was nominated during my time with Huddersfield,' revealed the 28-year-old Yorkshireman. 'It's a great honour, possibly the highest you can get. Although it's an individual award, I also think it's a reflection on the way the whole team played.'

It said a lot for Watford's Kevin Miller's ability that he was chosen in front of Paul Jones, and when the sides met at Edgeley Park on April 14th they showed just how talented they both were. Jones, in particular, was magnificent, making three outrageously good saves after John Jeffers put County in

ARMSTRONG COMES CLOSE TO SCORING AGAINST WATFORD.

the driving seat after 54 minutes. He initially beat away a shot from Kevin Phillips, flung himself with the agility of a gymnast to tip away a Craig Ramage header and finally thwarted Stuart Slater. No wonder Slater sunk to his knees in disbelief.

On the Ramage save, Jones confessed later: 'I knew Watford had scored a goal from a corner the previous Saturday. I was about to go the other way when I remembered the goal had gone in at the near post. It's what I'm paid to do anyway.' Both the

THE CONTEST HEATS UP: DAMON SEARLE (LEFT) AND ANDY MUTCH (BELOW) TAKE ON WATFORD. PAUL JONES (BOTTOM LEFT) PUTS IN A 10-OUT-OF-10 PERFORMANCE.

Manchester Evening News and *Stockport Express* awarded Jones 10 out of 10 in their post-match marks.

There was, however, a down-side to the night. Luis Cavaco had his tibia and fibula broken in an early challenge from Craig Armstrong which, at the time of writing, has taken longer to mend than was first diagnosed. His replacement was Jeffers, who danced round Nigel Gibbs before aiming a shot into the bottom right-hand corner of Miller's net. 'It was not the best way to come into a match but it gave me great personal satisfaction scoring the only goal.'

The win elevated County into second place, one point adrift of Bury but with a game in hand. It was their highest league position for thirty months and kept them firmly on course for Division 1 for the first time in seven decades. Unfortunately, all the hard work to fill an automatic promotion slot was undone in the next two away trips as the games at Gillingham and Preston ended in 1–0 defeats to put the celebrations on hold.

Dave Jones described the opening 45 minutes at the Priestfield Stadium as 'Our worst 45 minutes of the season. The second was one of our best and we virtually camped out in Gillingham's half.' County failed, though, to deny Steve Butler the winner from an Andy Hassenthaler corner, and Chris Marsden, who had returned after a five-match suspension, almost salvaged a point with a late free-kick. To make matters worse, Bury and Brentford had both triumphed the night before.

The trip to Deepdale meant a nostalgic return for North End old boy, Captain Fantastic Mike Flynn. However, since his last visit, the completed

AGONY FOR LUIS CAVACO, STRETCHERED OFF

Tom Finney Stand made an impressive sight — in contrast to the rest of the ground. Over 10,000 saw County squander plentiful opportunities and concede a sucker goal to Ian Bryson in the 79th minute. Armstrong and Charlery missed glaring openings again while the former should have had a penalty. Explained Dave Jones:

We can't put this defeat down to bad luck: it was down to bad finishing. It was criminal on our part. The amount of chances we wasted, the game should have been well and

STEVE SOUTHART

truly over before they scored. I had a bit of a moan afterwards, but at this stage of the season moaning can be counter-productive.

Suddenly, County were in danger of becoming the best team in the division not to make the grade, and an injection of confidence was urgently needed. Enter Brett Angell, rushed back into action and named as substitute for the match with York on April 22nd. Explained Angell:

> It was frustrating missing the matches I did, even though I knew I was fortunate to be back so soon. Had I been injured earlier in the season when it was less hectic, I might only have missed three or four games. If it hadn't been for the cup games, I reckon we would have won the league well before the end of the season.

It showed just how sorely Angell had been missed when, thirteen minutes

TOM BENNETT: (ABOVE), INSTRUMENTAL IN THE VICTORY OVER YORK. (RIGHT) HIS CRUCIAL HEADER THAT BROUGHT THEM LEVEL.

DES HINKS

STOCKPORT COUNTY FC
THE FRIENDLY FOOTBALL CLUB

DES HINKS

PROMOTION IS TANTALISINGLY CLOSE AS COUNTY FACE
WYCOMBE: RED-HEADED ARMSTRONG SCORES (ABOVE)
AND CELEBRATES WITH CHRIS MARSDEN.

after replacing the luckless Charlery, he headed a match-winner — his nineteenth goal of the campaign in County's 64th match. The roar of relief reverberated round the ground. After an invaluable 2–1 victory that pushed the Hatters back into second place, the manager chose to chastise the supporters.

> This is a time for backing the boys, rather than constantly having a go. It's not all about performances, but against York we put on a show and got the result which was a bonus at that point in the season.

York did their best to shred a few more nerves by taking a 20th-minute lead through ex Oldham Athletic player Neil Tolson, a chance that was served up on a platter by Jim Gannon and Tom Bennett, though Bennett atoned with a nodded equaliser seven minutes later. 'I was gutted at letting them score so it was a relief to find the net,' he sighed. And it was Bennett's

DES HINKS

STOCKPORT EXPRESS

WHAT'S THE SCORE? ARMSTRONG TURNS TO HIS FANS AFTER HIS FOURTH-MINUTE GOAL AGAINST WYCOMBE.

possible that victory for County and defeats for Brentford, Luton and Crewe would make the games at Chesterfield and Luton academic.

When the players ran out to warm up, it appeared that Dave Jones had flaunted league regulations by signing a new man after deadline day. Closer inspection revealed Alun Armstrong had hit the bottle — of hair dye: the Blond Bomber had become the Red Baron. Chris Marsden was another changed man, finishing the match against York as an expectant father and starting against Wycombe as proud dad to baby Matthew. Despite seventeen hours in the delivery room at Jessop Hospital, Sheffield, Mazza refused the boss's invitation to step down.

'It was an incredible experience and I felt totally drained,' said Marsden after seeing his girlfriend Natasha give birth. 'I felt like coming off at half-time, but the boss wanted me to stay on. It was a relief when I heard the final whistle. It was a funny time and it was hard to concentrate on the football.'

Angell came in for the suspended Charlery and off they went. Within four minutes, Armstrong's luck in front of goal had changed as dramatically as his barnet. Kieron Durkan flicked on Flynn's throw and Armstrong swivelled smartly to register his first goal since January. 'It was a great relief to score,' he smiled later. 'I'd changed my boots; I'd tried everything to end my drought.'

County started as they had done against in the Plymouth home game and Gannon saw a header rebound into play off the bar. Wycombe played their part in a rip-roaring game, with Dave Carroll always prominent, but they were rocked back again on the

drive that deflected into Angell's path for the winner.

County had scored two goals in a match for the first time in nine games. They also knew that by winning two of the last three matches promotion was guaranteed, regardless of what their rivals might do. 'It suddenly dawned on me we could go straight up,' agreed Dave Espley, and the realisation also struck home with the rest of the town.

The final home game against relegation-haunted Wycombe Wanderers attracted the biggest league crowd of the season, and all but a few hundred in the near-9,500 attendance were rooting for County. The Railway End was given over to the home fans for a change, with Wycombe's chosen few housed in the Vernon Stand. It was

half-hour. Again Flynn's throw created mayhem and, in his attempt to be first to the ball, Michael Forsyth headed past his own 'keeper. Wanderers refused to throw in the towel and only the reflexes of Jones denied Keith Scott and then Forsyth. They also had three players cautioned in the opening half, such was their commitment.

The half-time interlude was an excuse for more cheering from the home faithful. Thirty years earlier to the day, County's Class of '67 secured promotion from the old fourth division thanks to a 2–2 draw with Notts County. Former vice-captain Eddie Stuart received one of the biggest cheers of the afternoon when he stepped on to the pitch with the trophy. Later that evening, fourteen of the '66–'67 squad, including Matt

Woods, Len Allchurch, Ken Mulhearn and Derek Kevan, assembled at the Acton Court Hotel for a celebratory dinner and night of nostalgia. Among the number was Trevor Porteous, who served the club in practically every capacity from groundsman to manager. Tragically, Trevor died just a couple of months after this get-together and before seeing his beloved County kick a ball in the first division.

● **Factfile:** County's highest-ever league placing in the club's history came in 1905–1906 when, under manager Fred Stewart, they reached tenth in the old second division.

THE CLASS OF '67: FOURTH-DIVISION CHAMPIONS, WITH TREVOR PORTEOUS (SECOND FROM LEFT)

STOCKPORT EXPRESS

Striker Bill Atkins was bowled over by the reception. 'How I'd love to be in Alun Armstrong's boots now. I used to love scoring in front of the old Cheadle Enders, and this new stand is something else. I'd have to score at that end every week now, the noise level and the reaction of the fans is unbelievable.'

When the Class of '97 re-emerged, Wycombe did their best to gatecrash the party. The penalty awarded them for handball may have been harsh, but they certainly deserved a lucky break. Carroll sent Jones the wrong way from the spot and left everything to play for. Said chairman Brendan Elwood:

> For me the last twenty minutes of the Wycombe game was the worst moment of the season. We were holding on desperately and I was praying Wycombe wouldn't get another goal. Compared to the Wycombe game, going to play at Chesterfield was easy on the nerves. That was do or die, and there was no point in worrying about it. As far as I was concerned, it was a question of 'let's get it on'.

County did cling on against the Berkshire battlers, but hope of a hat-trick of defeats for their rivals soon disappeared: Brentford and Crewe did slip up, but Luton kept in touch.

Forty-eight hours later and all the anxiety, nerves, worry, panic, dread, apprehension — call it what you will — was to be replaced with joy, exultation, rapture, satisfaction, delight and delirium. It was fitting that the two most talked-about teams outside the Premier League, FA Cup semi-finalists Chesterfield and Coca-Cola Cup semi-finalists Stockport, should meet at Saltergate for such an important fixture. Anywhere between 2,000 and 4,000 fans made the trip across the Peak District for the history-making night.

Matt Horn, *Stockport Express* sports editor, knew it was to be County's evening.

> Before the game I decided to go and get something to eat. When we beat Chesterfield in the Coca-Cola, I'd gone to a kebab house near the ground. Coming out of the shop that night was County's match announcer Kenny Boxshall. And who should I bump into again on this occasion — Kenny Boxshall. I remember saying to him, 'This is a lucky omen, we're going to win again.'

Des Hinks, like many of his fellow supporters, will never forget the night of April 28th: in Des's case, partly for the wrong reasons. Having travelled to every game, home and away, including the pre-season trip to Portugal, Des eagerly anticipated the Chesterfield match. Imagine his horror then when his customary press pass hadn't been allocated because the box was full. Stood outside the main entrance with Steve Bellis, they heard a huge roar go up inside the ground. 'Us or them?' Steve asked. The accompanying chants soon told them the glad tidings. 'It was ironic that, after travelling thousands and thousands of miles and seeing first-hand every County goal, I should miss the one that got us promoted to the first division,' says Des. Within five minutes Des was inside, courtesy of director Dave Jolley, and watched history in the making.

For the record, the team selected that night was: Paul Jones, Sean Connelly, Lee Todd, Tom Bennett, Mike Flynn, Jim Gannon, Kieron Durkan, Chris Marsden, Alun Armstrong, Brett Angell and Kevin Cooper. Tony Dinning came on for Bennett and Ken Charley replaced Angell. Andy Mutch didn't get a kick.

The goal came from the head of Brett Angell — his 20th of the season

STOCKPORT EXPRESS

THE ONE THAT MATTERS: BRETT ANGELL NETS THE GOAL THAT SENDS COUNTY INTO THE FIRST DIVISION.

STOCKPORT EXPRESS

STOCKPORT EXPRESS

STOCKPORT EXPRESS

GOING UP: THE CLIMAX OF STOCKPORT COUNTY'S FINEST SEASON

— after a good cross from Alun Armstrong and a pass from Lee Todd to begin the move. Beamed the scorer:

I never expected to enjoy a night like this when the surgeon's knife went into my knee. I enjoyed promotion with Southend, but this is something different. People wrote us off because of the number of games we had, but we kept going and deserve it because we have come from the back and timed our run to perfection. Wimbledon and Barnsley have shown the way and there's no reason why we can't follow them in the future. At the beginning of the season my career was at the crossroads after being loaned out by Sunderland, but Stockport gave me my chance and I can hardly believe what has happened since.

Angell nearly made it 2–0, but his lob was pushed onto the bar by the Chesterfield 'keeper. For the first thirty minutes, County controlled the game, but Chesterfield still harboured play-off hopes and gained momentum either side of half-time. Kevin Davies, the three-goal hero of Chesterfield's cup upset of Bolton Wanderers, set up Marcus Ebdon, but Paul Jones saved a vicious low shot with his feet.

'A world-class save,' drooled John Sainty later. 'But that's the way he's played all season. He's been the difference between us going straight up and possibly even missing a play-off place.' Jones was to make one further inspirational save as, despite the wind advantage, County laboured to stay on top. Referee Carl Finch piled on the agony by adding on seven minutes of injury time before blowing the final whistle to spark the greatest celebration scenes in the club's life.

HERE WE GO! THE CELEBRATIONS CONTINUE IN THE DRESSING ROOM.

STOCKPORT EXPRESS

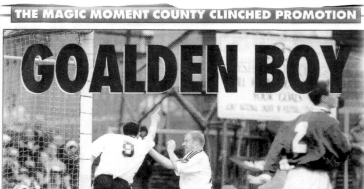

MANCHESTER EVENING NEWS

THE MAGIC MOMENT COUNTY CLINCHED PROMOTION

GOALDEN BOY

FIRST Division-bound Stockport superbly struck a further blow for soccer's minnows in the year of the underdog.

County march up confidently with local neighbours Bury, although

By Peter Gardner: Chesterfield 0 Stockport 1

Brett's Angell's 20th goal of the season confirmed County as partners to go straight up with Bury, ironically in the shadow of Chesterfield's famous twisted church spire which had looked down on them this season.

floated in a cross from the right. Marcus Ebdon saw his chance, cut in from the left and finished with a wicked low shot that Jones saved with his feet to leave County assistant boss John Sainty maintaining: "It was a world class save."

because we have come from the back and timed our run to perfection."

Angell's piercing headed winner came in a back-to-front move that started with a clearance by keeper Paul

Alun Armstrong ran from the half-way line and slid on his belly for twenty yards towards the away end; Mike Flynn tried to vault over into the same end while the chairman risked ruining his snappy suit by racing half the length of the field to join the party.

Back in Manchester, GMR presenter Jack Dearden was conducting a phone-in on the mother and father of all parties. He took one call from three supporters calling on a mobile from Saltergate. Such was the cacophony they couldn't hear Jack's questions and he could hardly hear their answers. Nobody seemed to mind.

Dave Espley was seated in the main stand with his father:

> We were away from the main celebrations but the atmosphere was still electric. I'm not one for getting pissed, so we eventually decided to make our way out of the ground. On the way back to the car, everyone was sounding their horns. I guess that what's it's like in Milan or Rome when Italy win the World Cup.

Back at Saltergate, the revelry was just beginning. Most of the players later moved on to the Fingerpost Hotel, a frequent haunt of the players and a constant source of County supporters. The celebrations lasted most

HEAD BOYS

MANCHESTER EVENING NEWS

GO GO COUNTY ... the Edgeley Boys celebrate last night   Picture by Andrew Yates

County hit the heights

By Peter Gardner

STOCKPORT are ready to shoot it out with Bury for the Second Division title.

The Shakers have their noses in front because of a superior scoring record.

And they will start favourites to take the title when they attempt to stretch their unbeaten home run to the final game when Millwall are Saturday's Gigg Lane visitors.

County, who clinched the second automatic place following a 1-0 Saltergate win over Chesterfield, thanks to Brett Angell's 20th goal of the season, must win convincingly at Luton to overtake Bury.

But boss, Dave Jones threw down the gauntlet today, claiming: "We're gunning for goals and glory. My message to Stan Ternent is that this battle ain't over yet."

The teams are level on points, but Bury have scored two more goals. Jones added: "We are on a roll.

"The pressure is off now that we are going straight up and we are going to Kenilworth Road looking for three points and as many goals as we can."

Stockport today got an official town tribute to mark their promotion. Mayor

of the night and much of the next day as well — and the next.

However, when everyone descended from cloud nine, there was still some unfinished business to attend to, as the small matter of the second division title had to be settled. County and Bury were neck and neck on points, with the Shakers having a better goal difference. County had to win at Luton, while Bury had to slip up at home to Millwall.

The trip to Kenilworth Road was designated 'hat day', both clubs being nicknamed 'the Hatters'. The omens were good when Kevin Cooper slotted a seventh-minute penalty, but Andy Fotiadis equalised and the Hatters versus Hatters clash ended 1–1. Bury defeated Millwall anyway, though it didn't seem to matter that the title hadn't been won. All that mattered was

County had won promotion and for the first time since 1937 would be playing in the first division. Chris Marsden insisted:

> If we can roll our sleeves up and perform week in, week out, I don't think we'll have any problems. I'm not saying it will be easier, but as a team we'll find it more suited to us because it's not played at such a hectic pace. I think you have to be mentally sharp as opposed to physically fitter. But if you can react quicker and be in the right place before the ball comes it can save you ten yards in running.

Fellow midfielder Tom Bennett risked a lot by dropping down a division after leaving Wolves, but admits: 'The gamble paid off. I want to stay at Stockport and help them not only play in the first division but to sustain something that the club has achieved over

IT'S ALL OVER! COUNTY SALUTE THEIR FANS AFTER THE LUTON MATCH.

DES HINKS

DES HINKS

Wigan and Chester manager Harry McNally. Elwood has promised at least £1 million for Megson to spend on new players if he sees fit. Said Elwood:

> I wasn't as surprised or as disappointed as others at the club when Dave left: I think I had resigned myself to him going. It was just a question of when. I have every faith in Gary emulating or even bettering what Dave has done for us. I have followed his career closely and I think we have made the right choice. I've only made two other managerial appointments while I have been at Stockport, and they didn't turn out to be too bad!

LEFT: PLAYER OF THE SEASON PAUL JONES WITH ECSTATIC FANS

the last five or six years.' County fans with long memories are only too aware of what happened the last time they played in the first division (old second division), back in 1937–38: they were relegated after just one season.

With Jones's departure to Southampton, some of the optimism has disappeared and that's not meant to be any reflection on the qualities of the next incumbent to the Edgeley Park hot seat, Gary Megson. The former Norwich and Blackpool boss becomes County's 27th post-war manager, who must quickly win over players and spectators alike. Megson, Manchester-born, has been given a two-year contract by Brendan Elwood. So too have his backroom staff of ex-Burnley and Manchester United midfielder Mike Phelan (a hard combination for County fans to swallow) and former

BELOW: ALL THERE IN BLACK AND WHITE: WHAT STOCKPORT FANS HAVE WAITED OVER SIXTY YEARS TO SEE

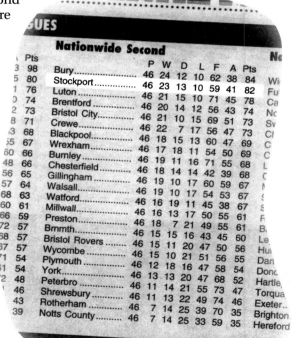

Nationwide Second

	P	W	D	L	F	A	Pts
Bury	46	24	12	10	62	38	84
Stockport	46	23	13	10	59	41	82
Luton	46	21	15	10	71	45	78
Brentford	46	20	14	12	56	43	74
Bristol City	46	21	10	15	69	51	73
Crewe	46	22	7	17	56	47	73
Blackpool	46	18	15	13	60	47	69
Wrexham	46	17	18	11	54	50	69
Burnley	46	19	11	16	71	55	68
Chesterfield	46	18	14	14	42	39	68
Gillingham	46	19	10	17	60	59	67
Walsall	46	19	10	17	54	53	67
Watford	46	16	19	11	45	38	67
Millwall	46	16	13	17	50	55	61
Preston	46	18	7	21	49	55	61
Brnmth.	46	15	15	16	43	45	60
Bristol Rovers	46	15	11	20	47	50	56
Wycombe	46	15	10	21	51	56	55
Plymouth	46	12	18	16	47	58	54
York	46	13	13	20	47	68	52
Peterbro	46	11	14	21	55	73	47
Shrewsbury	46	11	13	22	49	74	46
Rotherham	46	7	14	25	39	70	35
Notts County	46	7	14	25	33	59	35

STOCKPORT EXPRESS

ALL HAIL THE CONQUERING HEROES: DAVE JONES (LEFT), BRETT ANGELL (BELOW RIGHT) AND LUIS CAVACO (BELOW LEFT) ENJOY THE ADULATION FROM A TOWN STARVED OF FOOTBALL SUCCESS FOR SO LONG.

STOCKPORT EXPRESS

STOCKPORT EXPRESS

COUNTY APPLAUD THEIR FANS AFTER THE LAST HOME MATCH OF THE SEASON AGAINST WYCOMBE. JIM GANNON (TOP LEFT) AND CHRIS MARSDEN (RIGHT) ARE STILL APPREHENSIVE, AS PROMOTION IS NOT YET SEALED.

STOCKPORT COUNTY FC

THE FRIENDLY FOOTBALL CLUB

DES HINKS

DES HINKS

DES HINKS

DES HINKS

BUT THE RELIEF ON THEIR FACES IS EVIDENT, AS PROMOTION CELEBRATIONS ARE IN FULL SWING. CLOCKWISE FROM TOP LEFT: ANDY MUTCH, LEE TODD, KIERON DURKAN AND ALUN ARMSTRONG.

STOCKPORT EXPRESS

PORTUGUESE STAR LUIS CAVACO, AND
(BELOW) CONVALESCING AT HOME AFTER
BREAKING A LEG IN THE CRUCIAL PROMOTION
MATCH AGAINST WATFORD IN APRIL

STOCKPORT EXPRESS

12 Tales from David Jones's Locker

BY TRADITION, STOCKPORT County managers don't remain too long in the Edgeley Park hot seat. There have been 37 of them in the club's 114-year-old history, including the present incumbent Gary Megson. Of the previous 36, all but ten have been in charge since the Second World War, and nine fell during the troubled times of the 1970s.

Fred Stewart, County's first-ever Football League boss, is easily the longest serving, with seventeen years in charge from 1894–1911. The average term of office is much shorter and so, in that respect, Dave Jones was no different to any of his predecessors when he quit for Southampton during the close season. But there *is* a difference, and everyone who followed County last season knows it. With the exception of Danny Bergara, none of Jones's predecessors came close to achieving what the Merseyside Messiah managed.

For a start, when club and manager have parted company in the past, it's usually been at the behest of the club, but on this occasion the divorce was different. The club wanted the marriage to continue; Jones decided the love affair was over. It lasted just over two years from the time the 41-year-old Scouser replaced Danny Bergara until the moment Southampton announced Jones was to be the successor to Graeme Souness. They simply made the Southport-based former Everton and Coventry defender an offer that he couldn't refuse.

In one season Jones helped put County on the football map and his own name on the wanted list of would-be employers. Southampton got their act together first and, from trying to persuade Jim Gannon to sign a new contract one minute, he was soon persuading Matt Le Tissier he had a future at the Dell.

STEVE SOUTHART

STOCKPORT EXPRESS

THE SMILE SAYS IT ALL: AS THE WHISTLE GOES AT CHESTERFIELD, THE PRESSURE IS FINALLY OFF.

Jones's departure was a shock to most, though the warning signs had been there in the latter part of the season as his exciting side flourished. Time and again he insisted he wanted players at the club who were ambitious. 'Because I'm no different,' was his frequent follow-up. And in one of his last interviews as Stockport manager, Jones gave out the same message:

All the players here are ambitious. Just as I am. I didn't want to stay in the second division, but now I am in the first I don't want to stay there either. It's perhaps unrealistic at this stage though to talk of going higher.

As it transpired, not that unrealistic.

The rhetoric was the same after his installation as boss of last season's Premier League strugglers.

Agreeing to become the new manager at Southampton was about one thing and one thing only — ambition. People who say I left Stockport because of money simply don't know me. Of course I will be earning more money at the Dell than I did at Edgeley Park but, with hand on heart, money was never an issue when I was offered the manager's job at Southampton. I saw one thing only and that was I had been given a chance to work with top-quality players at a club in the Premier division.

I've been asked a hundred times whether the job of managing a Premiership club has come too soon. There is no answer to that question. All I know is Southampton gave me an opportunity that I couldn't afford to turn my back on. If I had turned them down, who knows when the next chance would have come along. When something like this falls into your lap, you don't ask yourself whether you are ready — you grab it.

Ironically, it was County's victory over the Saints in the Coca-Cola Cup quarter-finals that eventually brought about his departure from Edgeley Park and enhanced his career prospects.

When I went for the interview at Southampton, the chairman Rupert Lowe told me he'd been impressed by the way Stockport had played football. He told me the fans won't tolerate a team that plays the long-ball system. Apparently, that's why Ian Branfoot had such a tough time at The Dell.

I like my teams to play open, passing football and I'm sure that will suit the fans at the Dell right down to the ground. When I took over at Stockport I told John Sainty I wanted everybody in the club from the youth team up to be comfortable on the ball and not panic when they got it.

But while Jones has become a Saint — and he'll always have a soft spot for

County — some supporters feel he's sinned by leaving Edgeley Park so hastily. While most wish him well, there's a section who feel he's hardly bettered himself by joining one of the Premier League's least glamorous clubs. Insisted Jones:

> The call to tell the chairman, Brendan Elwood, I was leaving was the hardest I have made. It was a big wrench to leave, and Stockport will always be important to me. I know it will be the first result I look for.
> I'm sure a few of the 'speccies' will feel upset I have let them down by leaving at this stage, but I would ask them to put themselves in my position. I have got them into the first division, I have made them a lot of money and they have got about £200,000 for me leaving.

Jones may now be considered among the top twenty managers in the country and it's certainly a long way from where he cut his managerial teeth. For that, he owes a debt of gratitude to Bryan Griffiths, one of the North-West's top non-league managers and presently in charge of Unibond League side Chorley. The two worked closely together at a succession of semi-professional sides and remain good friends. Indeed, Griffiths was among the early well-wishers when Jones took over at Southampton. Said Griffiths:

> Dave was always ambitious as I remember. He used to say: 'I'll learn all I can from you, but if the opportunity comes along I'll go.' I didn't mind that, because at least he was being straight and that's something you'll always find with Dave.

They first teamed up after Jones returned from a spell playing football in Hong Kong with a club called Seiko. Jones had spent two years in the Far

DES HINKS

East and came back for a spell at Preston North End before hanging up his pro boots with over 300 league games to his credit. Explained Griffiths:

> Dave came to Southport where I was manager hoping to extend his playing career, but he'd had ligament problems during his days in the Football League at Coventry and the trouble flared up again. As a result, he began to help me on the managerial side. When I moved to Mossley, he came with me and we had quite a successful spell, winning a number of trophies.
> Then, after a few years at Seel Park, we both went to Morecambe. At the

FEARS ABOUT STOCKPORT'S INABILITY TO HOLD ON TO JONES WERE ALREADY IN EVIDENCE IN JANUARY AMIDST THE CELEBRATIONS AT THE DELL.

MANCHESTER EVENING NEWS

■ DELIRIOUS . . . Stockport's super heroes celebrate their stunning Coca-Cola Cup win in the Dell dressing room

HANDS OFF MIDAS MAN

STOCKPORT chairman Brendan Elwood is to seek urgent contract talks with his hot-property manager Dave Jones.

Elwood issued a hands-off warning after County had won 2-1 at Southampton last night to storm into a two-leg Coca-Cola Cup semi-final with Middlesbrough next month.

It was County's third Premiership scalp of season, following Blackburn and West

By Trevor Baxter

Ham, and Jones has masterminded the giantkilling nets without a contract.

Jones said: "I haven't got a contract and have never had one. The chairman spoke to me a couple of weeks ago but we haven't sat down and negotiated anything.

"I think I might want to say," quipped

the Merseysider with the Midas touch. "I've always said I want players at this club who are ambitious and I'm no different. Who is to say we can't beat Middlesbrough?"

County stage the first leg of the semi-final against Juninho & Co on February 19.

Wales today put County keeper Paul Jones on standby for their friendly against the Republic of Ireland in Cardiff on February 11.

■ Match report and pictures - page 7

time, Morecambe were low in their division, but we managed to take them to a cup final against Colne Dynamos at Ewood Park. It was then John Sainty asked whether Dave would like to join him at Stockport County. He asked my opinion and I told him he should go for it. As an ex-League player, you don't always get that many chances to get back into the big time.

So, he went to Stockport with my best wishes. The non-league can be a good stepping stone, and I'm sure his experiences at Southport, Morecambe and Mossley helped him during his days at County. It's made him humbler than some in his profession and also closer to the supporters.

While at Southport, the football was secondary to Jones, realising he couldn't

support himself and his family on memories from his playing days. Revealed Griffiths:

Dave took a job with social services and, as time went on, took all the necessary exams. On the strength of that, he learned how to communicate with people, and that's why he's so good on the man-management side: he knows how to handle players and how to get the best out of them. With Dave around, there was always a good rapport in the dressing room. The players were relaxed and that helped me in what I was trying to do. He has a good sense of humour and gets the respect of the players in his own way.

We bounced ideas off one another. I certainly learned from him, and I hope he picked up a few ideas from me. I like to think we got on well together, because at non-league level you don't want moody people alongside you.

Working as he did enabled him to get an insight into what life was like on the other side. He could see now that most non-league players worked during the day and then trained 120 per cent on Tuesdays and Thursdays. This was a new experience for Dave. During his time as a pro, everything was probably done for him and he ended up with time on his hands. It was so much different in the non-league. He's come a long way, but I'm made up for him and I'm sure he's got a lot more to offer.

They often say nice guys always finish second but, though Dave has a ruthless streak in him, this is one nice guy who has made it to the top.

Jones is the first to admit he isn't afraid to seek advice. At the end of last season he explained:

You are always learning in your job and I always listen to others. Before the season began, I had a sit-down with Alex Ferguson and he was very helpful. I also learned from speaking to men like Stan Ternent at Bury. I try to take all the good things and throw the bad things away.

Jones arrived at Edgeley Park from Christie Park in July 1990, quickly moving up from youth team coach to chief coach. Liverpool-born, he brought with him a welter of experience, having started his career at Goodison Park as a fifteen-year-old schoolboy. After signing professional terms, he stayed with the Toffees until 1981 when a £275,000 fee took him to Coventry City. The former England Youth and Under-21 international spent three years at Highfield Road before suffering the knee injury that was to shorten his playing career and take him prematurely into management.

There were a few raised eyebrows when Jones succeeded Danny Bergara, but John Sainty had made it plain he wanted to stay as number two. And Jones was popular with the players: in fact, Mike Flynn only signed a new contract because Bergara had left and Jones was put in charge.

In total, Jones was in charge of County for 131 matches, from his first game at Shrewsbury on April Fool's Day 1995, to the 1–1 draw at Luton Town on 3rd May 1997. County won 64 of those games, drawing 35 times and losing the rest.

But it's the final 67 matches that will go down in history. 'I have never been involved in a season like it,' he stated. 'It was a major relief to avoid the play-offs, because we didn't need another three games.' Along the way Jones collected two Manager of the Month awards and was a genuine contender for Manager of the Season.

Had things worked out differently, however, he might have been facing the prospect of season 1997–98 on the dole. County's appalling start, as documented elsewhere in the book, suggested Jones's head was on the chopping block.

> The papers were putting two and two together and making five. After six games I was losing my job. But the chairman never put me under any pressure and there was never any panic. Supporters were slagging me off because I wasn't running up and down the touchline ranting and raving, but that's not my style. I rant and rave, but I do it behind closed doors or in training.

A 3–1 victory over Plymouth scotched rumours once and for all that Jones would be leaving. 'We could have scored ten that day and beaten anybody: Liverpool, Manchester United — anyone.' The Jones juggernaut was off and running all the way to Division 1.

> No one really talked about us as promotion hopefuls for a long time because we were always behind in the number of games. But we always knew that if we won the matches in hand we would be in with a good shout. We kept going and, to be fair, the only real setbacks were at Gillingham and Preston.
>
> At Gillingham we looked shattered, but I didn't say it at the time or the players might have started to believe it. But after the defeat by Preston, we came back and got the three straight wins that we knew would get us up. It was a fantastic achievement and, whatever else I might do in my career, getting Stockport into the first division and into the Coca-Cola Cup semi-finals I'll remember forever.

STEVE SOUTHART

last, but for me he was excellent. He treated the players like adults, and that made for a good dressing room atmosphere. It was a bit of a shock when I saw the news on Teletext, but Dave is ambitious and this is a chance to manage a Premier League side.

Like Jones, Tom Bennett returned from holiday to discover Jones had moved on. Said Scotsman Bennett, a £75,000 buy from Wolves:

> It was great news for him, but I would have liked to see him stay at Stockport. He was a great boss for me and resurrected my career. He brought me to the club and stuck by me when he could have dropped me in my first season. I will always be grateful to him. He made me a more confident player and allowed me to express myself.

The man charged with the responsibility of emulating, or even bettering, Jones's achievements is Manchester-born Gary Megson. Said the ex-Norwich City and Blackpool chief:

> I keep being told Dave Jones will be a hard act to follow. But it's going to be a different act now. We're in the first division and it's going to be a tough league with some massive clubs. However, Stockport are there on merit, and hopefully it will be onwards and upwards.
>
> On my part, I left Blackpool on good terms: it wasn't a case of leaving Blackpool for any negative reasons; it was a case of all the positive things on offer at Stockport. They used to be very much the third club in the area behind Manchester United and City, but now they're very much a club in their own right and I would urge the people of Stockport to carry on giving us their support.

How can you forget nights at Middlesbrough, Southampton and Chesterfield?

Jones's departure, together with his backroom team of Sainty, Gary Gillespie and Joe Jakub, was a body-blow to County. But life goes on. He leaves behind a legacy that his successor can be grateful for. 'There's a great squad of players, a good ground, excellent training facilities and great supporters,' said Jones. That squad was reduced by two, however, with the departures of Lee Todd and Paul Jones to The Dell. Before discovering that he would be following his manager to the south coast, Paul Jones commented:

> As players we have got to get on with the job. He is not the first manager to leave suddenly and he won't be the

Helping Megson, son of former Sheffield Wednesday midfielder Don, is former Manchester United and Burnley star Mike Phelan and Harry McNally, one-time manager of Chester and a well-respected name in the lower divisions.

> Mike and I have tons of enthusiasm, though we lack a bit of experience, but that's a quality Harry possesses in abundance. Hopefully it will be a winning combination. There is already a good squad of players here, and obviously I know what they can do because we played them twice in the second division last season. But we're always in the market for quality if it comes along at the right price.

The appointment of Megson and co. caught County fans off-guard, almost as much as the outgoings of Jones and his team. Joe Royle, Sammy McIlroy, Gordon Cowans and John Deehan were names in the frame before chairman Elwood announced the new man. Said Elwood:

> I have followed Gary's career with interest because I know his father very well. He is a young manager of great potential, and it helps when you know the person taking over is of good character. The list of applicants for the job were as long as my arm and, as chairman, appointing a new manager is the biggest decision a chairman can make. This is only the third time I've had to do it and the other two appointments did quite well for us. I'm really optimistic Gary can continue the progress we have made over the last few years.
>
> There will be funds made available to strengthen the squad. I'm not prepared to say how much, but let's say £1 million would be a starting point. I have wished Dave well and the parting has been amicable on both sides.

I thanked him for what he did at Stockport. Some critics have suggested we could have done more to keep him at the club. But what could we have done? He always wanted to move to a Premier League club and Southampton offered him that chance. We wish him and John Sainty well but we must look to our future.

Thanks to Dave Jones, that future is brighter and more optimistic than at any other time in the last 114 years.

DES HINKS

STEVE SOUTHART

STEVE SOUTHART

IT'S A GOAL! TEAM-MATES TOM BENNETT (ABOVE LEFT), KEN CHARLERY (ABOVE RIGHT) AND CHRIS MARSDEN (RIGHT) RUSH TO CONGRATULATE KEVIN COOPER'S VITAL GOAL AGAINST CREWE IN APRIL.

STEVE SOUTHART

1996-97 Facts and Figures

PRESENTED IN THIS SECTION is the full round-up of the glorious 1996–97 season, with all League, FA Cup, Coca-Cola Cup and Auto Windscreen Shield appearances and goal-scorers.

WHERE ARE THEY NOW? THREE MEMBERS OF THE PROMOTION SQUAD WHO HAVE SINCE MOVED ON. BELOW: GORDON COWANS, NOW WITH RIVALS BURNLEY; RIGHT: LEE TODD, CURRENTLY PLAYING PREMIERSHIP FOOTBALL WITH SOUTHAMPTON; AND LEFT: KEN CHARLEY, WHO MADE A MOVE IN THE OPPOSITE DIRECTION TO THIRD-DIVISION BARNET.

MATCH NO.	DATE	COMPETITION	OPPONENTS	RESULT	SCORE	HALF-TIME	LEAGUE POS.	SCORERS AND TIMES	ATTENDANCE
1	Aug 17		Crewe Alexandra	L	0–1	(0–0)	22		(4,310)
2	Aug 20	ccc 1,1	CHESTERFIELD	W	2–1	(1–0)		Mutch 20, 53	(3,088)
3	Aug 24		Notts County	D	0–0	(0–0)	21		(5,271)
4	Aug 27		AFC BOURNEMOUTH	L	0–1	(0–1)	23		(3,446)
5	Aug 31		Bristol Rovers	D	1–1	(0–1)	22	Jeffers 73	(6,380)
6	Sept 3	ccc 1,2	Chesterfield	W	2–1	(0–0)		Ware 76; Mutch 84	(3,334)
7	Sept 7		Watford	L	0–1	(0–0)	22		(7,208)
8	Sept 10		WREXHAM	L	0–2	(0–1)	23		(4,244)
9	Sept 14		PLYMOUTH ARGYLE	W	3–1	(2–1)	22	Gannon 1, 10; Armstrong 51	(5,087)
10	Sept 17	ccc 2,1	SHEFFIELD UNITED	W	2–1	(2–0)		Flynn 24; Bennett 40	(4,004)
11	Sept 21		York City	W	2–1	(0–0)	20	Angell 48, 51	(3,061)
12	Sept 24	ccc 2,2	Sheffield United	W	5–2	(3–1)		Gannon 25; Armstrong 30, 80; Bennett 33; Angell 61	(6,285)
13	Sept 28		GILLINGHAM	W	2–1	(1–1)	16	Armstrong 10; Morris 50 og	(6,049)
14	Oct 2		Millwall	W	4–3	(1–1)	10	Durkan 24; Armstrong 60, 90; Gannon 63	(7,537)
15	Oct 5		Burnley	L	2–5	(0–2)	13	Angell 56; Mutch 75	(10,332)
16	Oct 12		PRESTON NORTH END	W	1–0	(1–0)	11	Angell 1	(8,405)
17	Oct 15		LUTON TOWN	D	1–1	(0–1)	11	Angell 58	(5,352)
18	Oct 19		Wycombe Wanderers	W	2–0	(1–0)	10	Angell 8, 86	(4,017)
19	Oct 22	ccc 3	Blackburn Rovers	W	1–0	(1–0)		Sherwood 23 og	(14,672)
20	Oct 26		Walsall	D	1–1	(0–1)	11	Durkan 90	(3,767)
21	Oct 29		CHESTERFIELD	W	1–0	(0–0)	10	Dinning 88	(4,831)
22	Nov 2		BRISTOL CITY	D	1–1	(0–1)	10	Bennett 83	(6,654)
23	Nov 9		Brentford	D	2–2	(0–0)	11	Angell 77; Cavaco 84	(5,076)
24	Nov 16	fac 1	DONCASTER ROVERS	W	2–1	(0–0)		Flynn 58; Mutch 60	(4,211)
25	Nov 19		BLACKPOOL	W	1–0	(0–0)	10	Bennett 70	(4,572)
26	Nov 23		Shrewsbury	L	2–3	(1–0)	11	Angell 6; Marsden 83	(2,865)
27	Nov 27	ccc 4	West Ham United	D	1–1	(0–1)		Cavaco 51	(20,061)
28	Nov 30		WALSALL	W	2–0	(1–0)	10	Angell 35, 51	(5,333)
29	Dec 3		Rotherham United	W	1–0	(1–0)	7	Durkan 35	(2,133)
30	Dec 7	fac 2	Mansfield Town	W	3–0	(1–0)		Kilcline 45 og; Durkan 53, 69	(3,354)
31	Dec 10	aws 1	Doncaster Rovers	W	2–1	(0–1)		Gray 69 og; Cavaco 70	(988)
32	Dec 14		PETERBOROUGH UNITED	D	0–0	(0–0)	6		(5,748)
33	Dec 18	ccc 4, r	WEST HAM UNITED	W	2–1	(2–1)		Dowie 23 og, Angell 27	(9,834)
34	Dec 21		Bury	D	0–0	(0–0)	6		(5,069)
35	Dec 26		Wrexham	W	3–2	(1–2)	5	Armstrong 18; Gannon 62; Dinning 65 pen	(6,736)

STOCKPORT COUNTY FC — THE FRIENDLY FOOTBALL CLUB — 1883

Angell, B.A.M.	Armstrong, A.	Bennett, T.	Bound, M.T.	Cavaco, L.M.	Charana, M. (Kiko)	Charlery, K.L.	Connelly, S.P.	Cooper, K.L.	Cowans, G.S.	Dinning, A.	Durkan, K.J.	Edwards, N.R.G.	Flynn, M.A.	Gannon, J.P.	Jeffers, J.J.	Jones, L.	Jones, P.S.	Landon, R.J.	Marsden, C.	Mike, A.R.	Mutch, A.T.	Nash, M.	Searle, D.	Todd, L.	Ware, P.M.	REFEREE	MATCH NO.
	10	4	6				2				†7		5	s	11		1		8	s	9		3		13	G. Singh	1
14	Δ10	4	6				2				•7		5	12	11		1		8		9		3		s	G. Cain	2
14	10	4	6				2				7		5	s	11		1		8		•9		3		s	R. Poulain	3
9	Δ10	4	6				2				•7		5	12	11		1		†8		14		3		13	M. Fletcher	4
•11	12	4	Δ6	†10			2						5	7	14		1				9		3	13	8	T. Lunt	5
s	10	4		†7			2			s			5	6	11		1				9		3	13	8	T. Heilbron	6
14	10	4	s	†7			2						5	6	11		1				Δ9		3	13	8	B. Knight	7
14	10	†4								12	13		5	•6	11		1		8		Δ9		3	2	7	J. Lynch	8
9	10	4					2			s	7		5	6	11		1	s	8				3		s	I.G. Cruikshanks	9
9	10	4					2			s	7		5	6	11		1	s	8				3		s	A.R. Leake	10
9	10	4		s			2			s	7		5	6	11		1	s	8				3			W.C. Burns	11
9	10	4					2			s	7	s	5	6	11		1	s	8				3			M.C. Bailey	12
9	10	4					2			12	7	s	5	6	11		1	s					3		•8	A.G. Wiley	13
Δ9	10	4					2			s	7		5	6	11		1		8		14	s	3			C. Wilkes	14
Δ9	10	4					2			s	7		5	6	11		1		8		14	s	3			G. Cain	15
9	•10	4		s			2			s	7		5	6	11		1		8		12		3			U. Rennie	16
9		4		12			2			s	•7		5	6	11		1	s	8		10		3			D. Laws	17
9		4		s			2			s	7		5	6	•11		1		8		10	12	3			A.P. D'Urso	18
9	10	4		Δ11			2				7	s	5	6			1		8		s	14	3			P. Rejer	19
9		†4		14			2			s	7		5	6	11		1		8		Δ10		3	13		S. Baines	20
9		4		14			2			6	7		5		11		1		8		Δ10	s	3		s	J.P. Robinson	21
9		4		•10			2			6	Δ7		5		11		1		8		12	14	3		s	T. Jones	22
9		4		12			2			6	Δ7		5		11		1	14	8		•10	s	3			G.R. Pooley	23
	10	4		s			2			s	7		5	6	11		1	s	8		9		3			T. Heilbron	24
9	10	4		14			2			s	Δ7		5	6	11		1		8		s		3			N.S. Barry	25
9	10	4		14			2			s	Δ7		5	6	11		1		8		s		3			E.K. Wolstenholme	26
9	10	4		14			2			12	•7	s	5	6	Δ11		1		8				3			H.C. Bailey	27
9	10	4		11			2			s	†7		5	6			1		8		s	13	3			A.R. Leake	28
9	10	4		†11			2			s	7		5	6	13		1		8		s		3			D. Laws	29
9	Δ10	4		•11			2			12	7	s	5	6	14		1		8				3			I.G. Cruikshanks	30
9				†10	14		2			12	6		5	6	Δ11		1		8			13	3		•4	M.R. Halsey	31
9	Δ10	4		11	14		2			s	†7		5	6	13		1		8				3			C.R. Wilkes	32
9	10	4		•11	s		2			12	7	s	5	6			1		8				3			U.D. Rennie	33
9	10			Δ11	14		2			4	7		5	6			1		8		s		3		s	M. Fletcher	34
9	10			11			2			4	7		5	6	s		1		8		s		3	•3	12	P. Richards	35

155

MATCH NO.	DATE	COMPETITION	OPPONENTS	RESULT	SCORE	HALF-TIME	LEAGUE POS.	SCORERS AND TIMES	ATTENDANCE
36	Jan 15	fac 3	Stoke City	W	2–0	(1–0)		Durkan 25; Armstrong 90	(10,287)
37	Jan 18		MILLWALL	W	5–1	(3–1)	4	Mutch 12; Armstrong 31 pen; 52 Flynn 35, Cavaco 46,	(7,502)
38	Jan 22	ccc 5	SOUTHAMPTON	D	2–2	(2–1)		Armstrong 25; Cavaco 26	(9,840)
39	Jan 25	fac 4	Birmingham City	L	1–3	(0–1)		Angell 82	(18,487)
40	Jan 28	ccc 5, r	Southampton	W	2–1	(0–1)		Angell 62; Mutch 82	(13,428)
41	Feb 1		BRENTFORD	L	1–2	(0–0)	8	Cavaco 47	(8,650)
42	Feb 4	aws 2	Burnley	W	1–0	(1–0)		Nash 20	(4,252)
43	Feb 7		Bristol City	D	1–1	(1–0)	8	Armstrong 26	(13,186)
44	Feb 11	aws 3	Bury	W	2–1†	(1–1)		Dinning 10 pen; Angell 99	(2,497)
45	Feb 15		SHREWSBURY TOWN	W	3–1	(0–0)	5	Angell 74, 75; Armstrong 87	(6,712)
46	Feb 22		Blackpool	L	1–2	(0–0)	6	Mutch 90	(5,772)
47	Feb 26	ccc sf,1	MIDDLESBROUGH	L	0–2	(0–0)			(11,778)
48	Mar 1		ROTHERHAM UNITED	D	0–0	(0–0)	9		(6,147)
49	Mar 4	aws 4	Crewe Alex. [won 5–3p]	W	1–1¶	(1–1)		Marsden 41	(3,529)
50	Mar 8		BURY	W	2–1	(1–0)	8	Mutch 2; Jeffers 46	(8,170)
51	Mar 12	ccc sf,2	Middlesbrough	W	1–0	(1–0)		Connelly 5	(29,633)
52	Mar 15		Peterborough United	W	2–0	(0–0)	8	Cavaco 46; Marsden 84	(4,857)
53	Mar 18	aws sf,1	Carlisle United	L	0–2	(0–0)			(7,053)
54	Mar 22		Notts County	W	2–1	(1–0)	7	White 30 og; Hogg 90 og	(4,238)
55	Mar 25	aws sf,2	CARLISLE UNITED	D	0–0	(0–0)			(8,593)
56	Mar 29		CREWE ALEXANDRA	W	1–0	(1–0)	4	Cooper 43	(7,411)
57	Apr 1		AFC Bournemouth	D	0–0	(0–0)	4		(5,476)
58	Apr 5		BRISTOL ROVERS	W	1–0	(0–0)	4	Cooper 85 pen	(5,689)
59	Apr 8		Plymouth Argyle	D	0–0	(0–0)	4		(5,089)
60	Apr 12		BURNLEY	W	1–0	(0–0)	4	Mutch 87	(9,187)
61	Apr 14		WATFORD	W	1–0	(0–0)	2	Jeffers 53	(7,164)
62	Apr 16		Gillingham	L	0–1	(0–1)	3		(4,485)
63	Apr 19		Preston North End	L	0–1	(0–0)	4		(10,298)
64	Apr 22		YORK CITY	W	2–1	(1–1)	2	Bennett 27; Angell 74	(6,654)
65	Apr 26		WYCOMBE WAND.	W	2–1	(2–0)	2	Armstrong 4; Forsyth 30 og	(9,463)
66	Apr 29		Chesterfield	W	1–0	(1–0)	2	Angell 5	(8,690)
67	May 3		Luton Town	D	1–1	(1–1)	2	Cooper 7 pen	(9,300)

↑ Key:
¶ decided on penalties
† decided on 'Golden Goal'

Key: →
● replaced by substitute number 12
† replaced by substitute number 13
Δ replaced by substitute number 14

STOCKPORT COUNTY FC — THE FRIENDLY FOOTBALL CLUB

Angell, B.A.M.	Armstrong, A.	Bennett, T.	Bound, M.T.	Cavaco, L.M.	Charana, M. (Kiko)	Charlery, K.L.	Connelly, S.P.	Cooper, K.L.	Cowans, G.S.	Dinning, A.	Durkan, K.J.	Edwards, N.R.G.	Flynn, M.A.	Gannon, J.P.	Jeffers, J.J.	Jones, L.	Jones, P.S.	Landon, R.J.	Marsden, C.	Mike, A.R.	Mutch, A.T.	Nash, M.	Searle, D.	Todd, L.	Ware, P.M.	REFEREE	MATCH NO.
Δ9	10	4		11			2			12	•7	s	5	6			1		8		14			3		A.P. D'Urso	36
10		4		11			†2			13	Δ7		5	6	14		1	12	8		•9			3		T. Lunt	37
9	10	4		11			2			s	7	s	5	6			1		8		s			3		R. Poulain	38
9	10	4		Δ11			2			12	7	s	5	6			1		•8		14			3		P. Jones	39
†9	10	4	s	11			2			8	Δ7		5	6	14		1				13			3		S.W. Dunn	40
9	10	4	s	11			2			8	s		5	6	7		1				s			3		W.C. Burns	41
	13	5		†8			12			4	7	1		6		14				•9	10	Δ11	3	2		T. Heilbron	42
9	10	4	s	11			2			8	Δ7		5	6			1				s	14		3		A.N. Butler	43
9		4	s	†11			2			8	13	1	5	6					14		Δ10	7		3		U.D. Rennie	44
9	10	4	s	Δ11			2			8	7		5	6	14		1				s			3		A. Bates	45
†9	10	4	s	Δ11			2			3	7		5	6	14		1		8		13			3		A.R. Leake	46
9	10	4		Δ11			2			s	7		5	6	14		1		8		s			3		D.R. Elleray	47
†9	10	4		Δ11			2			s	7		5	6	14		1		8		13		3	3		T. Jones	48
†9	10	4		12			2			6	•7		5	s	11		1		8		13			3		R.D. Fumandiz	49
s	•10	4		†7			2			6			5	12	11		1		8		9	13		3		G. Cain	50
14	10	4		†7			2			6			5	s	11		1		8		Δ9	13		3		P. Jones	51
s	10	4		†7			2			6			5		11		1		8		9	13		3		M.R. Halsey	52
14	Δ10	4	s	†7			2			6	13		5		11		1		8		9			3		K. Lynch	53
9	•10	4	s	13			2				7		5	6	†11		1		8		12			3		E.K. Wolstenholme	54
Δ9	10			13			2	•11	12		†7		5	6			1		8		14			3		N.S. Barry	55
	Δ10	4				9	2	†11	12		•7		5	6	13		1		8		14			3		D. Laws	56
	10	4	s				2	11	8		7		5	6	s		1			12	•9			3		F.G. Stretton	57
	•10	4		14		9	2	11	8	s	Δ7		5	6			1				12			3		A.G. Wiley	58
	Δ10			†7		9	2	11	8	4	13		5	6			1				14		s	3		D. Orr	59
	Δ10			7		9	2	†11	•8	12	13		5	6			1				14			3		I.G. Cruikshanks	60
	•10	4		Δ7		9	2	11	†8	13			5	6	14		1				12			3		D. Allison	61
		4				9	2	7	•8	s	14		5	6	Δ11		1		12		10			3		P. Taylor	62
	10	4				9	2	12		s	Δ7		5	6	•11		1		8		14			3		M. Brandwood	63
12	10	4				9	2	•11		13	Δ7		5	†6			1		8		14			3		C.J. Foy	64
•9	10	4					2	11		13	7		5	6	14		1		8		12			3		J. Robinson	65
†9	10	•4				13	2	11		12	7		5	6			1		8		s			3		C.T. Finch	66
Δ9	10	•4				14	2	11		s	†7		5	6			1		8		13			3		A.N. Butler	67
30	38	43	4	19	0	8	45	11	6	12	36		46	38	25		46	0	34	0	15	0	7	39	4	League App	
4	1			8	2	2		1	1	8	4			2	10			2	1		1	17	3	3	2	Substitute	
8+2	11	11	1	7+1			11			2+2	9		11	9+1	6+2		11		9		3+1	0+1	2+1	9+1	1	Coca-Cola App	
3	4	4		3			4				0+3	4	4	4	1+1		4		4		1+2				4	FA Cup App	
4+1	3	4+1	1	3+2	1+1		5+1		1	0+1	4+1	4+2	2	5	4		3	0+1	4		4	1+1	3+2	2+1	1	Auto Wind. App	

157

1996-97 Scorers

	LEAGUE	FA CUP	COCA-COLA CUP	AUTO WINDSCREEN SHIELD	TOTAL
BRETT ANGELL	15	1	3	1	**20**
ALUN ARMSTRONG	10(1p)	1	3		**14**(1p)
ANDY MUTCH	5	1	4		**10**
LUIS CAVACO	4		2	1	**7**
KIERON DURKAN	3	3			**6**
TOM BENNETT	3		2		**5**
JIM GANNON	4		1		**5**
KEVIN COOPER	3(2p)				**3**(2p)
TONY DINNING	2(1p)			1(p)	**3**(2p)
MIKE FLYNN	1	1	1		**3**
JOHN JEFFERS	3				**3**
CHRIS MARSDEN	2			1	**3**
SEAN CONNELLY			1		**1**
MARTIN NASH				1	**1**
PAUL WARE			1		**1**

TOP SCORERS: BRETT ANGELL (LEFT) AND ALUN ARMSTRONG

Stockport County: A Brief History

WHEN A CLUB CAN BOAST A history stretching back 114 years, it's inevitable there will have been plenty of memorable seasons and magical moments.

Unfortunately for Stockport County, the low spots have usually overshadowed the high points. In the last seven years, great strides have been made to shed an unwanted and detested image of a club bereft of achievement and ambition. The culmination of that hard work came on Monday, 28th April 1997 when County achieved promotion to Division 1 for the first time in sixty years. During the season, the club also achieved a best-ever showing in the 37-year history of the Coca-Cola Cup, still better known as the League Cup.

What follows is a potted history of the last 114 years.

1883 Formed as Heaton Norris Rovers after meeting by members of Wycliffe Congregational Chapel at Wellington Road South

1890 Name changed to Stockport County

1892 Lost 8–1 to Bury in their inaugural attempt in the FA Cup

1900 Became champions of the Lancashire League and joined the Football League as members of Division 2; first league game September 1st v Leicester Fosse: drew 2–2

1902 Moved to Edgeley Park

1904 Lost Football League status after four consecutive appeals for re-election

1905 Bounced straight back into Division 2 after topping the Lancashire Combination

1921 Became first club to be relegated from Division 2 to the new Division 3 (North)

1922 Finished champions of the new division and stepped up a flight

1926 Relegated

1934 Defeated Halifax Town 13–0 in Division 3 (North); remains biggest league victory

1935 Reached fifth round (last 16) of FA Cup, losing 5–0 to West Brom; defeated Walsall in final of Division 3 Cup

1937 Promoted to Division 2 as champions

1938 Relegated

1946 Wartime cup game against Doncaster Rovers lasted 202 minutes before bad light caused abandonment

1950 Reached FA Cup fifth round again, losing 2–0 to Liverpool

1958 Finished ninth in final season of Division 3 (North) and allocated place in new third division

1959 Relegated to fourth division; beat West Auckland Town 6–2 in FA Cup

1967 Promoted to Division 3

1970 Relegated to Division 4 and stayed there for 21 years

1972 Reached fourth round of League Cup; re-elected

1974 Re-elected

1976 Re-elected

1985 Re-elected

1990 Lost to Chesterfield in play-off semi-finals

1991 Promoted to Division 3

1992 Lost to Stoke City in Autoglass Trophy final; lost to Peterborough in third-division play-off final

1993 Lost to Port Vale in Autoglass Trophy final

1994 Defeated Premiership team QPR in the FA Cup third round; lost to Burnley in second-division play-off final

1997 Promoted to first division; reached Coca-Cola Cup semi-finals, losing 2–1 on aggregate to Middlesbrough

EDGELEY PARK, COUNTY'S HOME SINCE 1902

TRANSFORMING KING'S CROSS

TRANSFORMING
KING'S CROSS

MERRELL
LONDON • NEW YORK

Sarah Butterfield,
*King's Cross, December
Afternoon, 2011*
oil on canvas
45.7 × 63.5 cm (18 × 25 in.)

PREFACE

The Great Northern Railway opened its London terminus at King's Cross in 1852 and helped to usher in a new age of travel. Lewis Cubitt's double-barrelled train shed, with one side for arrivals and one for departures, fronted by a monumental twin-arched, yellow-brick façade, is a masterpiece of rational design. Opened sixteen years before its exuberant Victorian Gothic neighbour, St Pancras station, King's Cross station has brought travellers and goods to and from the capital for more than 150 years.

When it became clear that ever-increasing numbers of passengers could be properly accommodated only by a transformed station and a brand new concourse, English Heritage's advice was to be bold. The 'bungalow' extension that had obscured Cubitt's elegant front elevation for forty years had to go. Instead, a structure of the highest design quality should be built, to enhance, not detract from, the architectural interest of this great historic building.

John McAslan's dramatic new Western Concourse and refurbishment of the Victorian station have helped to create a railway terminus fit for the twenty-first century. In doing so, McAslan and engineers Arup have underlined the brilliance of Cubitt's original design and revealed his gloriously elegant front façade.

This book tells the story of a terrific project, and of those who have made it happen by bringing together the highest architectural, engineering, logistical and building skills. The finished building is a tremendous achievement that effortlessly brings old and new together in a way that present and future travellers will enjoy, and value, for many decades to come.

British engineers invented the railway, and railways changed the world. Network Rail, its architects, its engineers and its contractors have demonstrated that our forefathers' heroic approach to station design is alive and well at King's Cross. They have also confirmed English Heritage's conviction that the great buildings of our past have a hugely important part to play in our future.

Baroness Andrews
Chair, English Heritage

LONDON'S NEW GATEWAY TO TRAVEL AND ASPIRATION

Edwin Heathcote

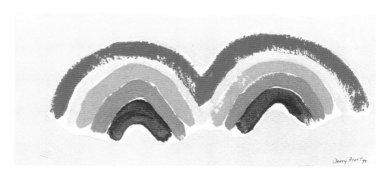

King's Cross station is one of the most superbly legible buildings in the world: its architecture is purely factual, and it explains itself unequivocally. There are two arches, one for arrivals and one for departures. A glass frontage makes the trains visible from the outside, and the platforms an extension of the public realm. The station is topped by a clock, reminding passengers that the railway runs on Greenwich Mean Time, which was adopted by the Railway Clearing House in 1847 so as to synchronize national train timetables. The station's architecture tells you everything you need to know. When the architect, Lewis Cubitt, delivered the terminus to the Great Northern Railway in 1852, the building represented a new kind of order and efficiency.

But after the station's completion that aura of order gradually frayed. The King's Cross area became one of London's apparently intractable socio-urban messes, an ill-coordinated and ugly tangle of road traffic and trains, with grumpy commuters, beggars and lost tourists thronging narrow pavements. A series of poorly thought-out 'temporary' extensions to the station, along with the long, deep sleep of the formerly derelict St Pancras station just to the west and the dead yards of the railway sidings within forbidding walls, all set cheek-by-jowl with dense social housing, created a kind of leftover urbanity, a dirty friction.

Above, left
A 1960s view of King's
Cross station, showing the
southern façade's canopy.

Above
A baby elephant and
its mother join their
circus troupe at the
station in 1927.

Yet here was an area that bounded both Bloomsbury, the heart of London's academia, and the youthfully arty and 'alternative' zeitgeist of Camden. The King's Cross area has the nation's best transport connections, and is also a place where interesting collisions of class, and of immigrants and embedded locals, had created a rich, improvised life from the straggling residues of seemingly defunct buildings. Today, industrial lofts mingle with hip bars and creative studios; the rate of cultural and commercial change has accelerated.

The trick, for the borough of Camden's planners and Network Rail, has been to envisage infrastructure not as an obstacle, but as a transport *and* civil utility. For decades, the King's Cross area was stymied by its endless goods yards and tracks, its old engine sheds and loading docks, and the no-man's-lands alongside them: decaying relics of an age of awesome engineering and national ambition that, until the turn of the millennium, seemed too distant, and too legendary, to comprehend.

Recent years have seen a remarkable resurrection of King's Cross station as a hub, in all the best possible senses. The British Library, completed to the west of St Pancras station in 1997 after a painful near-quarter-century gestation, has proved one of the city's great public buildings; Colin St John Wilson's monumental design anchored the area in the tradition of Bloomsbury academia, subsequently reinforced by the refurbishment of the Wellcome

Trust buildings half a mile along Euston Road. And now, as this book goes to press, we witness the first site scrapings of the vast Francis Crick Institute scientific research centre on a lot behind the library. That educational tradition has been further emphasized by the conversion of the huge granaries behind King's Cross station into a new home for Central Saint Martins College of Arts and Design, an anchor-point in the meshing of this disparate collection of post-industrial architectural salvage into a promising landscape of learning.

But the most profound transformation has been made in barely visible engineering, in the complex web of rail and Underground facilities that snake above, beneath and around King's Cross station in what is one of the world's most extraordinary archaeologies of transport.

At St Pancras, the flamboyant Victorian Gothic architecture of the Midland Grand Hotel has been resurrected (as the St Pancras Renaissance London Hotel) into a series of urbane spaces that overlook the platforms below William Henry Barlow's gorgeously generous barrel-vaulted St Pancras train shed (1868). From here, trains whisk passengers over to France via the Channel Tunnel. It took the inheritors of the much-derided British Rail to create a twenty-first-century station that is as stripped back and intelligent as it is sophisticated and elegant. The St Pancras redevelopment is a self-effacing piece of work that revivifies the existing structure with panache.

Left
Aerial view of the King's Cross station project nearing completion in 2011, seen from the north, with the Regent Quarter development immediately to the left (east) and the massive King's Cross urban development at the bottom right of the photograph.

Opposite
The dramatic canopy structure of the station's new Western Concourse, funnelling upward just feet away from the restored Grade I-listed Western Range building.

The operational, architectural and structural transformation of King's Cross station, led by Network Rail, designed by John McAslan + Partners and engineered by Arup, is the most notable component of this extraordinary transport revival. The rationalization of the immensely complex station infrastructure has produced an outcome of real clarity, with the station re-emerging as a piece of architecture with clear urban intent: a civic transport hub, rather than the series of obstacles it once was.

The semicircular canopy of King's Cross station's new Western Concourse echoes the curve of the Great Northern Hotel next door (which is being revived as a boutique hotel) and has created a grand new covered public space to counterbalance the planned resurrection of the Cubitt plaza in front of the station.

This is genuine public architecture that will touch countless lives, an exemplary demonstration of how architecture can have great, and ramifying, effects. Some 55 million people will use King's Cross station each year, and for many it will be the gateway to London. The challenge has been to produce a transformation that is also a connective piece of city reflecting the diverse character of the area; to create a new district that meshes with, and energizes, the area's historic grittiness and tightly knit urban grain. There was no room for a 'blandscape' of freestanding newness here.

Important architecture in the King's Cross area: Colin St John Wilson's British Library (above, left), and the elaborate neo-Gothic façade of what was originally St Pancras station's Midland Grand Hotel, designed by George Gilbert Scott.

Above
The nineteenth-century grain warehouse north of King's Cross station has been sympathetically remodelled and modernized by architectural practice Stanton Williams, becoming the new site for Central St Martins College of Arts and Design.

Above, right
A night view of the King's Cross train shed, photographed from the north.

Overleaf
A north-facing panorama showing, from left (west), the layered levels of the British Library, St Pancras station and King's Cross station, with the King's Cross development area between and to the north of the stations.

London's extraordinary urban complexity has made it difficult for the city to create ambitious, multi-modal infrastructure and architecture in its historic streets. The rebirth of King's Cross station proves that it can be done. The scheme is a bold and illuminating re-ordering of the last remaining dark urban void in central London. The railway terminus's electrified rails, embedded in this great tableau of historic and twenty-first-century architecture at the corner of Euston Road and York Way, are helping to spark the station, and this part of London, back to life.

15

MAKING TRACKS THROUGH TIME

Peter Hall

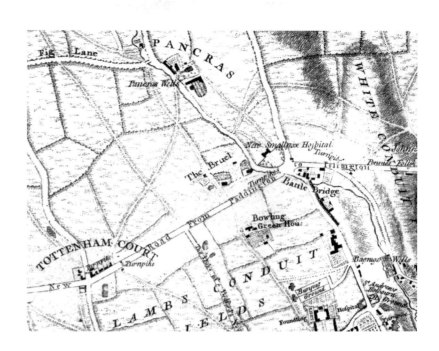

A map from 1769 of
the Battlebridge area –
later renamed King's
Cross – showing the
New Road turnpike.

To understand fully the significance of the King's Cross station story, a
short history lesson on the evolution of modern London's transport system
is in order.

There were four critical events, starting with the opening of London's first
bypass. London began to develop new aristocratic suburbs west of the historic
City of London, such as Covent Garden, St James's, Mayfair and Marylebone, in
the seventeenth century. By the middle of the eighteenth century the historic
Roman road into the City, the Oxford Street–High Holborn–Cheapside route, had
been enveloped by these suburbs, and a toll bypass, the New Road turnpike,
was created between the City of London and Paddington in the north-west.
But the turnpike was also a device to stimulate further real-estate development
in the area immediately to the north of the suburbs, and by 1800 London's
relentless residential growth had already lapped up to the New Road; today,
as Marylebone Road, Euston Road, Pentonville Road and City Road, the route
forms the northern boundary of London's central business district.

A second definitive point came in 1811, when the architect John Nash
proposed to develop a new street, Regent Street, as a processional way, lined
with magnificent residential terraces, between the existing royal park of
St James's, by Buckingham Palace, and a new park to be named after the
Prince Regent (later George IV) to the north. This effectively established

a bridgehead of high-class residential development that crossed the New Road. To the more airy west of the new park, elite development proliferated; to the smoke-ridden east, it was a very different story.

A third key factor was the construction, as part of Nash's grand design, of the Regent's Canal immediately behind his stately Regent's Park terraces, which made the area alongside it popular for industrial establishments and warehouses. Almost inevitably, the area east of the new park soon began to deteriorate. To the west and south, the big estates (the Bedford, Crown, Portman and Portland estates) fought successfully to maintain the quality of their developments; but immediately to their north and east, the local aristocratic landowners – Lord Somers, Lord Southampton and the Marquis of Camden – were indifferent.[1] In 1826 the Duke of Bedford's agent had to make his estate a gated community 'so as to shut out the low population of Somers Town' immediately to the north, on the other side of the New Road.[2]

Railway tracks as Victorian dividing lines

Even as Somers Town was being built, it instantly degenerated into a notorious slum, cleared and rebuilt only from 1928 onward.[3] So in 1835, the Southampton estate next to it did not present determined opposition to Robert Stephenson's new London and Birmingham Railway, the terminus of

An artist's impression of the construction of the Metropolitan Railway, passing under Euston Road near King's Cross station. The undergound line, the world's first, opened in 1863.

Lavishly dressed mid-nineteenth-century travellers at Paddington station, as portrayed in a copy of William Powell Frith's *The Railway Station* (1862).

which was sited at Euston, immediately east of Somers Town, while Stephenson was compelled to tunnel under the Eton estate immediately to the north.[4] And this was symptomatic of a wider divide: once the railway was open at Euston, to be followed rapidly by others near by, it became a major dividing line, separating an aristocratic-bourgeois west from a working-class and slum-ridden east.

Then came the fourth critical event in the development of London's public transport: in 1846 a Royal Commission decreed that the new railways could not extend south of the New Road. So the Great Northern Railway (GNR) and the Midland Railway (MR), seeking the nearest point of access to the City of London, had to terminate immediately east of Euston: the GNR at King's Cross (1852) and the MR at St Pancras (1868). But, while all this was happening, a campaign led by the City of London solicitor Charles Pearson forced a critical modification of the prescription of 1846: the world's first underground railway, the Metropolitan Railway of 1863, which took rail passengers, in a few minutes, from all these stations (and from Paddington station, which had opened in 1838) to the heart of the City.

In 1866 a direct connection was made from the GNR at King's Cross station to a widening of the Metropolitan line (known in railway parlance as the Widened Lines), allowing trains from the north to run into the City.

The Gare du Nord in
Paris, opened in 1864.

Furthermore, a tunnel under the new Smithfield meat market, the Snow Hill
tunnel, created a direct north–south link through the City and across the
Thames, to connect with south and south-east London.

Thus, London never developed a grand *Hauptbahnhof* (central station)
as there is in Cologne, Munich or Zürich – but neither did Paris, Berlin,
Madrid or Moscow, which similarly kept their new rail termini outside their
historic centres. In London a ring of termini quickly developed along the
line set by the Royal Commission in 1846. As well as those along the New
Road to the north of the City, some stations (Liverpool Street, Fenchurch
Street, Cannon Street, Blackfriars and the now-closed Broad Street) formed
a tight collar on the east and south edges of the City, which was by then
overwhelmingly the business heart of London, while others were further to
the south and west: London Bridge, Waterloo, Charing Cross and Victoria.

By 1884, some twenty years after the original Metropolitan Underground
line opened from Paddington to Farringdon, it had been progressively
extended – after huge technical, financial and organizational travails – into
a complete Circle line serving all these railway stations apart from the two
south of the river, London Bridge and Waterloo. This, plus the Snow Hill
Tunnel, formed the basic railway infrastructure of late Victorian London,
tying together the main termini into a great single system of interchange.

The rail-side approaches
to King's Cross station in
the post-war years.

London's answer to the Hauptbahnhof

In the following years, from 1890 to 1907, a series of new deep-level
Underground lines was constructed. Originally designed for short-distance
travel into the centre, they did not go out of their way to serve the rail termini.
But two of them interchanged at King's Cross: the City and South London
Railway (now the Bank branch of the Northern line) and the Great Northern
Piccadilly and Brompton Railway (today's Piccadilly line). In 1969 they were
joined by a third, the Victoria line, the first Underground line to be completed
under central London since the Edwardian era.

This extraordinary concentration of transport infrastructure had an
important consequence: the closeness to one another of Euston, King's
Cross and St Pancras stations offered a powerful substitute for a continental
Hauptbahnhof, effectively the nearest thing London had to a grand central
city terminal complex. And from these stations, radiating out, their networks
have a huge and growing geographical sweep: north-west to Birmingham,
Liverpool and Glasgow, north to Edinburgh and Aberdeen, north-east to
Cambridge and King's Lynn, south-east to Ramsgate and Margate, south to
Brighton and west to Heathrow; and further afield through the Channel Tunnel
to Brussels, Paris and Avignon (and, before long, various rail bureaucracies
permitting, to Amsterdam, Cologne and Frankfurt).

Another sequence of events has made this dominance historically manifest on the ground. In the 1980s the decision was made by the then-nationalized British Rail, and its young Network SouthEast manager Chris Green in particular, to reopen the Snow Hill tunnel, which had closed to passenger service in 1916. This created Thameslink, a new long-distance commuter line that extended 50 miles north to Bedford, and via the King's Cross area south to Brighton. Opened in 1988, it immediately proved a huge success, constrained only by the inadequacy of the exhumed Victorian station infrastructure.

Thameslink was soon extended into a much more ambitious network. Today's Thameslink Programme is designed to cater for longer trains to serve new or reconstructed stations to a wider variety of places – notably from Peterborough and Cambridge via an as-yet incomplete section of tunnel linking the East Coast Main Line to the domestic platforms beneath St Pancras International. The Thameslink Programme has been partially completed in time for the 2012 Olympics, and, with the rebuilding of London Bridge station now approved, will be completed in 2018.

The Handyside Bridge of 1893, which passed over the main-line platforms of King's Cross station, was carefully dismantled during the station's renovation and has been donated by Network Rail to the Mid-Hants Railway.

The crucial high-speed line decision

In 1993 came the critical decision to terminate the Channel Tunnel high-speed rail link in a rebuilt St Pancras station, replacing an earlier proposal for a through station under the site. To compensate for the loss of potential through services on to the Midlands and north of England, the winning proposal from London & Continental Railways included a through connection bypassing St Pancras immediately to the north of the station; this has been built but has not yet been made operational.

A brilliant solution to the difficult issues of accommodating the new international services into St Pancras station's historic structure was devised by the lead architect, Norman Foster, working closely with Alastair Lansley, the architect for Rail Link Engineering, which managed the construction of the Channel Tunnel Rail Link: the Victorian train shed would be extended to accommodate the Eurostar trains (three times the length of the Midland trains they displaced) in a new, uncompromisingly modern structure that would also house the Midland trains on its west flank and the new high-speed domestic services to Kent on the east. The new Thameslink station would be housed under the Midland tracks. The resulting complex, described by the travel writer Simon Calder as 'the greatest cathedral of the railway era', opened to great fanfare and acclaim in November 2007.[5]

St Pancras International. Its twenty-first-century modernizations lie under the magnificent arched vault of William Barlow's train shed of 1868.

A view from the mezzanine of King's Cross station's innovative Western Concourse on its opening day in March 2012.

Equally important, though less heralded, was the work done underneath all this emerging magnificence by Transport for London's interchange team, led by John McNulty, to create an entirely new system of subsurface pedestrian circulation linking all the Underground lines with the St Pancras and King's Cross rail termini. This consists of a vast pedestrian gyratory in which passengers circulate either through subways or, most spectacularly, at ground level through the main concourse of St Pancras station itself. This system was revealed at the opening of the new King's Cross station on 19 March 2012.

The new architecture and renovation of King's Cross station, by John McAslan and Arup, receive appropriate eulogies elsewhere in these pages. But what also needs emphasizing is the way this scheme completes the entire logistical design of the combined complex of stations. The magnificent new semicircular Western Concourse was designed to fit within the highly idiosyncratic outline of the Grade II-listed Great Northern Hotel adjoining it, the shape of which, in plan, was a pragmatic Victorian architectural response to the constraint of the now disused 'Hotel Curve' formed by the rail connection of 1866 from the GNR to the Widened Lines lying underneath. Thus, the new Western Concourse is designed to complete the great subsurface pedestrian circulation system by creating an airport-style one-way pattern of movement through the station: people departing enter through the new concourse, and over the magnificent new pedestrian bridge that spans the Grade I-listed train shed; and people arriving exit through the old main entrance at the front.

There is one last element in this amazingly complex logistical jigsaw, and it will be the last to be completed, taking perhaps another decade, perhaps another two. It is the regeneration by the development company Argent of the entire King's Cross Railway Lands, the old freight terminus complex immediately north of the station and above the tracks that lead through a short tunnel known as the Gasworks Tunnel. Passionately, even ferociously debated over two decades, the broad regenerative shape of the development is now evident as the visitor comes out from the Underground circulation system through King's Cross station's northernmost exit, signposted to Regent's Canal.

The first piece of the Argent development opened for business in September 2011: the new Central Saint Martins College of Arts and Design, the cornerstone of the University of the Arts London, housed in Lewis Cubitt's Grade II-listed Great Northern Grain Warehouse and in modern extensions designed by the Stanton Williams architectural practice. In front, a new open space next to the canal is newly in place. The first residential

A visualization of King's Cross station (with the twin barrels of its train-shed roof flanked by its long Eastern Range, towards the top left of the image), in relation to the area's regeneration masterplan area to the right (north).

buildings are also emerging, to be followed by a score of blocks – some residential, some containing offices, plus shops, restaurants, cafes and bars – that will make up this totally new quarter of London. And its special quality is already evident: this is bound to become a new creative district that will attract start-up businesses, some doubtless founded by St Martins graduates, some by other individuals attracted by the ambience of the area. The future social, cultural and commercial values of this new quarter of London are incalculable, but one thing is certain: it is going to surprise. It will complete the development of this amazing station complex and give a massive boost to the regeneration of the area around it.

1 Prince, H., 'North-west London 1814–1863', in *Greater London*, ed. Coppock, J.T., and Prince, H., London (Faber and Faber) 1964.

2 Kellett, J.R., *The Impact of Railways on Victorian Cities*, London (Routledge & Kegan Paul) 1969.

3 Clarke, L., *Building Capitalism: Historical Change and the Labour Process in the Production of the Built Environment*, London and New York (Routledge) 1992.

4 Prince, H., *op. cit.*; Kellet, J.R., *op. cit.*

5 Calder, S., 'A Renaissance Arrives at St Pancras', *The Independent*, 12 February 2011.

ALL CHANGE! THE TRANSFORMATION OF KING'S CROSS STATION

Jay Merrick

An aerial view of King's Cross station and its twin-barrelled train shed (at the centre of the image), with St Pancras station to the left (west), taken in 2010, showing early works on the semicircular King's Cross Western Concourse site.

The transformation of London's Grade I-listed King's Cross station is a *grand projet* in the European tradition, and a key element in what is Europe's biggest single urban-regeneration scheme. The station project combines modernization, restoration, sophisticated construction techniques and new architecture of the highest quality. King's Cross station is more than one of Britain's greatest railway termini: it has become the gateway to the wider regeneration of 30 hectares of derelict post-industrial land to the north.

The station's rebirth, commissioned and led by Network Rail, designed and masterplanned by John McAslan + Partners, engineered by Arup and delivered by a host of supporting contractors and subcontractors, is also the latest and most dramatic signal of big changes in the early decades of the twenty-first century in the way we will travel, and live, in Britain.

The twenty-first century's new culture of movement

Transport and infrastructure renewal are no longer background concerns in our growing cities. They are having an increasingly important impact on daily life and on the way Britain is perceived internationally. In London, and elsewhere in Britain, we can expect only urban growth, matching a macro trend that has already concentrated half the world's population in cities; this figure is projected to have risen to two-thirds by 2030.

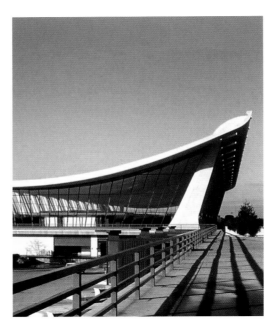

From 36,000 feet, sitting in the cabin of an aeroplane, one could hold this stark fact at bay, and, despite the rigours of passing through most airports, we have surely become accustomed to thinking that flying is the most effective and strategically important way to travel. In 2012, we may think fondly of such iconic railway termini as New York's Grand Central station and the Milano Centrale. But our greater interest in air travel reflects a postwar zeitgeist fuelled by package holidays and occasional flashes of brilliant airport design by such architects as Eero Saarinen. From the late 1950s, airports developed a strangely romantic image, and proved that transport hubs could be a pleasure to use. Great airports, such as Osaka's Kansai, designed by Renzo Piano and opened in 1994, and Richard Rogers's new terminals at Barajas airport in Madrid, opened in 2006, have continued that tradition in the face of the turgidly chaotic ennui that now characterizes so many international airports.

On terra firma in Britain, one of the most densely populated countries in Europe, another reality bites: in terms of transport and movement of people, the Earth's surface is where the toughest challenges lie. In 1993 Grimshaw Architects' Eurostar terminal at London's Waterloo station (closed in 2007 when the St Pancras terminal opened) hinted at the shape of innovations to come in Britain. Across the Channel, the quality of station design and infrastructure

The public's perception of travel as having both romantic and modern qualities was originally prompted by such great railway stations as Grand Central in New York (1913; above, left), and by the design virtuosity of Eero Saarinen's Dulles International Airport, near Washington, D.C. (1962).

In the twenty-first century, the design of airport and railway stations has often been hugely ambitious. Madrid's Barajas airport (2006; above), with its wave-form roof, and Avignon's super-svelte TGV station (2001) are two of the most striking examples.

renewal on French high-speed lines has been of exceptional quality. Now Britain's forthcoming High Speed Two line from London to the north of England promises to move the travel experience bar just as high in terms of speed and connectivity, in the same way that on London's Underground the Jubilee line extension in 1999 delivered a quantum leap in the standards of both subsurface travel and the Underground station architecture that serves tens of millions of people every day.

The modernization of King's Cross station by Network Rail and its architects, engineers and contractors marks a paradigm shift in the rail operator's strategic thinking and its architectural ambition: a commitment to Britain's future ability to generate enterprise and innovation, coupled with a programme designed to integrate the best the twenty-first century can offer with the finest the nineteenth has already provided. Ultimately, however, it took London's successful bid for the 2012 Olympic Games to focus a collection of several smaller King's Cross station projects into one grand vision.

At the neighbouring St Pancras station, remodelled and extended in 2007 by London & Continental Railways, the glint of large-scale modern interventions within the historic fabric is as eye-catching as William Barlow's famous train shed (1868), its beautiful roof nearly twice the span of the King's Cross station

vaults. At King's Cross, the intention was always to re-present Lewis Cubitt's Victorian architecture, to de-clutter its historic fabric and combine it with state-of-the-art interventions. There was an even more fundamental idea: that King's Cross station should contribute significantly, and coherently, to the energies of the urban regeneration around it. The station's Eastern Range building forms part of the western edge of the massive Regent Quarter regeneration zone, and to the north is Argent's vast urban-regeneration development. Below ground, the multi-modal transport situation is equally dynamic: six Underground lines, and their combined King's Cross St Pancras concourse, lie beneath part of the south-western segment of King's Cross station.

The potential value of better transport networks should not be seen in relationship only to London. The economics commentator Aditya Chakrabortty has highlighted research by Manchester University's Centre for Research on Socio-Cultural Change, which found that between 2002 and 2008 businesses in the City of London paid taxes worth £193 billion, about half the amount contributed by the manufacturing sector. Thus, if Britain's manufacturers and non-financial services industries are to remain competitive, the quality of regional passenger and freight rail transport must improve, too.

London inevitably sets the country's standards for change. If the strong international perception of London as a pre-eminent world city is to continue,

A freight service operated by Direct Rail Services passes through the Scottish Highlands' Loch Moy area. On the day this photograph was taken the train reached Inverness on time, whereas the nearby A9 trunk road was closed because of snow.

A 1990s appraisal by John McAslan + Partners mapping the main pedestrian and traffic routes through the King's Cross area, as well as urban connections stretching south as far as the River Thames below Aldwych and Temple, and north into Finsbury Park.

it will depend as much on transport efficiency as on the capital's long-established magnetism as Britain's cultural and financial powerhouse.

King's Cross station has taken fifteen years to emerge from its complex chrysalis of change, and the process has been unavoidably tortuous. The vision for change at King's Cross triggered a ripple effect of subsequent design, and civic, visions. The project was not, by any means, a tidy progression of client's brief, followed by gradually refined design and engineering proposals.

Indeed, historically, nothing has been straightforward about the redevelopment of either King's Cross or St Pancras stations. Sir Neil Cossons, former chairman of English Heritage and current chairman of the Royal College of Arts, has noted that in the 1960s there had been talk of the potential destruction of St Pancras, or of the creation of some fusion of the operations of King's Cross and St Pancras, but the Victorian Society and the poet John Betjeman led the fight to secure St Pancras's future by campaigning successfully for its Grade I listing.

In 1987–88 a massive new scheme for the development of King's Cross station was driven by British Rail's proposal to insert a Eurostar terminal underneath the station, and at right angles to it. This was shown in designs commissioned by the London Regeneration Consortium (LRC),

A 1990s development masterplan for the King's Cross–St Pancras area (left), commissioned by the London Regeneration Consortium, and the development scheme conceived by Argent (opposite), agreed by the London Borough of Camden in 2007 and now being implemented. Comparing the two provides an insight into changing attitudes to appropriate forms of major inner-city urban regeneration.

the predecessor to Argent's current King's Cross urban-regeneration development. (The Eurostar terminal, of course, was in the end sited at St Pancras.) But it was only in 2005, when London was awarded the staging of the 2012 Olympics, that Network Rail's King's Cross station scheme accelerated and became more ambitious, both operationally and architecturally.

From that point, the scoping of the King's Cross station project, and its design, involved regular consultations or collaborations with more than twenty statutory authorities and public-interest groups. The attention to detail required to preserve a Grade I-listed structure was imperative, but the transformation of the station also depended on the understanding and ultimate support of key organizations, notably Camden Council and its then planning director, Peter Bishop; the Greater London Authority; and the historic buildings watchdog, English Heritage, under Paddy Pugh, head of advice and grants. These organizations, and their specialist teams, understood the benefits of marrying preservation and restoration with urban regeneration.

Before any of the physical work could begin, a bewildering number of land transactions and funding arrangements had to be resolved in order to provide Network Rail with the land on which to build, and the work sites needed to support construction activity; the land owner, CTRL, and the site

A portrait of Lewis Cubitt, the architect of King's Cross station, painted in 1845 by William Boxall.

developer, Argent, needed clean title to support their development; and all parties had to resolve complex funding and construction responsibilities. This was all pulled together in an unwieldy legal document, likely in time to be forgotten, but pivotal in unlocking the scheme's potential.

And while the bureaucracy associated with government departments in making use of public money often adds time, complexity and, rather paradoxically, cost, the King's Cross team have been universally complimentary about the light but effective touch of their colleagues in Michael Hurn's major projects team at the Department for Transport. The positive working relationships forged over the years developed into a mutually supportive partnership.

How very different it had been for Lewis Cubitt! After being commissioned by the directors of the Great Northern Railway, he designed and built King's Cross station in 1852 in little more than a year. The can-do Victorians had already tracked the country with extraordinary rapidity. The world's first public railway opened in 1825, on some 27 miles of line between Stockton and Darlington in north-east England. Other railways followed, and by 1838 5.4 million people were travelling by train. By 1862, a decade after Cubitt delivered King's Cross station, Britain's stations and termini teemed with 170 million rail users. And in London early railways fed a huge growth in

population, which between 1841 and 1900 – less than sixty years – surged from 2 million to 6 million.

Today's national station-use figures are astonishing: Britain has more than 2500 stations, which handle about 2.1 billion passenger entries and exits a year. As for King's Cross station, it currently handles about 45 million passengers a year, and that figure is expected to rise to 55 million in the medium term. Together, King's Cross, St Pancras and their Underground station deal with nearly 90 million travellers a year.

The twenty-first-century version of Cubitt's masterpiece is a bold fusion of restored historic fabric, state-of-the-art modernization, and innovative contemporary architecture and engineering by McAslan and Arup. The station's Western Concourse is arguably the most striking piece of new British transport architecture since Foster Associates' Stansted Airport in 1991, and Grimshaw Architects' London Eurostar terminal at Waterloo station two years later.

The importance of the King's Cross project as a whole is magnified when seen in the wider context of recent transport development initiatives, such as the extension of the Underground's Jubilee line (1999). London's £16 billion Crossrail scheme, linking west and east London, is cut from an equally ambitious cloth. It is Europe's biggest single construction project and, when completed in 2018, will make travelling across London faster and easier

London's new generation of transport interchanges includes North Greenwich Underground station (Jubilee line, 1999; above, left), the forthcoming Bond Street Crossrail station (shown above in a visualization), and Blackfriars rail station with its 'solar bridge' across the River Thames (shown opposite in a visualization).

for 200 million passengers a year, generating billions for Britain's economy. The project will upgrade thirty-seven stations, and create eight new subsurface stations and 13 miles of twin-bore tunnels under central London, with new subsurface stations along the main spine route at Paddington, Bond Street, Tottenham Court Road, Farringdon, Liverpool Street, Whitechapel and Canary Wharf. The trains will each carry up to 1500 passengers, and twenty-four trains per hour will run in each direction between Paddington and Whitechapel.

Network Rail's massive improvements to King's Cross station, and the concurrent redesign and reconstruction of the Thameslink Programme at Farringdon and Blackfriars, plus the work to transform London Bridge station, are designed to transform the experience of passengers travelling to, from and through central London. These projects are creating more space for passengers, and for trains going to more destinations. This will reduce pressure on other networks, and provide more pleasant and reliable travel options. These schemes are being built on a scale only previously seen in the nineteenth century, when mass-transit railways were first imagined and constructed.

The completion of King's Cross station and the start of Crossrail's projects have made room for the next big debate on transport strategy: high-speed rail networks in relation to airports. Norman Foster's proposal for a Thames hub

airport, jutting into the Thames estuary and linked by dedicated high-speed lines to Britain's biggest cities, has been countered by Terry Farrell's scheme for a so-called constellation rail hub in west London that would connect five existing airports. Their stark disagreement is fertile; it illuminates the need for thoroughly examined, out-of-the-box ideas about national strategies for transport and infrastructure.

The end of the line, and the beginning of urban change

The reinvention of King's Cross station is a key part of this dynamic cat's cradle of transport evolution in Britain, and not just in terms of the movement of people. The well-designed changes to the station and the public realm around it have also helped to energize urban, demographic and commercial shifts in the wider community.

The station and the forthcoming public plaza in front of it (which will be about the size of Leicester Square) lie at the junction of four main roads, including the extremely busy Euston Road. This makes the station the de facto gateway to the £2 billion regeneration scheme for the King's Cross area, a phased development that will eventually create more than 743,000 square metres of mixed-use space in new buildings and modernized Victorian industrial hulks.

In the past twenty to thirty years, large-scale developments have given parts of London a new look, and new purposes. Such schemes as Broadgate (above, left) were dependent on existing transport infrastructure. The creation of Canary Wharf (above) required new transport interchanges.

Other developments in London, such as Paternoster Square (above), were responses to wartime damage or to the need to replace outdated post-war developments with more contextually led regeneration schemes. The layout of buildings and spaces in the visualization of the King's Cross urban regeneration (above, right) makes an interesting comparison.

A key point about the station modernization and the King's Cross development as a whole is that they go against the grain of the kind of planning and development that was common in the 1980s, and that still generally applies in Britain's towns and cities. Such projects as the Broadgate development in the City of London, Paternoster Square by St Paul's Cathedral and Canary Wharf in Docklands were undoubtedly an innovative kind of corporatized placemaking, essentially land-clearance exercises that led to major changes in infrastructure: old buildings around Liverpool Street station, including the former Broad Street station, removed; docks altered at Canary Wharf; and new buildings (some of considerable architectural merit) slotted in.

In the 1990s a development masterplan for King's Cross, St Pancras and the area north of them proposed something similar: that the hefty Victorian buildings on the wasteland north of King's Cross station be razed and replaced with a park surrounded by medium- and high-rise buildings. But almost exactly the opposite has happened. At King's Cross station and in the area around it, historic buildings and infrastructure have been salvaged, adapted, extended and modernized to give them an entirely new lease of life. The modernization and extension of the station has worked with, rather than against, the existing infrastructure.

And so, King's Cross station has become the most obvious landmark for energetic social and commercial change in a part of London long regarded as a miasma of social and economic deprivation. In 1838 Charles Dickens referred to the Foundling Hospital at King's Cross in *Oliver Twist*. Had George Orwell written *Down and Out in Paris and London* in the 1970s rather than in 1933, King's Cross would surely have provided some of its scenes. It certainly did for the Ealing comedy film *The Ladykillers* (1955) and for the Bollywood film *Dilwale Dulhania Le Jayenge* (1995). Nevertheless, even at the turn of the millennium, the King's Cross area remained synonymous with urban blight and lives lived on the very edge of degradation and ruin. Peter Hall's essay, which starts on page 18, sets out the historical urban and transport scene relating to King's Cross meticulously.

Because of their pivotal position in terms of surface and subsurface transport routes, King's Cross station and Argent's King's Cross urban development offer conclusive proof that the adaptive re-use of historic buildings is an excellent way to give regeneration zones a more meaningful, physically characterful sense of both continuity and change. Network Rail, Argent, and their teams of masterplanners, architects and engineers have shown that history has a future. And the area's refreshed character, its mix of revived old and spanking new, has retuned the vibe in this once reviled

Below
Poster advertising
The Ladykillers (1955),
the Academy Award-
winning Ealing comedy
filmed in and around
King's Cross.

quarter of London. Even only an hour's stroll through the streets around King's Cross station reveals clearly the extent of social, cultural and commercial change: the garishly polychromatic Nido student tower in Pentonville Road and the just-completed Central Saint Martins College of Arts and Design; the Gagosian Gallery in a tough nineteenth-century building in Britannia Street, harbouring the work of superstar artists; the London Wildlife Trust's Camley Street Natural Park; children playing in Coram's Fields; small terraced houses in the once ever-so-humble Keystone Crescent, just around the corner from the station, selling for £750,000; newspaper production and classical music at King's Place; vulnerable youngsters learning how to make more of their lives at the New Horizon Youth Centre and Copenhagen Youth Project; and, very soon, tens of thousands of professionals, householders and art students thronging into the King's Cross development. And at the centre of it all is the glistening canopy of King's Cross station's Western Concourse, and the hurly-burly of people coming and going.

How Cubitt's nineteenth-century marvel was transformed

Many may not be aware of the greatness of Lewis Cubitt's obdurate, pared-down railway architecture, which the design critic Stephen Bayley has described as a brilliant example of Victorian matter-of-fact architecture. And

great it is: each of the two round-arched train-shed roofs spans 22 metres. In today's postmodern, anything-goes architectural environment, the station's main façade of plain undecorated brick seems wonderfully straightforward, expressing nothing more than the diagrammatic cross section of the train sheds; this terse architectural clarity is very nearly Modernist in manner. Between the façade's two monumental arches is a 37-metre-tall clock tower, the only deliberately 'grand' element of Cubitt's design, which will be fully restored by 2013, along with the main façade. We can think of the Great Northern Railway's London terminus as the architecturally calm yin to the decoratively outré yang of St Pancras station, a mere 50 metres to the west.

John McAslan + Partners and Arup have been intimately involved in the design of the project as a whole since it began in 1997. McAslan's design team was led throughout that fifteen-year period by its principal, John McAslan, with a series of associates, initially Adam Brown and, from 2005, by Hiro Aso and Simon Goode as project directors, Aidan Potter as design director and Pauline Nee as historic buildings adviser. Arup's engineering team was originally headed by Tony Marriott, who passed the baton to a team headed, successively, by John Batchelor, John Turzynski and Mike Byrne. McAslan and Arup have collaborated for many years, and both practices are renowned for

Two views of King's Cross station from the 1960s: the Main Train Shed illuminated at night, seen from the platform of the former York Road station (above, left); and a view from the steps of the old Handyside Bridge, looking south along the platform next to the Western Range.

A study model of the Western Concourse structure.

transformations of historic buildings – among them McAslan's Roundhouse and Peter Jones in London, and De La Warr Pavilion in Bexhill-on-Sea; and Arup's work on London's Tate Modern and St Pancras station, and the Rijksmuseum in Amsterdam. The fact that McAslan, Arup and English Heritage had worked together on culturally important projects involving transformations of historic buildings was crucial: it generated confidence and mutual trust in both the design of major interventions at King's Cross and the fine details of restorations.

The designers worked closely with the Network Rail construction teams. The key players in Network Rail's team included a succession of three chief executives: Sir John Armitt, who initiated the scheme; Iain Coucher; and Sir David Higgins, who oversaw the station's completion along with the group board director, Simon Kirby, and programme director, Ian Fry. The latter was responsible for the delivery of a project that addressed a massively challenging set of design and engineering tasks, and other complex factors that influenced the phasing, timescales and, in some cases, the final result of the planned work.

Throughout the construction programme, it was imperative that the existing station continue to serve the public with minimal intrusion or disruption. This challenge, faced by Network Rail senior programme manager Kevin McGeever, rather resembled trying to decorate a hallway using only the

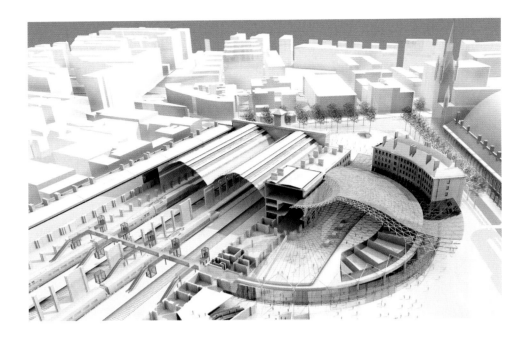

letterbox as an access point. That image gives a flavour of the challenges imposed by the site, which was very small for the scale of the project being undertaken, and bounded on two sides by other construction projects and on a third by one of London's busiest roads.

Beneath the site, London Underground was still completing its huge Northern Ticket Hall, which provided the station's new Western Concourse with a high-quality interchange with the Underground. But it also created major complications for the design and construction teams in terms of structural arrangements and when work could commence.

These factors dictated the order in which initial works could be carried out. The works included alterations to the Eastern Range, into which staff and functions were temporarily transferred during the restoration of the Western Range; upgraded platforms, with a new bridge over the main-line tracks; complex operational upgrades; and large-scale conversion and expansion of the Victorian vaults beneath the platforms so that they could carry state-of-the-art servicing systems for the station and surrounding developments. There was also the creation of a new platform beneath the Eastern Range building, a vital precursor to the work required within the Main Train Shed.

These works also included the design and construction of a new and substantially enlarged concourse to replace the infamously grim structure

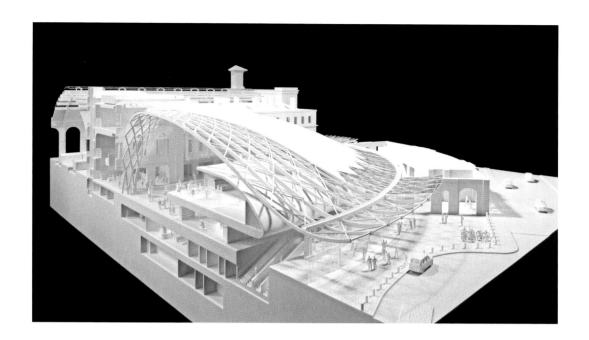

A cross-sectional model of the station and London Underground projects, which was exhibited by John McAslan + Partners at the Royal Academy of Arts, London, in 2011.

that has projected from the southern façade of the station since the 1970s. The 'unmasking' and precise restoration of this façade was of particular importance to English Heritage, Camden Council and numerous amenity groups, including the Victorian Society. There was the historically sensitive repair of the Grade I-listed train shed to deliver, too. But the project's single most significant design and engineering challenge was the creation of a new concourse three times the size of the existing 1970s one, to handle comfortably passenger movements for the foreseeable future as well as the immediate needs relating to seventeen peak-time train movements per hour on the station's twelve main-line and suburban service platforms.

McAslan and Arup investigated three potential solutions for Network Rail. The first was to create a vast new concourse in the southern half of Cubitt's train shed. This would have involved pushing the platforms 120 metres to the north and widening a tunnel under the Regent's Canal. The projected £1 billion cost of this option – not to mention the destruction of listed industrial archaeology – ruled it out. A second proposal was to insert a massive mezzanine structure inside the train sheds, but this too was ruled out as being overly complicated in terms of heritage and people movement.

The preferred solution in operational, architectural and placemaking terms was to position the new concourse on the western side of the station,

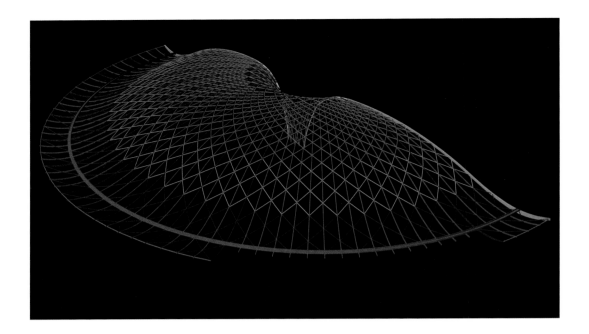

where the original Victorian entrance to the station had been. But even this approach faced three major constraints: the existing Grade I-listed Western Range façade had to be retained; so, too, did the curving, Grade II-listed façade of the Great Northern Hotel 40 metres to the west; and, lastly, London Underground – with Arup as lead designer – had already begun building the subsurface Northern Ticket Hall to service its King's Cross St Pancras station, and the ticket hall passed directly beneath the footprint of the proposed new Western Concourse for King's Cross station.

This meant that Arup and Tom Hyland, Network Rail's project engineer, had to ensure that the supporting columns of the concourse canopy hit the ground at seventeen very precise points that 'fitted' the irregular subsurface structural grid of the Underground's ticket hall. Furthermore, the design of the canopy had to avoid funnelling significant weight into the foundations of the Western Range and the Great Northern Hotel, and could barely touch their façades in the process.

London Underground's start on the subsurface construction of its Northern Ticket Hall before the construction of King's Cross Western Concourse was not the only complicating factor. In addition, the modernization of St Pancras station, along with extensions to the Underground and Thameslink concourses, was also well under way, and had a direct, and challenging,

A parametric analysis by Arup of the anticipated stresses in the 1200-tonne Western Concourse roof. This was an early application of building information modelling, in which building modelling software is used to increase productivity in building design and construction. Shown here are the primary radial beams overlaid with the diagrid lattice.

A model of the diagrid lattice roof showing its relationship with the Grade I-listed façade of the Western Range.

bearing on the planning, designing, construction and phasing of the King's Cross modernization.

These constraints were ultimately a blessing, because they demanded highly innovative architectural and structural solutions. And this led to the design of the semicircular Western Concourse, the remarkably expressive form of which has become one of Network Rail's first genuinely iconic structures of the twenty-first century. The canopy's vivid trajectory springs upward in a splayed funnel of columns, within a few feet of the Western Range. The potential effect of this on the historic architectural composition and physical integrity of Cubitt's original Booking Hall entrance was of great concern to English Heritage, and that is why the new concourse was designed to be structurally independent of the Western Range building and all adjoining structures.

The canopy's lightweight steel diagrid shell structure is supported by branching columns at its perimeter, creating a cavernous space oversailed by a dramatic, wave-like double arch. The elegance of the canopy belies the fact that its structure is actually composed of modular and repetitive elements, which can be rapidly assembled. The structure is almost Victorian in the way it demonstrates that pragmatism and apparent simplicity can give birth to clear, graceful architecture.

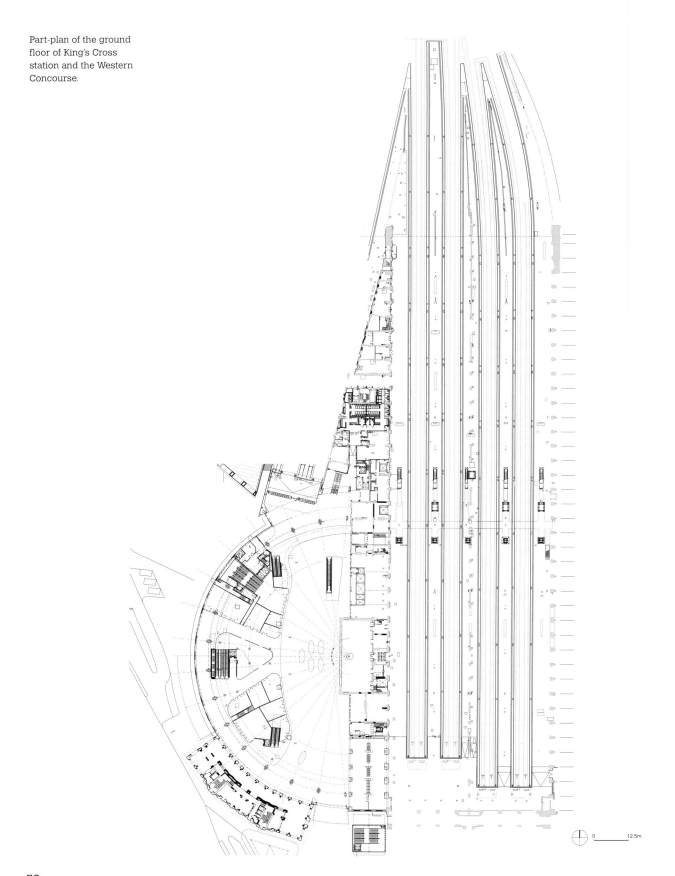

Part-plan of the ground floor of King's Cross station and the Western Concourse.

0   12.5m

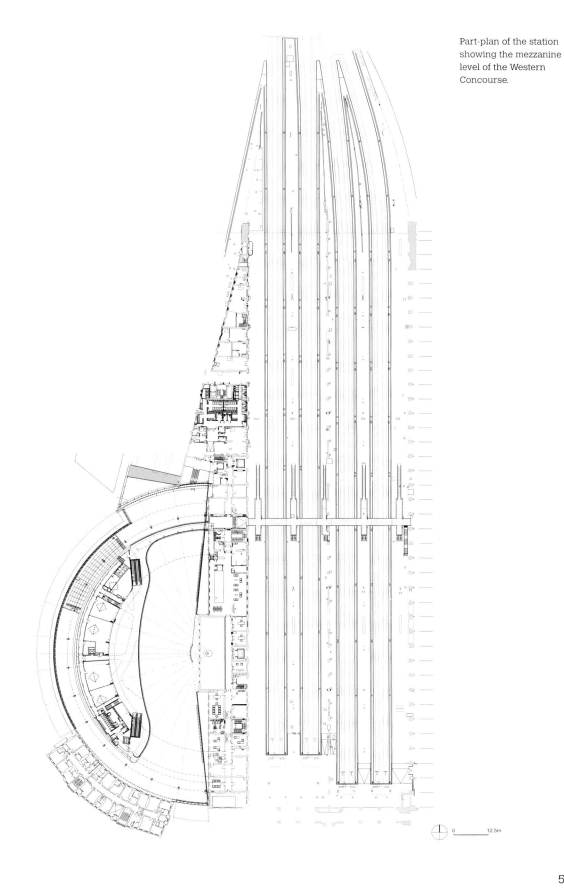

Part-plan of the station showing the mezzanine level of the Western Concourse.

0   12.5m

A model by John
McAslan + Partners
of the primary radial
members of the Western
Concourse roof, resting
on one of the perimeter
tree columns.

Visualizations of roof
glazing assemblies,
designed to optimize
levels of natural light
inside the Western
Concourse.

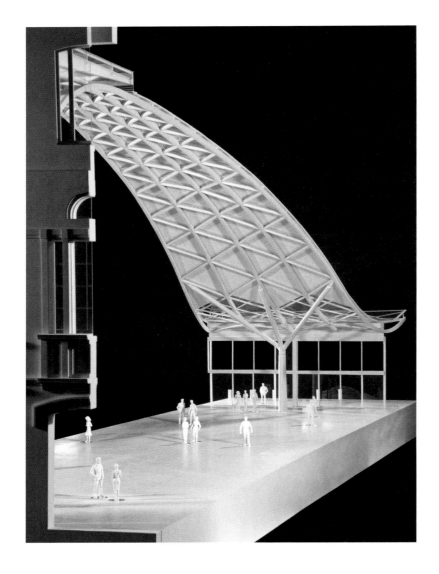

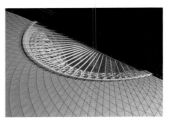

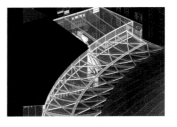

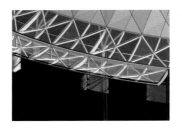

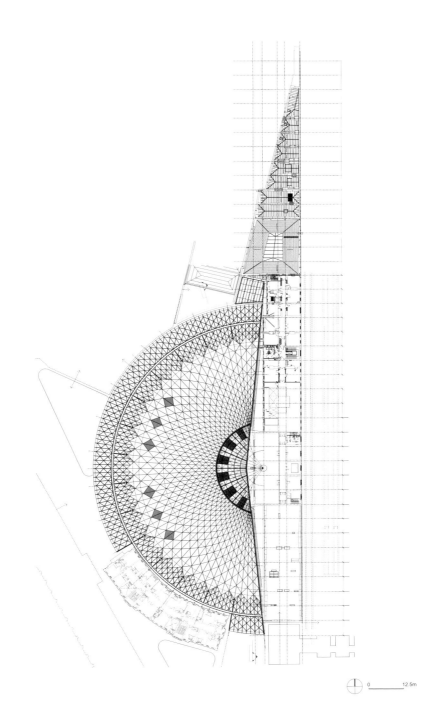

0   12.5m

Even so, there were major challenges for Simon Morgan, Network Rail's Western Concourse project manager, to deal with. Until the roof became self-supporting, its erection required one of the most extensive scaffold constructions ever seen in Britain. It was a structural wonder in itself.

Internally, the two-level concourse has a semicircular ground-level plaza. Above the plaza, beneath the sweeping western edge of the canopy, a raised mezzanine balcony, coated with more than five million small, gleaming circular ceramic tiles, contains shops and cafes, and an elevated, curvilinear walkway; this passes through the Western Range building to the new 65-metre-long bridge that sails over the nine main-line platforms and carries passengers, by escalator and lift, to and from trains. The design of the bridge's components, and its visual impact within the historic train shed, were also a matter of acute interest to English Heritage, and took the architects eighteen months to refine.

But what a compelling architectural and structural result. The glass-and-steel canopy over the new 140-metre-wide concourse radiuses outwards like a wave, rising to 20 metres at its highest point, just below the line of the Western Range parapet. The canopy is the largest single-span structure in Europe. Its form recalls the parabolic structures designed by the Italian master Pier Luigi Nervi, and Eero Saarinen's TWA terminal in New York's JFK airport.

A visualization of the 'lost' Parcels Office atrium that was rediscovered during a survey of the Western Range; access to the atrium had previously been blocked off.

The soaring structure of the Western Concourse roof (above) rising by the entrance to the Grade I-listed Booking Hall (above, right), shown here during construction; the space had previously been used as a plant room.

The mixture of refurbishment and modernizing alterations to the Western Range buildings was equally challenging, in a very different way. Because the buildings had been constructed at different times, and for different purposes, architectural interventions had to accommodate a range of different original construction methods and varying storey heights, and also allow connections to new structures.

The renovation and modernization of King's Cross station's Western Range is an object lesson in the way in which pragmatism and respect for the heritage of the whole site have been brought into focus. Few passing through the station will be aware of the contribution made to its architecture by a single bomb dropped by the Luftwaffe during the Second World War, which tore a substantial gap in the original building and blocked any direct link between the southern and northern ends. The Network Rail team had to find a solution to London Underground's need for a large ventilation duct from the new Northern Ticket Hall below. This was resolved by building the vent in the bomb gap, which also meant that floors could be added to give access around its structure. Network Rail also specified a sympathetically designed shell around the duct: a heritage cloak, no less.

In the Western Range, Arup's innovative engineering allowed the invisible insertion of new structures supporting the four-storey Victorian

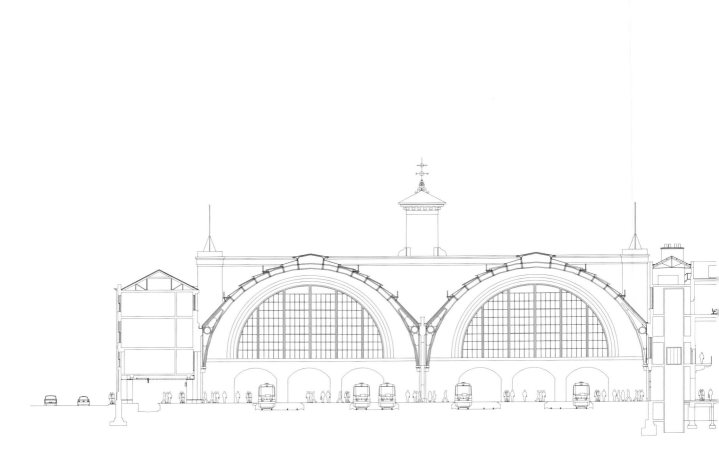

0   2.5m 5m   12.5m

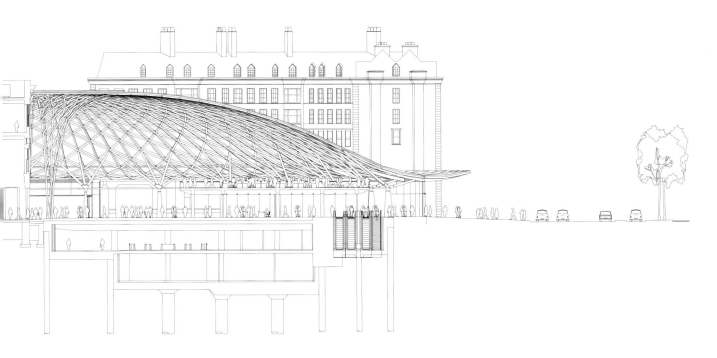

A south-facing section drawing showing, from left, the Eastern Range, the train-shed vaults, the Western Range and the Western Concourse, with London Underground's Northern Ticket Hall construction beneath it. Behind the Western Concourse is the façade of the Great Northern Hotel.

This east-facing section shows the Western Concourse structure and the Western Range behind it. Beneath them lie the London Underground Northern Ticket Hall and the escalator barrels. The Underground's Northern line platform is visible on the far right.

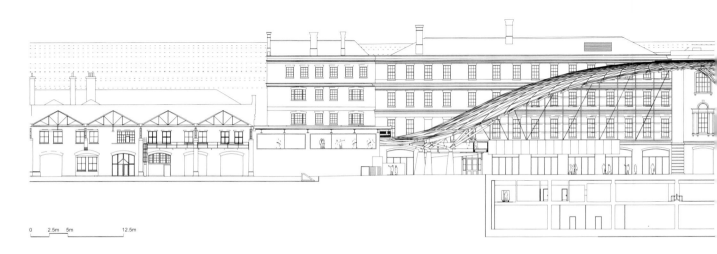

0   2.5m   5m   12.5m

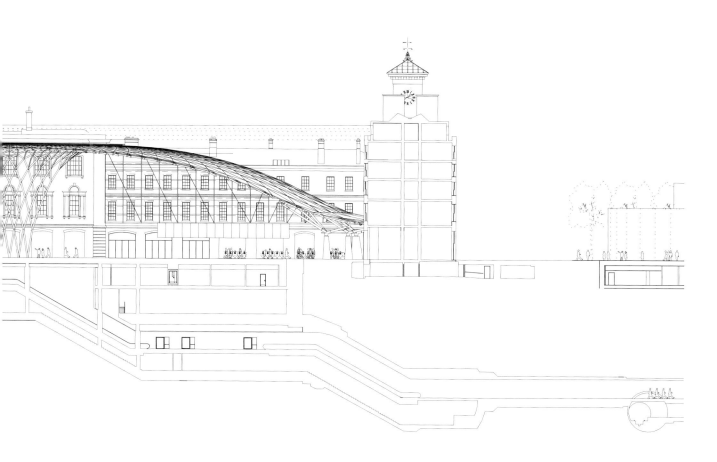

View looking north in the
refurbished Main Train
Shed (above, left); the
new wayfinding and train
information systems
from the new bridge in
the Main Train Shed.

building, as well as providing lifts and modern mechanical and electrical
services. This has brought clarity to internal circulation and functions for
the first time in many decades, and created room for a wide gate-line in the
Western Range. Subtly applied design and engineering have also reinstated
delightful, but previously blocked off, Victorian spaces, such as the original
Booking Hall and the Parcels Office atrium – the latter rediscovered during
a routine site inspection.

The modernization of the historic Booking Hall required the removal of
an original mezzanine floor and the enclosure in glass of a balcony walkway,
and strengthening work on the historic iron girders. The balcony is supported
by decorative iron brackets inter-spanned by restored sandstone slabs.
The sympathetic structural solution has also provided new balcony posts
and strengthening to the stone slabs without affecting the craft aesthetic of
the balcony. The creation of the new gate-line at the south-west corner of the
Western Range required an equally deft engineering solution.

By comparison with the complexity of the Western Range, the long and
narrow four-storey Eastern Range is original in its entirety, with a simple and
repetitive architectural and structural rhythm. The essential tasks here were
discreetly to integrate new functions and building services and to carve out
an impressive, brick-walled reception area at the southern end of the building.

One of the new entrances to the Western Concourse.

The McAslan product-design team, led by Jasmine Wadia, also designed a coherent 'family' of wayfinding signage and information systems, in order to create a unified visual language relating to passenger movement in the station. This ostensibly low-key series of interventions has created a strong sense of de-cluttered space in the station.

The treatment of the Great Northern Hotel is another example of the partnership culture that developed as the concept of the programme evolved. With projected major increases in passenger numbers and through-flows, an architecturally quirky nineteenth-century hotel directly in front of the station's new main entrance might have been a major obstacle to progress. The Network Rail team, working with the Department for Transport, hotel owner Argent, its architects and designers, and English Heritage and Camden Council, developed an innovative solution: the ground floor of the hotel has been 'arcaded' in order to allow a free flow of passengers through its base, while retaining the full form and function of the building above the arcade.

Ultimately, then, the range of architectural and structural interventions in the King's Cross station project has brought together historically sensitive repair, modernizing interventions and moments of striking innovation, all of which has depended on an exemplary collaborative process over a fifteen-year

period between client, designers and contractors. Network Rail's support of the architect's vision has been crucial: it has given King's Cross station a new future, allowing the architecture and engineering of the transformation to draw from, and reinforce, the bold precedents set by Lewis Cubitt more than a century and a half earlier.

The funnel structure of the Western Concourse roof. It fans 20 metres into the air, stopping just below the parapet of the Western Range.

A view across the past, and into the future

The works described here can be regarded only as snapshots of what has been achieved in an immensely complex process of operational change. The project generated well over 1000 jobs, almost six million man hours of work and an excellent construction safety record. But King's Cross station tells us a story that is, ultimately, about more than the renewal of a great Victorian railway terminus. The station, and its rapidly changing locale, is nothing less than a preview of the new dynamics of movement and place that will become familiar in London and Britain's bigger cities in the next decade or two.

The modernization and extension of Cubitt's celebrated train shed and station buildings remind us that the challenge of moving many millions of people through our biggest towns and cities every day has become as important to the future of Britain's economy, and to its sense of public purpose and well-being, as the financial performance of the City of London.

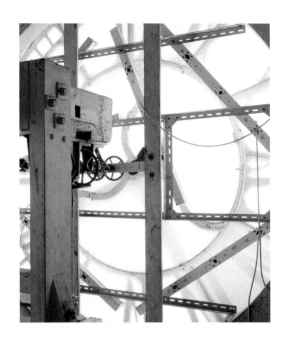

Above
The original Victorian mechanism of the station tower clock.

Overleaf
The massive scale of the transformations at both King's Cross and St Pancras, two stations embedded in a complex urban environment.

In the early weeks of 2012, standing by the high parapet wall that divides the station's clock tower from the glazed vaults of the train shed, it was hard not to wonder what Cubitt would have made of it all: the gleaming splash of the Western Concourse designed and engineered with such brio by McAslan and Arup; the small electric motor affixed to the Heath Robinson arrangement of tarnished nineteenth-century gears that once ticked the station clock's hands onward; the glinting photovoltaic arrays fixed to the crowns of the train-shed vaults, absorbing sunlight to contribute to the station's electricity supply; and, half a mile to the north, beyond the train shed, the bustle of construction activity on the King's Cross regeneration site . . .

All change!

SETTING THE STAGE FOR CHANGE

The King's Cross and St Pancras area has been targeted for redevelopment since the first major urban regeneration scheme for the district was mooted in the 1980s. The transformation of the Grade I-listed King's Cross station is a key supporting element in a new regeneration scheme that is the biggest of its kind in Europe.

The rebirth of the station as a twenty-first-century transport hub for Network Rail and London Underground combines modernization, restoration, new architecture of the highest quality and placemaking. The station is the gateway to Argent's £2 billion King's Cross mixed-use regeneration scheme on 30 hectares of derelict post-industrial land north of the nineteenth-century train shed. Immediately east of the station lies the substantial Regent Quarter redevelopment.

The modernized station, and these urban regeneration projects, have triggered extraordinary changes in the wider King's Cross area. For more than a century, and until relatively recently, this part of London was synonymous with profound social and economic deprivation. Today, the changes in and around the station have helped to make it a hot spot of creative and commercial aspiration.

1 The public realm The rebirth of King's Cross station has contributed to the civic quality of its thresholds and the urban spaces around its western and southern edges.

2 The Eastern Range This pragmatic building once carried three storeys of offices over the station's cab road. Its modernization has left its key features untouched.

3 The Main Train Shed and bridge An additional platform has been created, and a bridge with stairs and lifts sails over the main-line platforms. Beneath them, Victorian vaults now carry servicing equipment.

4 The Shared Service Yard This subsurface facility ensures that deliveries and services can be handled 'backstage', freeing space at ground level. The service yard will be shared by the station and neighbouring new office buildings.

5 The Western Range The creation of a new gate-line, Booking Hall and other facilities was complicated by the fact that the nineteenth-century buildings had different structures and storey heights.

6 The Western Concourse The most strikingly designed piece of British transport architecture for two decades has set an iconic benchmark for station and multi-modal hub developments.

The public realm

The transformative effect of the modernized King's Cross station is about a great deal more than massively improved travelling conditions. The station lies at the southern edge of the King's Cross regeneration area, at a famously busy three-way junction that includes the Euston Road. And so the treatment of the public realm in front of the station, and along its western flank where it meets Pancras Road, is of critical importance to the way the station contributes energy, and a new sense of place, to the flows of people passing through and around it.

The most obvious contribution to the character and civility of this pivotal part of London will be the creation of a new plaza, about the size of Leicester Square, in front of the station. And the station's new Western Concourse adds porosity and vitality to the Euston Road–Pancras Road junction, and will be used not only by millions of Network Rail and London Underground travellers every year, but also every day by thousands more people making their way to and from work or home in the King's Cross regeneration area.

A visualization of King's Cross station's forthcoming southern plaza, with St Pancras station in the background.

The Eastern Range

The Grade I-listed Eastern Range, 240 metres long and only 12 metres wide, was originally designed as three storeys of offices suspended over the station's cab access road. The modernization of this pragmatic architecture involved consultations with English Heritage, and has balanced twenty-first-century operational needs with the imperatives of conservation and the retention of historic architectural features.

The major interventions included the discreet integration of new functions and building services into the building's fabric, and the creation of a reception area at the southern end of the range, where Victorian brick walls, iron beams and columns have been refurbished. These features are juxtaposed against the new laminated-metal-mesh glass cladding of the lift core, granite slab flooring, monolithic reception desk and glass mezzanine-level bridges. The building's grand Victorian stairwell, with its original ornamental iron banister and glazed bricks, has been highlighted by a new lighting scheme. Unseen are the photovoltaic power converters and grey-water recycling tank that lie beneath the building.

Below
The Eastern Range building during renovation (left), and a cross-sectional diagram showing the new platform and highlighting the narrowness of the 12-metre wide building.

Opposite
The restored and modernized Eastern Range entrance and reception area.

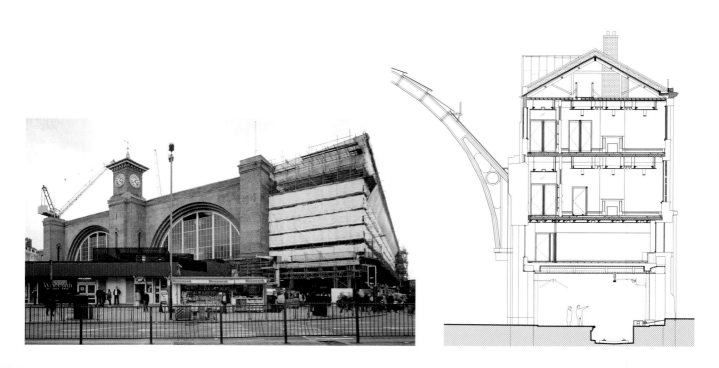

The Eastern Range
entrance during
construction.

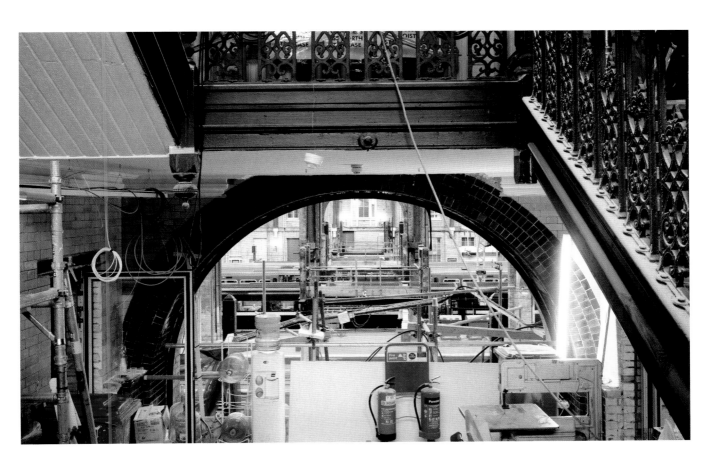

A view from the main stairwell of the Eastern Range, looking into the train shed.

Part of the new plant room
within the roof space of
the Eastern Range.

Air-handling units are
housed in new dormer
structures on the Eastern
Range roof, concealed
below parapet height.

Handmade replacement
wooden windows and
stone sills in the bays
of the Eastern Range.

Full-height glazing in the vaulted openings in the Eastern Range walls affords expansive views of the train-shed interior.

Below and opposite
The robust Victorian
character of the
Eastern Range is
highlighted by the
contrast between the
original fabric and
the crisply designed
mezzanine walkway.

Opposite and below
The stairwell of the
Eastern Range, with its
restored glazed bricks
and original ironwork
balustrades.

A newly formed corridor
in the Eastern Range
runs for 200 metres,
and carries a new
building-services zone
in its ceiling.

The Main Train Shed and bridge

Several key modernization and restoration tasks were undertaken in the Main Train Shed. There were renovations and weather-proofing of the two vaulted roofs, meticulous repairs of sections of original Victorian brickwork, and the addition of photovoltaic arrays to supply top-up electricity to the station. A new platform was created in the Eastern Range – a vital precursor to other work in the train shed – and other platforms were upgraded, and a new bridge was built over the main-line tracks, with integral stairs and lifts. Given the bridge's alignment through the historic train shed, the project was closely monitored by English Heritage, and the detailed design of its system took the architects many months to refine.

There were also complex operational upgrades in the train shed, and large-scale conversions and expansions of the Victorian vaults beneath the platforms so that they could carry state-of-the-art servicing systems for both the station and surrounding regeneration developments.

Below, from left
A view of the Main Train Shed, with the Eastern Range to the left, from the signal-box rank; post-war platform barriers; parcels handling on Platform 8 in *c.* 1970, with Handyside Bridge in the background.

The interior of the Main Train Shed, seen from scaffolding on the Eastern Range. Work on the train shed had not started at this point, and the old roof's lack of transparency is evident.

Below
The reconstruction
of Platforms 2 and 3,
with its new escalator
pier and lift structure.

Below
The reconstruction
of Platforms 2 and 3,
with its new escalator
pier and lift structure.

Opposite
View looking north in
the refurbished Main
Train Shed.

Below and opposite
The Main Train Shed roof
has required stripping,
strengthening, repairs
and redecorating, and
a new support structure
for re-glazing.

Below and opposite
The historic details of
the station's southern
gable and clock tower
were an important
part of the repair and
restoration programme.
Completed works to these
elements were revealed
in February 2012.

Below and opposite
Work on the Main
Train Shed roof has
transformed levels
of natural light inside
the station.

The Shared Service Yard

A key development in the operational efficiency of King's Cross station cannot be seen by station users or pedestrians. It is a major but hidden piece of civil engineering that lies under part of the Western Concourse, and it has transformed the way in which goods and services are delivered to the station.

The development of the station's masterplan eliminated the street-level deliveries on which King's Cross had relied for decades. Working closely with developer Argent, which owned land on the western side of the station, Network Rail created a ramped access to the subsurface Shared Service Yard; this now serves platforms via a tunnel and goods lifts, and also Argent's development north of the station. Furthermore, plant and utilities are no longer housed in outlying buildings. Network Rail also wanted to eliminate a key operational problem: the congestion caused by passengers and delivery vehicles having to share the same space.

In conjunction with new freight lifts and rehabilitated 1930s parcels tunnels, the new subsurface yard ensures that all service traffic into and out of the station is handled efficiently, without obstructing passengers. Incoming utilities, and all the services that make up the 'guts' of the station, are also housed here.

By the 1990s, platform crowding was posing major operational problems (below), which have been eliminated by the massive new subsurface Shared Service Yard (shown opposite during construction).

The subsurface Shared Service Yard under construction (below) and completed (opposite). Shown below is the framework around the access ramp connecting the yard to ground level. The yard will also supply the urban-regeneration development that will be constructed near by at a later date by the developer Argent.

The Western Range

The renovation, restoration and modernization of the Western Range brought pragmatism and care for the station's historic fabric into a shared focus. Unlike the Eastern Range, which has a single, continuous form, the buildings of the Western Range were constructed at different times, for different purposes, with different structures and storey heights.

Innovative engineering allowed the invisible insertion of new structures supporting the buildings, and provided lifts and new mechanical and electrical services. For the first time in more than half a century, there is a clarity to the Western Range's internal circulation and functionality. One crucial gain was the new space created for a wide gate-line.

Subtly applied design and engineering has also reinstated delightful, but previously blocked-off, Victorian spaces, such as the original Booking Hall and the Parcels Office atrium – the latter rediscovered during a routine site inspection that revealed a long-forgotten gap created by a wartime bomb. This now embeds a large vent funnel rising from the London Underground concourse and ticket hall that lie beneath part of the Western Range.

The original Victorian Booking Hall was exposed during the modernization of the station. The space had previously been subdivided into two floors containing plant rooms, storerooms and offices.

The elevated walkway in the Booking Hall is supported by original Victorian cast-iron brackets, shown here during their restoration.

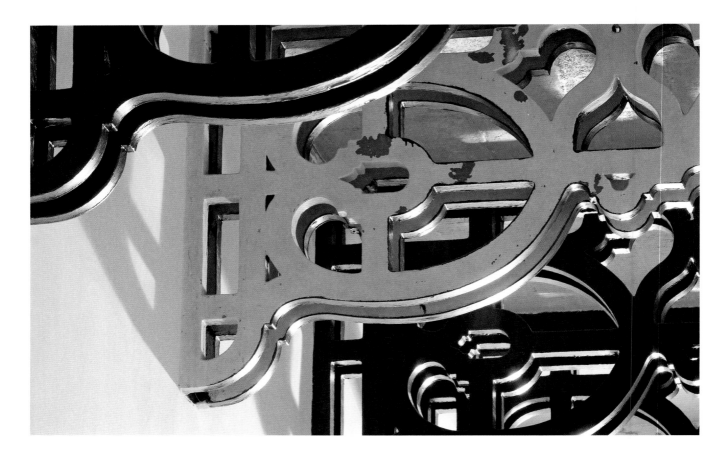

Looking out from the
Booking Hall into the
Western Concourse.

The formation of the
Western Range's southern
gate-line required a
particularly complex
engineering solution to
support the building's
upper storeys. The result
is an impressive, highly
expressive space for
passenger movement
between the Western
Concourse and the Main
Train Shed.

The entire station was
photographically mapped,
and visual details were
used to assess the level
of repairs required.
The blank space in the
centre of the image is
the section containing
the Western Range's
so-called 'bomb gap' of
1941 (see page 57).

A large vertical shaft was constructed in the 'bomb gap' in order to ventilate the Underground network beneath the new structure. This intervention required particularly close cooperation between Network Rail, London Underground and their respective project teams.

The 'lost' Victorian Parcels Office atrium of the Western Range before its renovation (left), and restored and in use as a pub (opposite).

One of numerous models constructed to investigate options for strengthening roof trusses and integrating building services in a manner appropriate to the historic nature of the old Parcels Office atrium.

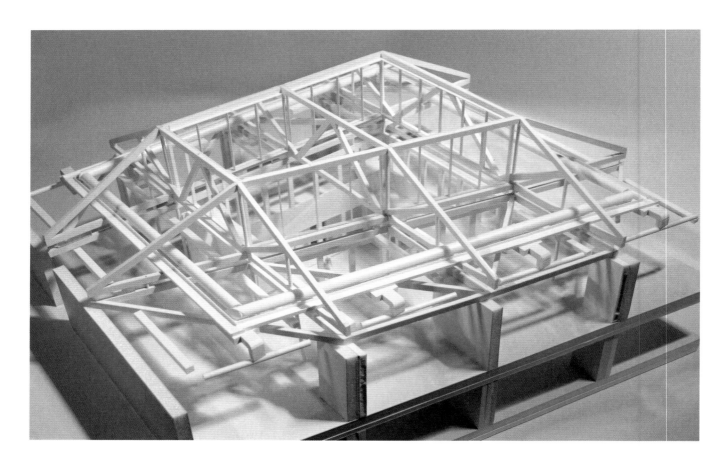

The Western Concourse

This element of the King's Cross transformation has created what is arguably the most vivid and innovative example of British transport architecture in a quarter of a century. The glass-and-steel canopy over the new 140-metre-wide concourse is the largest single-span structure in Europe. It radiuses outward like a wave, rising to 20 metres at its highest point, just below the line of the Western Range parapet.

The façade of the Grade I-listed Western Range had to be retained, as did that of the curving Grade II-listed Great Northern Hotel 40 metres to the west. The canopy's modular diagrid shell structure could therefore not funnel significant weight into these buildings' Victorian foundations. The canopy's supporting columns hit the ground at seventeen very precise points that fit the structural grid of London Underground's Northern Ticket Hall, above which the concourse sits.

Above a semicircular ground-level plaza, beneath the sweeping western edge of the canopy, is a raised mezzanine balcony, coated with more than five million small circular ceramic tiles. The mezzanine contains shops and cafes, and from it an elevated walkway passes through the Western Range to the new bridge across the main-line platforms.

Below and opposite
Network Rail began
work on the Western
Concourse after
the handover of London
Underground's Northern
Ticket Hall 'lid' in 2008.
Work by developer
Argent on the concave
façade of the Great
Northern Hotel also had
to be coordinated with
construction work on
the Western Concourse.

Left
London Underground's Northern Ticket Hall roof, which covers the surface alongside the Western Range of King's Cross station. The site above the subsurface Shared Services Yard is in the foreground.

Opposite
Construction of the self-supporting mezzanine-level structure within the Western Concourse.

Below and opposite
Off-site fabrication of
elements of the Western
Concourse roof ensured
consistent high quality.
Equally essential was
the close design
collaboration between
Arup, John McAslan +
Partners, Network Rail
and its contractors.

124

Below and opposite
The curving bulkheads
for the mezzanine level
were fabricated near
Dumfries, Scotland.
Their finish involved
the application of
millions of circular
white ceramic tiles.

Below, opposite and
following pages
The prefabrication of
elements of the Western
Concourse roof enabled
rapid construction,
but some 1500 tonnes
of scaffolding were
required to support
it during its erection.

A panoramic view of the construction of the Western Concourse roof, which measures some 140 metres at its widest point. The roof edge meets the Great Northern Hotel, but is structurally separated from the hotel's Victorian façade.

A view of the Western Concourse roof during construction (opposite), with the Great Northern Hotel and the tower of St Pancras station rising in the background; the first aluminium panels being fixed to the roof structure (right).

*Below, opposite and
following pages*
Aluminium panels
being fixed to the
Western Concourse roof
structure. More than
2000 glass and aluminium
panels were used in the
roof's assembly.

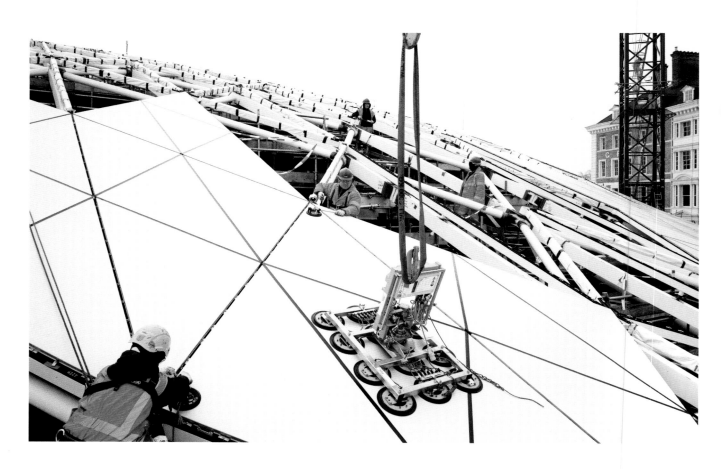

View of the Western
Concourse after its
opening, from the parapet
of St Pancras station.

Opposite
A view of the interior of
the Western Concourse
from the southern
entrance.

Right
Detail of one of the
sixteen tree columns in
the Western Concourse.

143

The fully operational
Western Concourse, with
the restored booking hall
(central entrances) and
southern ticket gate-line
(far right).

Overleaf
An aerial view of the
Western Concourse
canopy during its
completion, with the
Great Northern Hotel,
scaffolded and
protectively wrapped,
between the edge of
the canopy and
Pancras Road.

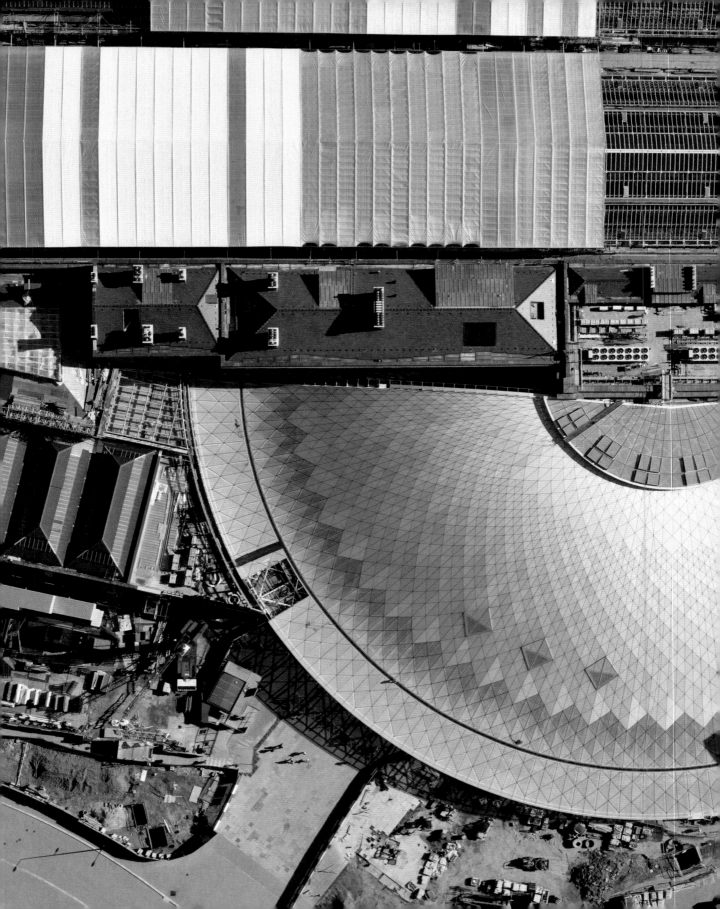

THE INSPIRING POWER OF CREATIVE CHANGE

Sir John Sorrell

In a year when the eyes of the world will be turning towards Britain, first for the Queen's Diamond Jubilee in June 2012 and, later in the summer, for the Olympic and Paralympic Games, it will be our civic buildings, doing what they do democratically and inclusively, that show the true character of our nation.

As a civic building, King's Cross station has many roles to perform. The transformation of the station, and of the neighbouring St Pancras station, represent a return to an almost Victorian approach to civic architecture: the idea of civic buildings as totems of a shared national ambition, rather than just functional civic objects.

There is no doubt in my mind that the restoration and transformation of King's Cross station will be a success. But on what basis should we judge this success? Conceived and led by Network Rail, the sensitive renovation and modernization of the existing buildings, and the new iconic diagrid shell roof over the Western Concourse, are an architectural and placemaking triumph. The station was delivered, on schedule and on budget, with key partners John McAslan + Partners and Arup.

The re-imagined King's Cross provides world-class passenger facilities that are highly efficient not only as a passenger interchange, but also in terms of energy use. The station will be safer and more comfortable, and easier to service. And it will have much greater passenger capacity, in order to accommodate future demand. Technically, and aesthetically, the project is going to deliver.

But there is also another, philosophical measure by which we should judge the success of King's Cross station in its new form. Shouldn't its impact be seen through the lens of British productivity and innovation? Might we consider judging the success of the project by the ways in which it inspires its users to carry into their own lives the station's quality, its detailing, its ingenuity and its elegance?

In the nineteenth century the British architects Joseph Paxton, Augustus Pugin, Alexander Thomson, Charles Barry and the designer of King's Cross, Lewis Cubitt, were expressing through their great buildings and engineering projects innovations that ultimately assisted the reach and influence of the British Empire. It was a national confidence that fed on, and created, innovation after innovation and allowed the likes of the engineers Isambard Kingdom Brunel and George Stephenson, and the scientist inventors Joseph Swan, Alexander Parkes and Charles Wheatstone, to shape history.

Little more than a century later, such projects as the renovation of King's Cross station will have a similar transformative effect. Coinciding with a moment when the British government is looking to the creative sector to spur the growth of new industries, the new station declares to everybody who uses it that British design can achieve great things. Originated and delivered with the flair, care, attention to detail and sheer quality that has been generated through its client, its architect and its engineer, this project embodies a spirit that goes far beyond that dry phrase, 'the built environment'.

Such projects define Britain as a creative island, inspiring young minds to become the next generation of designers and innovators. And my belief is that, with some 55 million people passing through King's Cross station each year, it will inspire many of its users to create, to build and to challenge convention usefully and successfully.

The legacy of King's Cross station and other such projects should be felt for generations. I believe it will be. The team of Network Rail, John McAslan and Arup has achieved something truly special.

CHRONOLOGY

1799
29 September: Lewis Cubitt is born. The younger brother of master builder Thomas Cubitt, he goes on to design many of the housing developments constructed by his sibling, and later designs King's Cross station. He dies in 1883.

1850
7 August: A first, temporary station is built by Great Northern Railway at Maiden Lane, north of today's King's Cross station; it closes in 1852.

1852
14 October: The present King's Cross station, designed by Lewis Cubitt, opens. Its location was determined by the Royal Commission on Railway Termini of 1846, which recommended that railways should not pass south of the New (now Euston) Road. The station's site was bounded to the west by a tributary of the River Fleet, establishing the route of Pancras Road and the subsequent curved footprint of the Great Northern Hotel.

1854
17 May: The Great Northern hotel, also designed by Cubitt, opens.

1863
10 January: The Metropolitan Railway – the world's first subterranean rail system – opens between Paddington and Farringdon. (The line is now part of London Underground's Circle line.)

1 October: The Suburban and City service is inaugurated; it uses the 'York curve' and 'hotel curve' tunnels beneath King's Cross station, subterraneously connecting the Great Northern Railway with Farringdon station.

1864–65
Improvements are made to the southern approach to King's Cross station; new railings and gates.

1865
The German Gymnasium is built in Pancras Road with a roof constructed from laminated wood trusses with cast-iron fillets, the same construction as the original King's Cross train sheds.

1866
1 January: York Road station opens just north of King's Cross station; it closes in 1977.

1868
St Pancras station opens just west of King's Cross; Pancras Road is subsequently realigned, disconnecting King's Cross station from direct contact with the adjoining streets. St Pancras is opened by the Midland Railway as the southern terminus of its main line, which connects London with the East Midlands and Yorkshire. At its opening, the arched train shed (designed by William Barlow) is the world's largest single-span roof.

The laminated timber ribs of King's Cross eastern roof barrel are replaced with wrought iron following structural decay related to condensation. The western barrel ribs are replaced in 1886.

1870–90
An additional floor is added to the Western Range's North Wing.

The suburban platform opens (to the west of the current Suburban Train Shed).

1874
18 December: The main-line local station opens; it later becomes the Suburban Train Shed.

1875
The Western Range is extended to the north, and a new engine shed for the local station is constructed to the west.

1878
1 February: The suburban station opens; it is extended in 1880 and rebuilt in 1895.

1879
A glazed 'cab arcade' is added to the southern elevation, the first of many buildings to encroach on the southern precinct; others include a post office, a left-luggage office and a mortuary. The cab arcade is demolished in 1969.

1894–95
The Suburban Train Shed is enlarged and re-roofed, and offices are built in a portalized structure over the east-side Cab Road taxi rank.

1906
The entrance to the Piccadilly line's Underground station in front of King's Cross station is built, in glazed red brick.

1924
15 December: An extended local station is opened.

1935

Entrepreneur John Laing builds a suburban 'show house' immediately next to the station forecourt, to showcase developments in the suburbs served by King's Cross.

1939

The Parcel Tunnel and British Rail-operated Red Star parcel office are constructed.

1941

11 May: The station sustains severe damage from aerial bombing during the night, resulting in the destruction of about 25 metres of the main roof's western barrel, and of the Western Range building north of the Booking Hall.

1955

The Eastern Range mezzanine is built.

1969–73

The Underground's Victoria line is built, as well as an underground ticket office beneath King's Cross station, and a new Southern Concourse is completed, sweeping away all previous buildings. Major reconfiguration of passenger facilities takes place along Platform 8.

1977

4 March: The suburban and York Road platforms are closed.

1987

18 November: A major fire breaks out in King's Cross St Pancras Underground station, killing thirty-one people. The fire starts in an escalator shaft serving the Piccadilly line; the shaft is burnt out, along with the upper-level entrances and ticket hall. As a result of the public inquiry, new fire-safety regulations are introduced and incorporated into London Underground's later works.

1997

30 June: The first novel in J.K. Rowling's Harry Potter series, *Harry Potter and the Philosopher's Stone*, is published; it includes several scenes set in King's Cross station.

John McAslan + Partners wins the international competition to design the redevelopment of King's Cross station.

2001

The Strategic Rail Authority is established under the Transport Act 2000 as a non-departmental public body to provide strategic direction for the railway industry; it is wound up in 2006.

2002

The client for the King's Cross station project changes from Railtrack to Network Rail (NR), after Railtrack falls into administration.

2003

The Strategic Rail Authority instigates changes to the design of the station, including the introduction of a new bridge link between the Western Concourse mezzanine and the new footbridge inside the Main Train Shed.

2005

6 July: London is awarded the 2012 Olympic and Paralympic Games.

7 July: Four suicide-bomb attacks take place on London's public transport. This initiates a further review of security measures at King's Cross station, from which the bombers had entered the Underground network.

The Department for Transport pledges sponsorship support for King's Cross station.

2006

28 May: Phase 1 of London Underground's King's Cross St Pancras station is opened. It provides access to St Pancras station via new passenger facilities created in St Pancras's undercroft.

Network Rail submits town-planning and listed-building applications.

The Strategic Rail Authority is abolished.

The 27-hectare King's Cross Central development scheme, planned to create more than 743,000 square metres of mixed-use space next to the station, is granted planning permission.

2007

14 November: The modernization of St Pancras railway station is completed.

Network Rail obtains full planning consent for the works at King's Cross station. Construction starts with Project 1 (Eastern Range building) and Project 4 (Network Rail Plant Room and Shared Services Yard).

2008

1 September: London Underground completes structural work on the roof slab of its new Northern Ticket Hall, allowing Network Rail's Western Concourse works to begin.

Construction starts on Project 2 (Main Train Shed roof).

2009

29 November: London Underground Northern Ticket Hall opens, completing the final phase of the new King's Cross St Pancras Underground station.

Works on the Eastern Range are completed, allowing staff to move out of the Western Range and work to commence on it.

Construction starts on Project 3 (Main Train Shed platforms) and Project 6 (Western Concourse and Western Range).

2010

The Network Rail Plant Room and Shared Service Yard are completed.

A spending review by the Department for Transport maintains sponsorship support for King's Cross station.

2011

September: Central Saint Martins College of Arts and Design relocates to the development site behind King's Cross station, at the old grain warehouse, adjacent refurbished historic buildings and new purpose-built studios.

The Western Concourse and Western Range building are completed.

2012

January–March: The Main Train Shed platforms are completed.

March: The new Western Concourse opens.

Summer: The Main Train Shed roof is completed.

July–September: London 2012 Olympic and Paralympic Games take place.

September: Construction to start on Project 7 (Southern Canopies and Southern Plaza).

2013

Winter: The Southern Canopies and Southern Plaza to be completed.

KEY TERMS

Approval in principle (AIP) A part of Network Rail's governance arrangements to ensure that adequate checks have been obtained on a project prior to granting authority to proceed with the subsequent stages.

Arup The multidisciplinary engineering consultant for the whole of the King's Cross station project, from the competition design through to actioning planning consent, and the engineering designer for the Eastern Range building, Western Range building, Western Concourse and Southern Plaza.

British Transport Police (BTP) The national police force for the railways, providing a policing service to rail operators, their staff and passengers throughout England, Scotland and Wales.

Closed-circuit television (CCTV) The broadcast and recording of the King's Cross station environment is part of the security strategy.

Commission for Architecture and the Built Environment (CABE) The organization, which has been the government's adviser on architecture, urban design and public space, has merged with the Design Council; the joint body is known as Design Council CABE. It champions well-designed buildings, spaces and places, runs public campaigns and provides expert, practical advice. It works directly with architects, planners, designers and clients.

Construction (Design and Management) Regulations 2007 (CDM) Regulations concerning the construction industry in the United Kingdom, introduced by the Health and Safety Executive's Construction Division. The regulations aim to improve safety in the industry, which in Britain employs more than two million people.

Construction Skills Certification Scheme (CSCS) A scheme set up to help the construction industry to improve quality and reduce accidents. CSCS cards are increasingly demanded as proof of occupational competence by contractors, public and private clients and others.

Corporate content management system (CCMS) Network Rail's internal information-sharing system and secure intranet.

Lewis Cubitt (1799–1883) The architect of King's Cross railway station (1852) and the associated Great Northern Hotel (1854), as well as a granary behind the station (now part of Argent's King's Cross Central regeneration scheme); he designed many of the housing developments constructed by his older brother Thomas Cubitt, a leading master builder. Another of his brothers was William Cubitt, Lord Mayor of London in the early 1860s.

Lewis Cubitt and his two brothers should not be confused with Sir William Cubitt, the eminent but unrelated civil engineer responsible for the Great Northern Railway's main line between London and Doncaster.

Cubitt House The site office and nerve centre for the construction stage of the King's Cross station project, sited north-west of the Suburban Train Shed and housing a collaborative project team, including Network Rail, Arup, John McAslan + Partners and contractors.

Customer information system (CIS) A system of electronic screens providing 'real-time' information on services to passengers and other users of the station.

Department for Transport (DfT) The government department that is the principal sponsor of the King's Cross station redevelopment programme; it is responsible for the English transport network and a limited number of transport matters in Scotland, Wales and Northern Ireland. The department is run by the Secretary of State for Transport.

Design for London (DfL) A design advisory department within the Greater London Authority.

Diagrid (diagonal grid) A design for constructing large spans, typically in steel, based on triangulated framing; it can be expressed as triangular structures with diagonal support beams. Triangulated beams, which are straight at King's Cross but can also be curved, together with horizontal rings, make up a structural system that is highly efficient.

English Heritage (EH) An executive non-departmental public body of the British government, set up under the terms of the National Heritage Act 1983 and sponsored by the Department for Culture, Media and Sport (DCMS), with a broad remit of managing the historic built environment of England; it advises the Secretary of State on policy and in individual cases, such as registering listed buildings and scheduled ancient monuments. English Heritage is the steward of more than 400 significant historical and archaeological sites.

Governance to Railway Investment Projects (GRIP) A process that describes how Network Rail manages and controls projects that enhance or renew the national rail network. It can be compared to the Royal Institute of British Architects' Plan of Work frameworks.

Great Northern Hotel A hotel built in 1854 next to King's Cross, designed by Lewis Cubitt, the designer of the station.

Greater London Authority (GLA) A strategic regional authority, presided over by the Mayor of London, with powers over transport, policing, economic development, and fire and emergency planning. Four functional bodies are responsible for the delivery of services in these areas: Transport for London, the Metropolitan Police Authority, the London Development Agency and the London Fire and Emergency Planning Authority. The planning policies of the Mayor of London are detailed in a statutory London Plan that is regularly updated and published.

Inter-discipline check (IDC) A review during the design development process to ensure coordination between the multidisciplinary design team members. Many IDCs will be held during the life of a project.

John McAslan + Partners The architectural practice appointed as lead architect and masterplanner for the whole of the King's Cross station in 1997 after winning the international competition to provide architectural consultancy services to the then client organization, Railtrack (now Network Rail).

King's Cross Station Redevelopment Programme (KXRP) The £550 million modernization programme for King's Cross station, one of London's most important terminus stations.

Listed Building Consent (LBC) The special approval sought for the alteration, extension or demolition of listed structures; this is done through the local planning authority, which, particularly for significant alterations to the more notable listed buildings, consults English Heritage.

London Underground Limited (LUL) The owner and operator of London's rapid-transit system, the world's first underground railway.

Main Train Shed The station structure designed by Lewis Cubitt, completed in 1852. The shed originally contained two platforms, one in the western vault for departures, the other in the eastern vault for arrivals.

Network Rail (NR) The owner and operator of most of the rail infrastructure in Great Britain; a statutory corporation created in 2002 as a 'not for dividend' private company limited by guarantee, following the administration of its predecessor, Railtrack. Network Rail does not run train services, which are provided by NR's main customers, the separate and mostly private-sector passenger-train and freight operating companies.

Northern Ticket Hall London Underground's new ticket hall for the expanded King's Cross St Pancras Underground station, opened in 2009 and located under Network Rail's new Western Concourse.

Office of Rail Regulation (ORR) The independent safety and economic regulator for Great Britain's railways.

On-board servicing (OBS) The facility that delivers catering services on board trains, starting with the delivery, storage and handling of associated goods at the station. As part of the modernization programme, the OBS facility at King's Cross has been completely overhauled in order to avoid crossover between servicing and passenger movements in the concourse and on the platforms – a move away from the conditions that existed previously.

Overhead line equipment The overhead wires and other fixtures required for the running of electric trains.

Personal protection equipment Clothing and equipment used by a person at work to protect against risks to health or safety; includes safety helmets, gloves, eye protection, high-visibility clothing, safety footwear and safety harnesses.

Programme Architect John McAslan + Partners was appointed as the Programme Architect for Network Rail (NR) at King's Cross station following the granting of planning consent. The role is underwritten by the statutory commitment made between NR and the local planning authority, the London Borough of Camden, that quality would be safeguarded during construction of the project.

Safety Directorate The section of the Office of Rail Regulation responsible for overseeing safety on Britain's railways.

Strategic Rail Authority (SRA) A body that provided strategic direction for the railway industry in Great Britain from its founding under the Transport Act 2000 until it was wound up in 2006; its functions were transferred to the Department for Transport Rail Group, Network Rail and the Office of Rail Regulation.

Suburban Train Shed A later addition to the original station, completed about twenty years after the 1852 opening and then rebuilt in 1895 north-west of the Main Train Shed. The Suburban Train Shed was made famous by the Harry Potter books' Platform 9¾, located between its Platforms 9 and 10.

Train operating companies Companies that provide passenger-train services in Great Britain, mostly through franchise agreements with the Department for Transport. They have existed since the network was privatized under the Railways Act 1993.

Transport for London (TfL) The local government body responsible for London's transport system, including London Underground, Docklands Light Railway, buses, trains, trams, river services and roads.

Western Concourse The new structure located to the west of King's Cross station, a semicircular volume that engages the Western Range building (the station's original main entrance).

Western Concourse mezzanine The double-storey building sitting within the Western Concourse, housing passenger, retail and operational facilities.

CREDITS

The team behind the
transformation of King's
Cross station.

Client
Network Rail

Architect and Masterplanner
John McAslan + Partners

Principal engineer
Arup

Engineers
Fourway Communication
Tata Group

Contractors
Carillion
Kier Construction
Laing O'Rourke–Costain joint venture
Morgan Est
Osbourne
Vinci Construction UK

Key subcontractors and consultants
Chapman Taylor
Cliveden Conservation
Design Rationale
Gormley Group
Houston Cox
Lee Warren
McGee
Mundy Roofing
NG Bailey
Pascall + Watson
Pyramid Construction
Schüco
Seele
Simplicity
Stanton Williams
Stonewest
Swift Horsman
Vitral UK

Major consultees and stakeholders
Argent
British Transport Police
Department for Transport
Design Council CABE
East Coast Main Line Company
English Heritage
First Capital Connect
First Hull Trains
Grand Central Railway
Greater London Authority
High Speed One
King's Cross Conservation Area Advisory
    Committee
Local resident groups and businesses
London Borough of Camden
London Borough of Islington
London Fire and Emergency Planning
    Authority
London TravelWatch/London Access Forum
London Underground
Passenger Focus
Station tenants
Transport for London
Victorian Society

CONTRIBUTOR BIOGRAPHIES

Baroness Andrews OBE is chair of English Heritage, the first woman to hold that position. She was a Parliamentary Clerk from 1970 to 1985, then became a policy adviser to Labour Party leader Neil Kinnock between 1985 and 1992. She served as director of Education Extra until 2002, and has been a government spokesperson for education, skills, health, work and pensions. She has served on a number of House of Lords Select Committees and, before taking up her appointment at English Heritage in 2009, was Under-Secretary of State at the Department for Communities and Local Government.

Sir Peter Hall is Bartlett Professor of Planning and Regeneration at The Bartlett, University College London, and president of both the Town and Country Planning Association and the Regional Studies Association. He is internationally renowned for his writings on the economic, demographic, cultural and management issues that face cities, and has been a planning and regeneration adviser to successive British governments. He is widely considered to be the father of the industrial enterprise zone concept.

Edwin Heathcote is the architecture and design critic of the *Financial Times*. He has written or co-written a number of books on architecture, including *Imre Makovecz: The Wings of the Soul* (1997), *Contemporary Church Architecture* (2007), *London Caffs* (2004) and *The Architecture of Hope: Maggie's Cancer Caring Centres* (2010). He is also the founder-director of the architectural hardware producer Ize.

Jay Merrick is the architecture critic of *The Independent*. He has also written on architecture and art for publications including *Blueprint*, *Art Review* and *New Statesman*, and contributed central texts to monographs on leading architectural practices. His novel *Horse Latitudes* (1999) contained the vision of a degraded Britain in the future in which movement, behaviour and urban areas had become increasingly constrained and compartmentalized.

Sir John Sorrell CBE is UK Business Ambassador for the Creative Industries, chairman of the London Design Festival and co-chair of the Sorrell Foundation, which works with thousands of young people each year to inspire their creativity and give them life and work skills. He was awarded the Royal Society of Arts Bicentenary Medal in 1998, and holds four honorary design doctorates and an honorary design fellowship. He is an Honorary Fellow of the Royal Institute of British Architects. His book *Creative Island* (2002) features inspired design from Great Britain. A new edition, *Creative Island II*, was published in 2009.

PICTURE CREDITS

Argent: 37, 52, 56, 104, 103.
Arup: 50.
Matt Brown: 43(l).
Richard Bryant: 87, 88, 89.
Ian Christie: 45(r).
Robert Cutts: 14(r).
Alan Delaney: 11(l), 70(c), 102(l), 118.
David Dennis: 33(r).
Ealing/Rank/The Kobal Collection: 44(b).
Steven Earnshaw: 42(r).
English Heritage/John Gay: 10(l), 11(r), 23, 25, 48, 70(l), 90 (all), 106.
Foster + Partners: 36.
Terry Frost: 9(t).
Getty Images: 20.
Google Earth Pro: 31.
Simon Hazelgrove, used courtesy of King's Cross: 16–17.
Hufton+Crow: jacket front, 4, 13, 15(r), 27, 45(l), 57 (all), 62 (all), 63, 64, 73, 79, 80, 81, 82, 83, 84, 85 (all), 93, 96, 97, 99, 100, 101, 105, 108, 109, 111, 115, 119, 142, 143, 144–45.
Lee Jackson: 44(l).
John McAslan + Partners: 3, 6, 35, 40(r), 48, 52, 53, 54(rt, rc, rb), 55, 56, 58–59, 71, 72(r), 92, 94(r), 95 (all), 98 (all), 102(r), 112, 117, 124 (all), 125 (all), 126, 127, 128.
Kier Construction: 12, 69.
Herry Lawford: 26.
Magnus D: 14(l).
Miller Hare, used courtesy of King's Cross: 29, 43(r).
National Portrait Gallery, London: 39.
Network Rail: 19, 34, 41, 98(l), 156.
Oxford Film & Television: 122.

Mark Power: 38 (all), 65, 72(l), 74, 75, 76, 77, 78, 86, 91, 94(l), 107, 110, 113, 114, 120, 121, 136, 140–41.
Andrew Putler: 47, 49, 51, 54(l), 70(r), 116.
Mirco Tobias Schaefer: 33(r).
Seanbjack: 42(l).
Simon: 22.
Sotheby's/akg-images: 21.
John Sturrock: 66–67, 129, 130–31, 132–33, 134, 135, 137, 138–39, 146–47.
John Sturrock, used courtesy of King's Cross: 15(l), 44(r).
Underwood & Underwood/Corbis: 32(l).
James Vaughan: 32(r).
Yisris: 40(l).
Zoological Society of London: 10(r).

First published 2012 by
Merrell Publishers, London and New York

Merrell Publishers Limited
81 Southwark Street
London SE1 0HX

merrellpublishers.com

For Arup:
Editors: John Turzynski, Mike Byrne,
Tom Foulkes, Sue Garland

For John McAslan + Partners:
Executive editor: John McAslan
Coordinator: Carol Choi

For Network Rail:
Editors: Hannah Staunton, Tom Fernley

British Library Cataloguing-in-Publication
Data:
Transforming King's Cross.
1. King's Cross Station (London, England)–
Conservation and restoration.
I. Merrick, Jay.
725.3'1'0942142-dc23

Trade edition ISBN 978-1-8589-4587-3

Produced by Merrell Publishers Limited
Designed by Alexandre Coco
Project-managed by Marion Moisy

Printed and bound in Italy

Jacket, front
The soaring structure of
the Western Concourse
diagrid roof.

Page 3
Drawing of the Western
Concourse roof.

Page 4
View of the interior of
the Western Concourse
funnel, roof and elevated
walkway to the Main
Train Shed.